About Island Press

Since 1984, the nonprofit organization Island Press has been stimulating, shaping, and communicating ideas that are essential for solving environmental problems worldwide. With more than 1,000 titles in print and some 30 new releases each year, we are the nation's leading publisher on environmental issues. We identify innovative thinkers and emerging trends in the environmental field. We work with world-renowned experts and authors to develop cross-disciplinary solutions to environmental challenges.

Island Press designs and executes educational campaigns in conjunction with our authors to communicate their critical messages in print, in person, and online using the latest technologies, innovative programs, and the media. Our goal is to reach targeted audiences—scientists, policymakers, environmental advocates, urban planners, the media, and concerned citizens—with information that can be used to create the framework for long-term ecological health and human well-being.

Island Press gratefully acknowledges major support of our work by The Agua Fund, The Andrew W. Mellon Foundation, The Bobolink Foundation, The Curtis and Edith Munson Foundation, Forrest C. and Frances H. Lattner Foundation, The JPB Foundation, The Kresge Foundation, The Oram Foundation, Inc., The Overbrook Foundation, The S.D. Bechtel, Jr. Foundation, The Summit Charitable Foundation, Inc., and many other generous supporters.

The opinions expressed in this book are those of the author(s) and do not necessarily reflect the views of our supporters.

DESIGN AS DEMOCRACY

DESIGN AS DEMOCRACY

Techniques for Collective Creativity

edited by

David de la Peña

Diane Jones Allen

Randolph T. Hester Jr.

Jeffrey Hou

Laura J. Lawson

Marcia J. McNally

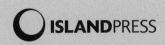

ISLANDPRESS

Washington | Covelo | London

Keywords: advocacy, analysis, assessment, budgeting, collaboration, community engagement, conflict, creativity, design, dialogue, diversity, empathy, empowerment, environmental justice, equity, ethics, evaluation, grassroots, implementation, improvement, local knowledge, mobilize, negotiation, network, organizing, participation, participatory design, partnership, perspective, photography, playground, politics, postconstruction analysis, power, public process, responsibility, sea level rise, sketching, structural change, teamwork, transformation, values, vision, workshop

Library of Congress Control Number: 2017940666

All Island Press books are printed on environmentally responsible materials.

Manufactured in the United States of America
10 9 8 7 6 5 4 3 2 1

Contents

Acknowledgments

As a book on participatory design techniques, it has required, among a host of things, active participation and thoughtful contributions from many people. We are indebted to each and every one.

We begin by thanking our families, who have inspired us by their creative actions, provided insights by their inquisitiveness, and enforced participatory decision making within our own households. They also patiently supported us when we left town for editor meetings, worked over holidays to get a draft out, and yammered in general about what we were learning in the process. Thankfully, they also kept our feet on the ground, reminding us that this kind of commitment to participation must be balanced with our larger lives. We thank you.

Beyond our immediate families, our extended family of community designers helped at critical points. A number of colleagues at CELA (Council of Educators in Landscape Architecture), EDRA (Environmental Design Research Association), ASLA (American Society of Landscape Architects), and the Pacific Rim Community Design Network offered encouraging support, timely criticism, and connections to community designers we didn't know. Many of the techniques included in the book came from members of these organizations.

This book would not have materialized if so many people from around the world hadn't enthusiastically contributed techniques and responded to our comments and suggestions. Thank you. Your work, some familiar, some new to us, provided the raw material for active debate and deliberation as we worked on the organization and big ideas of the book. We hope you are as excited about the result as we are.

Chip Sullivan, you are amazing. It was a great pleasure to be on the inside of your drawing process. We are thrilled with your drawings. They bring life and brilliance to our work in a way that only you know how to do. Thank you.

Our university departments and affiliations have provided us with the financial, collegial, and staff assistance needed to have three face-to-face work retreats and to print the book in color. We are grateful to the School of Environmental and Biological Sciences at Rutgers University; the Department of Landscape Architecture and Environmental Planning at the University of California, Berkeley, including the Student Community Design Fund and the Beatrix Farrand Fund; the Office of Research and the College of Agricultural and Environmental Sciences at the University of California, Davis; and the Department of Landscape Architecture at the University of Washington, Seattle.

We are also grateful to our students and the young people with whom we have worked in professional offices. Many of you have been involved in the creation and shaping of our participatory techniques. Similarly, we thank those of you who, as community members and clients, have tested the utility of the techniques we include in the book.

And finally, we would like to thank Island Press. Courtney Lix, you inspired us with your commitment to the project as well as performing the first edit and helping us navigate the title and cover. Elizabeth Farry, you kept us organized and have been amazing at keeping all of our contributors on the straight and narrow. Sharis Simonian, we have been lucky to have you at the production helm. Thank you and everyone at the press for recognizing the importance of design as democracy and bringing the book to life.

Introduction

REFORM! RE-FORM!
Together We Design

Participatory design is hands-on democracy in action. It is up close. It is personal. It is grounded in the everyday places and lives of people. For over half a century it has guided us in understanding communities, honoring difference, creating vibrant neighborhoods and ecosystems, challenging environmental injustice, and fostering citizenship. Yet, in spite of our creative potential as designers, we tend to draw upon the same palette of techniques that were developed 50 years ago, without adapting or innovating for the contexts we now encounter. This complacency has come at a cost. Familiar techniques are now rote and stagnant. Formalized and calcified into contemporary practice, they offer predictability for clients but hold little promise for grassroots community transformation.

For participatory design to be truly democratic it cannot remain a standardized public process. This task requires more than just conventional design skills—it challenges designers to seek meaningful, ethical, and effective ways to design with communities. It needs to move beyond conventional processes that are formulaic, closed, abstract, superficial, and monofunctional. Participatory design must become contextual, open, experiential, substantive, and holistic.

To renew participatory design we need to reform and to re-form. Reforming means tackling abuses, rethinking old methods, and seeking more just outcomes. Re-forming means forming again, and again, and again. It is a continuous process of shaping and reshaping civic landscapes so they can be informed and inhabited by deep democracy. To accomplish these ends, participatory design must not only have good intentions, it must also refine its democratic techniques. Innovative techniques can strengthen meaningful relationships between communities and designers, help revitalize participatory design as it breaks barriers to collective creativity, and open doors to possibilities that are yet unimagined.

This book provides a framework for addressing the forces that shape participatory design. It highlights design techniques that go beyond standard practices and charts a path toward designing together that is truly transactive, transformative, and tenacious. Some of the techniques have been tested by time; others are notable for their timeliness. They are all deeply connected to their spatial, temporal, and social contexts, as is evident in the case stories that accompany them. As a collection of practices they describe an ambitious, adventurous, and assertive approach to participatory design.

A PROCESS OF TRANSACTIONS

Democratic design is transactive—it facilitates a process of give-and-take between community members, designers, technical experts, and power brokers. If done well, participants exchange critical information that others do not have but need, as well as opinions others may not share but need to understand and respect. Through this process more than information and opinions is exchanged. Participants experience empathy as they learn to walk in each other's shoes. Shared language is found as knowledge flows from the community, as local and outside technical expertise mix. Everyone gains knowledge beyond their limited experiences. We teach each other. We become smarter together. This initiates thinking multimodally across boundaries of discipline, race, and class. This empowers communities and sustains stewardship.

Transactions don't only exist where consensus comes easy. It may be easier to avoid interpersonal confrontation, but we learn as much or more by making space for contention so that shared values are articulated and conflicting ones are exposed. Further, when we find deep-seated problems, we avoid fixing symptoms and instead attend to the heart of the matter. We address oppression, exclusion, inequity, and inaccessibility because we understand that even in the design of the smallest park we are shaping the moral capacity of our living democracy. We do not resolve or mediate disagreements until we have discussed, digested, and ruminated on them. We find a calming effect from exhuming and ordering new information together. We consider the alternatives that are evoked by the process. We evaluate them. And most often our transactive exchange produces a design that none of us could have imagined alone. The unimaginable breakthroughs that we witness are the result of collective creativity.

As we design together to achieve our objectives we build community capacity to act effectively, to work with allies, and to negotiate. We act civilly and sometimes disobediently along the way. We strengthen our democracy through what John Friedmann called "the radical openness required by dialogue." Transactive design truly means that we design together. There are no strangers and no spectators in deeply democratic design. Everyone must contribute in order to optimize the outcome.

THE GOAL IS TO TRANSFORM

Transactive design doesn't exist for its own sake—the goal is to transform. Done well, the resulting transformations can touch multiple dimensions—individual, social, and physical. While physical change often receives our conscious attention, transformations at a personal level be just as profound. Individual participants change as they gain new information, skills, and perspectives. We learn from each other, and that transforms us in ways small and large, subtle and dramatic. We may gain confidence, become empowered, or experience the joy of creating. When we finish we may see our community, others, and ourselves differently. These personal transformations may seem to be the expected by-products of participation, but they can also be deliberately pursued as objectives in and of themselves.

Similarly, an entire community may be transformed and may begin to act collectively in more enlightened and tolerant ways. Local groups become civically responsible, considering both immediate needs and long-term consequences. They gain knowledge and experience that enhance their capacity to work together and with professionals to address issues in the community. They articulate guiding principles, set priorities, and map directions with near and far vision. Transformative design also facilitates connections between members of the community, catalyzing innovations that spur local economic activity or fostering alliances that reallocate political power. Residents may gain access to work or necessary services. New community identities may be formed, and commitments to inclusive processes solidified.

Finally, the physical condition of the community can be dramatically altered by transformative design. Facilities may be built that better reflect local conditions. Social spaces may be enhanced through improvements in the public realm. Groups previously marginalized may have better access to places that have become more welcoming and tailored to their needs. The community's most deeply held values may be directly expressed in the cultural landscape. Sacred places may be protected and celebrated. New places may be created that encourage flexibility, reuse, and innovation. Lost lands may be recovered. Ecological diversity may be preserved. Much of this work may be done with the hands and the dedicated time of community members themselves, building ownership, place, and sociability from the assets that were inherent to the place all along.

It Takes Tenacity

Getting to know ourselves and communities, putting knowledge to work, collectively identifying issues, finding creative solutions, and testing those solutions—we think of these as the core competencies of the participatory designer. But they aren't always enough. Oftentimes the right thing to do is thwarted by other potent interests: a selfish economic motive, the grasping of long-held power, a fear of change, an aversion to risk, or a lack of optimism. Finding the right thing to do is hard enough, but having power means being able to do it—being effective. The tenacious designer knows that efficacy requires understanding the political, economic, and cultural contexts in which projects proceed or are scuttled. It means mapping out not only neighborhoods, watersheds, and bus routes but also power hierarchies and community networks, schedules, and stories that resonate. It means thinking systematically and creatively about how to proceed—it means formulating strategies.

Strategic thinking comes easily for some designers, especially those with years of experience who intuitively read political landscapes. They know from trial and error when to use the media, when to go to a politician, when to get better technical information, when to muddle through, when to take a field trip, when to resist or negotiate. For others wading into the political realm for the first time, a tried-and-true framework to organize a campaign may prove a wise initial step. Even the most ardent step-followers, of course, will deviate when a crisis arises or when technical data are unavailable, consensus can't be found, political resistance threatens a good plan, or something just isn't working. A contested process can wear down even the most seasoned activist. But to transform, we must stay the course for the long term.

We must hold fast and firmly together with intention and attention. As obligatory public participation has become commonplace and institutionalized, powerful interests have appropriated once-radical techniques, resulting in watered-down, controlled, and manipulated outcomes. Today we are awash in participation, yet citizens still find their right to design their own communities elusive. This is because even minor reform menaces powerful systems; more significant transformation sets a threatening and destabilizing precedent, portending a different society. The work we do is not all consensus and cooperation. Yes, we must know how to cooperate, to negotiate, and to compromise, and how to do so constructively and effectively. But in many cases, confrontation and conflict are unavoidable. Democratic designers do not consider *conflict* a dirty word, but rather a time-honored means to honorable ends. Nonetheless, enabling and managing conflict requires courage, diplomacy, skill, and tenacity.

Democratic design redistributes power, and as those closer to the grassroots gain an effective voice, others must necessarily yield some power. Those at the grassroots may also be skilled at design, challenging the very authority of the professional. Indeed, the power of design professionalism depends, in large part, on claiming to be elite experts with superior aesthetic judgment, but participatory design threatens to devalue that distinction. As a result, participatory projects struggle to overcome marginalization by the profession. Even worse, design professionals who cater to corporate or state interests serve those patrons by resisting the empowerment of the less powerful, the just allocation of land uses, the redistribution of economic resources, and the approval of grassroots improvement plans. Corporations, states, and design institutions must continually be reminded that participation makes cities and economies stronger, and that participation in design is not compromise but, rather, enrichment. This is the truth that democratic designers deliver, and we must constantly express it through our actions and through the proven quality of the designs that we arrive at together.

PARADOXES OF DEMOCRATIC DESIGN

To effectively practice democratic design is to embrace the many paradoxes we encounter and represent. Reconciling our values with those of others is but one of the paradoxes we must acknowledge. We are set apart by the strength and passion of our values, even as we seek to facilitate others' self-expression. We may be motivated to include the excluded, give space for cultural difference, preserve endangered species, advance resilience, or create deeper democracies. But these are not always mainstream motivations, and in fact often conflict in communities where we work.

In democratic design we assume multiple roles that are ever shifting, conflictual, and sometimes contradictory. Some assert that facilitation in participatory design tends toward manipulation. We check our own motivations and positions of power but do not sacrifice the potential of instigation in the process. We avoid working against our values, not by ignoring or denying the paradoxes but by holding them in our awareness. There are many more paradoxical roles we balance. We listen between the lines and teach. We follow and lead. We connect to others' minds and hearts. We are insiders and outsiders. We give life to conflict and mediate conflict. We are powerless and powerful. We are expert and ignoramus. We draw what others say and what we think. We work in groups and in isolation. We recapture and create. We shape order and disorder. We work at small and extra-large scales. We set aside and confront. We obey and disobey. We reform and rebel. Do we do all of this at once? No, but we likely do each in due time. We are convinced that specialization can be dangerous. Utilizing the power of opposites is the essence of transactive, transformative, and tenacious design. To be effective, democratic designers must be able to sense when to employ all of the above oppositions with equal skill and enthusiasm. This does not require super-heroic powers; adventurous flexibility and daring persistence will suffice.

How to Use This Book

As designers we can enhance transformations with a well-conceived process and thoughtfully developed techniques that are appropriate to the task. *Design as Democracy* is written with this intention in mind, for anyone who wants to meaningfully engage people and place in the design process—community members and leaders, landscape architects, architects, and planners—as well as educators and students. It is a collection of techniques and stories that contain seeds to reform and re-form that can be applied to many places and contexts, assembled to help achieve more successful outcomes. We expect that they will be used and adapted by readers to serve their efforts to improve communities.

The book is divided into nine thematic chapters, organized in roughly chronological sequence through the design process, but not strictly so. It should be useful to read the entirety from beginning to end to grasp or reacquaint yourself with the whole process of democratic design. In some ways, we have conceived the book to be used as a cookbook, with step-by-step instructions and descriptions of how recipes have been created from or adapted to local ingredients and traditions. Just as with any real-world design project, we expect readers to improvise, to skip ahead, to flip through, or to focus on one especially salient case story. Each chapter title combines words unconventionally, calling attention to the nuances of the process. An opening essay directly addresses that part of the process and introduces the techniques. The techniques themselves come from the responses to a call we made in 2015, asking designers to offer their most effective participatory methods. We offer this collection of best practices from many corners of the world. The authors of each technique describe the intention, lay out a set of instructions, illustrate a case story of how it has been used, and reflect on its merits and challenges. We have consciously honored the tension between the universality of the techniques and the particularities of the stories. Even as we acknowledge that every situation requires different approaches and begets a different outcome, we still chart a path for others to follow, however loose and improvisational. Additionally, none of the techniques stands alone, but, rather, each exists as part of a bigger participatory process.

Chapter 1, "Suiting Up to Shed," describes how to mobilize a project, how to determine roles of community members and designers, and how to expose assumptions about the underlying site and community issues. Chapter 2, "Going to the People's Coming," shows how the responsibility for participation can be borne both by community members and by designers who commit to learning about a place and its people by spending time there and interacting in the mundane activities of everyday life. In Chapter 3, "Experting: They Know, We Know, and Together We Know Better, Later," we highlight techniques where local knowledge and professional expertise are given equal weight, then negotiated, and distinctions between the two are challenged. "Calming and Evoking" is explored in Chapter 4 as a way of exhuming, ordering, and interpreting information to allow designers and the community to articulate thoughtful, well-informed solutions. In Chapter 5, "Yeah, That's What We Should Do," we focus on techniques that bring to light underlying issues in ways that catalyze new visions and create certainty about the best course of action. Chapter 6, "Co-generating," introduces the process in which different parties and participants come together to generate explicit designs that can be implemented. Chapter 7, "Engaging the Making," highlights techniques that offer participants and stakeholders the chance to engage in construction— the physical manifestations of projects. In Chapter 8, "Testing, Testing, Can You Hear Me? Do I Hear You Right?" evaluation is described as a transactive process used before construction to assess the likely meshing of potential and effective solutions. The techniques in Chapter 9, "Putting Power to Good Use, Delicately and Tenaciously," provide the analytic tools to dissect, develop, and exercise power to make community improvements.

This book captures decades of insights from some of the most experienced figures in the field as well as innovative approaches by emerging democratic designers. Many of the contributions hail from academic contexts, a fertile testing ground, but they are equally applicable in professional and grassroots contexts. The book occasionally references historically central works, such as Alinsky's tactics, Halprin's Take Part methods, Davidoff's construct of pluralism in planning, and Hester and McNally's 12-step design process. Our book is not intended to replace these or other valuable frameworks, but rather to extend into promising terrains for participatory design by drawing from practices in a wide range of social, cultural, and geographic contexts.

The old techniques that gave birth to modern participatory design are still in play, just as they were 50 years ago, but we also need to master new modes, roles, and tactics that will make our shared practices more empowering. This book itself is an open, democratic way of sharing techniques and stories that should spark additional approaches that will reinvigorate democratic design, reforming and re-forming the way we design together. We know that most of our collective efforts to radically transform communities will render only modest reforms; occasionally they will achieve their stated goals; and infrequently, perhaps only a few times in our lifetimes, they will surprise us by taking on lives of their own, contributing to deep structural change. We strive for all these outcomes and more.

1

Suiting Up to Shed

Participatory designers provide a personal perspective that has the potential to greatly influence design outcomes. Upon hearing about a project designers begin generating ideas, and these initial ideas often help us determine what needs to be investigated, how to approach the work, and which questions to ask. Suiting up to shed focuses on techniques that prepare the design team for self-conscious, aware engagement.

A commitment to engage with community means that the team, collectively and individually, is a participant with formative experiences, values, and ideas. To suit up is to ready yourself and your team for the role you will play given the project at hand, but also to shed the pretense that participatory design is a neutral process and the designer is a neutral facilitator. As such it is important to figure out who you are, whom you are working with, and what you expect to be the underlying site and community issues. But how to do this? What will help you check your expectations and open yourself to seeing the community's values and uniqueness?

GETTING OURSELVES READY

Slowing down at the very beginning offers opportunities to test assumptions, ground information, and build a stronger network of participants and collaborators. Many community-based projects are complex in nature and require multiple perspectives and skill sets. The team's roles, relationships, expectations, and structure need to be mapped out. Similarly, the team needs to articulate the design process it will use and then communicate this to all members so that they will know when and how they can plan to take part. This often involves the team pretesting its standard procedures—from how data are collected to design generation—to better tailor them to the particularlity of people and place.

ME RELATIVE TO YOU

In addition to getting our initial impulses on the table we need to know the lens through which we see and respond to a place and its people. This lens consists of our values, which are often the root of what impelled us to become designers in the first place. However, our values may or may not mesh with those of the community. There are techniques for drawing out a designer's own inspirations, personal working style, demographic profile, spatial preferences, and everyday life behavior patterns. Whether you are an experienced designer with many past projects to draw from or a young designer just starting out, part of the unique contribution you bring to a project comes from within.

Once we are clear on who we are, we can see our position in society relative to the cultural and economic context of the community in which we plan to work. This in turn equips us with empathy rather than sympathy. This distinction is important because designers can find themselves in communities with acute needs that have been repeatedly ignored. Although providing technical assistance to a community in need is a critical role of participatory design, responding with sorrow or pity hampers one's effectiveness. Sympathy, even when it is grounded in understanding, can subtly convey to residents that only the designer's expertise counts. Another pitfall lies in creating a patronizing process that diminishes the community's self-worth.

TECHNIQUES TO SUIT UP AND SHED

The techniques in this chapter are about preparation as much as participation. Some are appropriate to undertake every time your team begins a project; some are personal explorations that you will need to work through if you haven't already done so. In "What's in It for Us?" Julie Stevens provides a technique to develop a team road map that members can rely on to anchor their involvement. Randolph T. Hester Jr., in "I Am Someone Who," offers a simple test of the designer's attitudes and practices to maximize the designer's effectiveness. Sungkyung Lee and Laura J. Lawson illustrate how a team can explore its assumptions about a locale in "Challenging the Blank Slate." The technique "Environmental Autobiography Adaptations" provides two alternative approaches to reconnecting with one's childhood places using self-guided hypnosis and environmental autobiography. In "Finding Yourself in the Census" Marcia J. McNally proposes a simple way to contextualize oneself by working up a demographic profile and then comparing it with similar data on the community. "Consume, Vend, and Produce" allows the designer to identify commonplace and frequently overlooked activities, while recognizing things that are out of the ordinary.

Technique 1.1

WHAT'S IN IT FOR US? DESIGNING A DURABLE TEAM

Julie Stevens

When it comes to community design, one person can't do it all—we need teams as dynamic as the communities with whom we work. However, it is difficult to assemble and maintain a team, especially for long-term-engagement projects that evolve in scope and require new inputs of skill and expertise. If you are the leader, you must continually evaluate the needs of the project, the abilities of teammates, and, most importantly, the human connections among members of the design team and community. Because successful teams often form around shared interests and ethics, determining mutual rewards—or team members defining What's in It for Us—can be a critical technique for developing and managing a team.

Instructions

1. In order to understand the expertise, skills, and resources needed, first map out the project. What is the purpose? What will you need to achieve it?

2. As the leader with the responsibility of building the team, clarify your own strengths and shortcomings in terms of organization, communication, project management, professional expertise, and so forth. You should know what is motivating you—what is in it for you?

3. Make sure you also understand what's in it for the community by working with community members. Methods to gather this information include informal interactions, formal administrative meetings, focus groups, and town-hall-style meetings.

4. Identify the skills and expertise needed on the team. Look for critical skills as well as different perspectives that come from diverse backgrounds and interests. As the project progresses, additional skills may be required.

5. Based on conversations with potential team members, fill out a "What's in It for Us?" worksheet (see sample provided), or, if appropriate, have the team members fill it out themselves. Use the worksheet to identify or select new team members and to refresh an existing team member's role.

6. Work with the team to establish ground rules, structure, and a positive working environment. Work toward consensus when possible, but at times it may be necessary for you, as a leader, to make decisions in the interest of time and progress. How does your team want to interact? When, where, and how often will you meet? How will the topics of each meeting be determined? How will the team communicate and how often? What are the expectations for individual members of the team? What are the team's expectations for the leader? Investing time in this

WORKSHEET 1-1: WHAT'S IN IT FOR US?		
Name	**What can you do for this project?**	**What can this project do for you?**
Intern A	Bring knowledge of construction tools and equipment, generally good energy and people skills, and superior design skills	Provides a very intense and at times personal glimpse into a completely unfamiliar life and helps the intern to see the needs and struggles of the world differently—to do good work for the right reasons
Intern B	Employ strong research and organizational skills and sensibilities about communicating with and relating to marginalized women	Allows the intern to dive into environmental justice issues that are not presented in most courses and not common in the profession
Extension specialist	Connect the team with educational content and resources and facilitate meetings	Allows the specialist to work with marginalized communities and earn the attention of the university administration eager to participate in such work
Prison sergeant	Help the project run smoothly, guide decision making, help other officers understand the value of the project	Makes the job easier, eliminates conflict, and places the sergeant in a position favorable to the administration
State politician	Connect the team with resources, promote a positive perception of the project in the statehouse	Enables connection with members of the community, especially those marginalized, and allows the politician to express concern about the health and safety of women in the state

process encourages all to claim an equal stake in the responsibilities of the team. These questions may need to be revisited from time to time as the team and project goals change.

7. Use your team to build a bigger team. Focus on finding well-connected collaborators who can liaise with the community or help secure resources. Potential team members may be affiliated with local businesses, government, and the community. They may also be specialists in an allied area or distant experts who help from afar.

8. Evaluate what is working and what is not. This step can be useful at various points of the collaboration and is effective during transitions. For example, we evaluate when starting a new phase of the project or when we have a new crew, in the middle, after the crew has had some time together, and at the end to inform future

Figure 1-1: After some time has passed on the project, the team members fill out index cards, answering, "What is working well?" on one side and "What is not?" on the other.

endeavors. Give each team member an index card and ask members to answer "What is working well?" on one side and "What is not?" on the other. Gather the cards and read through the answers while a team member records them on a flip chart. Build themes and threads to discuss openly with the group. Transfer the themes to another chart and add a column for action items and another to assign team members to each item. This is a good time to revisit the What's in It for Us? worksheet. What skills and expertise are missing in the current team? Who might fill these gaps? Does a team member's role need to be refreshed?

Case Story

The Environmental Justice in Prisons Project of Iowa State University has worked with the Iowa Correctional Institution for Women (ICIW) in Mitchellville, Iowa, since 2011. The initial request from the Iowa Department of Corrections (IDOC) was for a five-month project to generate planting plans for the newly expanded minimum- to maximum-security prison. We took a more holistic approach and generated ideas for therapeutic and production gardens, outdoor recreation, and native habitat. At the end of our first phase, we gathered ICIW and IDOC administrators, offenders, and project architects and engineers and decided to continue the partnership, which is ongoing. Each year, the team and focus become more complex as we deepen our understanding of the prison community and strengthen our partnership.

With the help of extension specialist and team member Susan Erickson I developed an assessment tool called What's in It for Us? to help manage our ever-evolving team. This was first developed to select interns for the summer design–build program, but I've used the tool with community members and research collaborators as well. With interns, I conduct a formal interview and ask them what they hope to gain from participation and what they offer to help meet the goals of the project. I also note social skills and personality traits, such as "good people skills," when appropriate. In some cases, I ask potential team members to answer, "What can you do for this project?" and "What can this project do for you?" Other times, I exercise my leadership role and answer these questions more discreetly based on conversations or interviews with individuals.

This assessment has provided clarity to the selection process and diversified the skills and expertise of the team, making project management and construction more positive and efficient. There are several good examples. As incarcerated women are released, new women are needed on the crew. By involving the sergeant early on, we established buy-in and were able to fill open spots quickly and with women who were really interested in the project. In another case, I nearly dismissed an application from a potential intern because his essay did not express any compassion for the prison population. In terms of what he offered to the project, I recorded that he had experience with construction tools and equipment. In terms of what the project could do for him, I recorded that this young, white man might benefit from a summer working with women from much less privileged and much more racially diverse backgrounds, which could open up new worlds as he engaged people both informally and through design. His inclusion on the team was validated when I saw him give an incarcerated woman a high-five after completing a difficult retaining wall.

Recently, our focus shifted to studying the impacts of the environment on the health and well-being of correctional officers. Many aspects of this project required knowledge beyond the reach of the research team. The chart helped us determine who was needed in order to fully understand this important topic. We connected with an environmental psychologist who is an expert on the impact of the environment on workplace stress and job commitment.

Figure 1-2: Building the Healing Garden for Special Needs. This one really warms my heart; I love to see the women and interns working so well together. If it weren't for their clothes and the razor wire in the background, you might not know it was a prison!

Figure 1-3: Recent view of the grounds of the Iowa Correctional Institution for Women.
Source: Kim Gaspari Photography.

Figure 1-4: The garden is maintained by a landscape crew of incarcerated women.

Reflection

The technique presented here is based on the revelatory process inherent in community design projects. It works best when the leader has spent ample time getting to know the place and its members and can make some assumptions about the skills needed and the capacity-building opportunities for the team, while also acknowledging ongoing evolution and reassessment. The partnership and resulting built work appear to be having impacts. Interns express changes in perception about incarcerated individuals. The ICIW staff psychiatrist reports improved mental health and lower medication needs for several incarcerated women on the landscape crew. An ongoing study reveals that 86 percent of women incarcerated report that the gardens help to relax and calm them, and 76 percent report that the gardens motivate them to make changes in their lives.

Technique 1.2

I AM SOMEONE WHO

Randolph T. Hester Jr.

This technique helps clarify the various personal values and beliefs that influence the designer. The goal is to honestly assess your own personality traits and reflect on what they suggest about your intentions for being involved in and the ways you might most contribute to participatory design. This exercise can be revisited over time as a means to reflect on your changing perspective. It is an updated version of the one first published in my book *Community Design Primer*. The case describes how the list of skills community designers need has changed over time and gives a brief example of how the technique was useful.

Instructions

1. Hand out the worksheet "I Am Someone Who" (next page) to your group for them to answer individually. Have them check yes, sort of, or no for each answer. Then ask them to add additional characteristics at the end of the checklist.
2. Next instruct group members to go back over the statements and circle the 12 that best describe them.
3. Instruct the group members to put a star next to the ones they feel most influence their approach to design.
4. Ask a series of questions to follow up. What most motivates them about community design or a specific project? What do their answers reveal about special skills they have for participatory design? What skills do they need to develop?
5. Instruct members to share the results with other people on the team and have someone who knows each member well give feedback about the statements circled and starred. Suggest that they do this exercise often (you should too).

Case Story

I first used this exercise when I was developing a plan for a schoolyard, a design–build project. The participants were parents, teachers, and children at the middle school I had attended two decades before, as well as landscape architecture interns. I wanted to know why the interns wanted to be involved and what they would be best at doing during planning. As it turned out several were self-proclaimed leaders, whereas others preferred shared responsibility. One was an experienced carpenter; another had been a playground supervisor. The interns created one of the most interesting play environments I had ever seen. One who was central to the success of the construction had few hard skills but had said she was patient with other people.

I am someone who... (complete sentence below)	Yes	Sort of	No
thinks that planning and design are separate activities.			
would enjoy helping people design their home and garden.			
is optimistic most of the time.			
thinks that a lack of community feeling is one of the most serious problems of modern life.			
can easily change my designs to reflect others' input.			
believes that experts know best when it comes to environmental issues.			
is willing to speak out even if my opinion is unpopular.			
believes that small changes can accumulate to produce big results.			
has a hard time working with people who have backgrounds different from my own.			
thinks that the design process extends beyond the time my project is built.			
would do a slightly misleading drawing in order to get my great idea adopted.			
often feels uncomfortable in unfamiliar places.			
would work in the federal bureaucracy for many years in order to get better public housing standards approved.			
does not like to have constraints put on my design.			
thinks the design process can empower people.			
would rather organize people to design their own community than design it myself.			
is patient with other people.			
would most often rather be with nature than with other people.			
is open to ideas from people different from myself.			
wants to use design to solve problems.			
thinks that the design process is more important than the product itself.			
is able to negotiate and compromise effectively.			
believes that the most important role for designers and planners is to preserve and create beautiful places.			
enjoys hanging out with people.			
would risk my job to fight what I considered to be an injustice to another person.			
is well organized.			

I am someone who… (complete sentence below)	Yes	Sort of	No
is a good listener.			
has a good sense of humor.			
has a strong sense of myself but is not overly egocentric.			
is a better follower than a leader.			
likes to engage in David vs. Goliath battles.			
believes in aiming for the best outcome rather than settling for something politically acceptable.			
firmly believes that meetings need an agenda.			
values respect more than fame.			
knows how to work with government officials.			
believes that social media are an important tool for communication.			
agrees that understanding how government works in a community is important.			
can mobilize anything.			
is most interested in big picture thinking.			
believes in doing my part.			
believes refreshments are key to good events.			
works to keep all participants in the loop.			
understands power should be mapped and tracked.			
has little patience for whiners.			
believes good participatory projects need good information.			
believes in native wisdom.			
believes technology has a place in participatory design.			
works best as a collaborator.			
understands that each project has its own pace but generally operates with a sense of urgency.			
is a strategic thinker.			
Add other key characteristics about yourself below:			

This first version of this exercise was brief—a dozen or so questions—but the responses helped us divide up the tasks based on what each of us was most skilled at doing and thus mobilize effectively. A few years later I conducted a survey of leading community designers around the country and asked them questions similar to those in the "I Am Someone Who" exercise to determine what principles guided the work they tried to accomplish, and what skills and personality traits they considered essential for success in participatory design. Collectively there was significant agreement about necessary skills, but the design motivations were far more varied. And the respondents had dramatically different strategies for achieving the same goals. I expanded the exercise accordingly.

I continue to use this exercise to help designers expand their democratic design capacity, thereby improving the outcome of dozens of projects. The exercise continues to evolve in response to the values and skills needed in participatory design. For example, the idealistic motivations of 1960s Great Society designers have been supplemented with the need to partner with nongovernmental organizations, be entrepreneurial, embrace science, and discover new avenues of radical practice.

Reflection

This technique helps emerging designers clarify motivations, skills they already have, and ones they need to develop. For more experienced designers, it is a useful annual checkup. For everyone it reveals fundamental motivations, and it often uncovers newfound skills. This is why it is critical to have blanks at the end of the list so that designers can define characteristics of their own identity and abilities. The blanks can reveal a unique skill that becomes the key to a project's success.

Responses often predict who will be an effective community designer. Some of the factors have remained unchanged since I first used this technique—good listeners, optimists who are concerned about diminishment of community and the rise of inequities. Other answers were added to the list with increasing awareness of the importance of attention to detail, power mapping, and other forms of expertise. Whiners made the list for the first time in this version.

"I Am Someone Who" reveals contradictions within community design. Many simply cannot answer whether process is more important than product. They insist on both. Others are either process- or product-oriented. The best community designers are often filled with opposing inclinations. It is especially empowering for democratic designers to be aware of these tensions and to reconcile the use of opposing values and strategies in design work.

Technique 1.3

CHALLENGING THE BLANK SLATE

Sungkyung Lee and Laura J. Lawson

This technique acknowledges that designers come to every project with knowledge that leads us to predisposed solutions. It gives us the opportunity to track where our ideas come from and determine if we can be receptive to new, community-based knowledge. By reversing the typical design process of inventory, analysis, and design we can check how readily available data, such as census information, topography, and urban form, will influence design instincts that may or may not be appropriate.

Instructions

1. Establish a leader within the design team. One person needs to know the intent of the exercise and lead the team through three rounds of thinking and mapping. The leader has to be willing to intentionally withhold the typical data that the team expects.

2. Prepare the "blank slate" at the beginning of the project. Develop a context map that shows minimal site features (city boundaries, major circulation, key natural resources) without giving any names or place signifiers. Make three copies of this map for each member of the design team.

3. The leader should instruct team members to work individually. For Round 1 they should draw their first ideas regarding the intended project (town plan, park system, etc.). Team members should be told to work from internal ideas and not get sidetracked by the lack of information. They should not be told anything about the place or the people. Note how imagination comes into play as the team dreams of the ideal location, size, and context for the intended intervention.

4. Put the first proposal (Round 1) aside and take a break so everyone can clear their mind. Then start Round 2 by revealing the community. Instruct the team to collect distant information from typical scientific or quantitative data sources, such as the national census, geological survey maps, and land use maps. Add relevant information to the base map, such as locations of major commercial areas and parks, demographic distinctions, or environmental considerations. Instruct team members to reconceptualize their proposal in light of what is learned.

5. Round 3 is about investigating local institutional information. Look at websites for the chamber of commerce, school district, parks department, nonprofit service organizations, and so forth. Add information to the map and then reenvision the project at hand.

Figure 1-5: With very little information, in Round 1 the designer explores her own assumptions about an open space system for East St. Louis.

Figure 1-6: Fortified with background information from diverse sources, in Round 3 the designer again reconsiders her ideas for an open space system.

6. Examine the results of the three rounds. As a last step, have team members hang up their three maps to see how internal ideas, distanced information, and local information are shaping designs. Are they getting more specific? Between the first and second rounds, how did socioeconomic information shape the designs? Did knowledge of income, race, or age change anyone's proposal? Between the second and third rounds, was insider information about local institutions informative? It may be helpful to write down reflections and discuss among the team so that this experience can be referenced later in the process.

7. Revise the base map and start the participatory process.

Case Story

For many years the University of Illinois East St. Louis Action Research Project (ESLARP) brought teams of faculty and design students to work with residents of this distressed urban community. Whereas East St. Louis was 98 percent African American and 37 percent of the residents were below the poverty level, the design teams tended to be white and from middle-class suburban American or international communities. For years East St. Louis has been notorious for crime and poverty; however, during its tenure the ESLARP program had worked with multiple resident organizations and tenacious individuals to improve community conditions. Underlying racist beliefs sometimes infused student expectations, so faculty developed preparatory exercises as a means to discuss race, class, and structural inequalities prior to the young designers' first trip to the city.

One year the landscape architecture studio was asked to work on several park projects in East St. Louis. Prior to the first visit, team members were given a blank slate map that included city boundaries, major highways, and key natural features, and then asked to design a park system that would serve an unnamed city of 35,000 residents. The results tended to be overscaled and included large swaths of "open space" connected by greenways and large parks along the riverfront. The green system helped organize the assumed, nearby land uses but tended to be passive spaces rather than programmed for activities.

Next, it was revealed that the context map was actually East St. Louis, and team members were asked to analyze the physical and social context based on census data, land use, environmental hazard maps, and locations of public services, such as schools, libraries, and parks. With this new knowledge, they developed new park system proposals. Most of the young designers considered assets to be the parks, river, and existing downtown, with liabilities being vacant land, highways, and industrial areas. Many of the proposals required tearing down and rebuilding large sections of the city. When asked what this would mean to the displaced residents, team members often felt that current conditions were so bad that no one would want to live there. Other members felt paralyzed due to the complexity of the socioeconomic problems and came up with minor proposals, such as recreation fields, better access to the river, and new community centers.

The team then read more about community organizations in East St. Louis. They visited the city for two days and talked with residents about their lived experience, their ties to the place, their commitment to improving their neighborhoods, and so on. Members quickly recognized the difference between their "expert" perspective ("Why would anyone want to live here?") and what residents said ("I want to make a safe community for my children and their children.").

As a result final proposals rejected solutions that covered the entire city and instead focused on projects to showcase neighborhood identities building on existing assets— schools, community centers, and churches they had visited. Because residents didn't feel connected to the river, solutions tended to be neighborhood-scale initiatives for parks, greenways, and stormwater abatement instead of citywide plans. In the end they were aware that they had listened to what the residents wanted, and they had responded as sensitized designers.

Figure 1-7: Vetting design ideas with a resident of East St. Louis.

Reflection

This technique exposes how sometimes "neutral" information leads to assumptions and design impulses that do not reflect the lived experience of residents. The technique is not intended to be shared with the community, but rather is a method of self-reflection prior to a participatory process. It may be most useful when the designers are working in a new context and with communities that are different from their own. Because the technique intends to encourage designers' reflection, it may work best in supportive teams that encourage discussion. For the same reason, the technique may not work if designers refuse to admit preconceptions, particularly their own race, ethnicity, or class biases.

Technique 1.4

ENVIRONMENTAL AUTOBIOGRAPHY ADAPTATIONS

Marcia J. McNally and Laura J. Lawson

Our connections to places have a stronghold on what we consider to be "standard" and what we envision when asked to design. For instance, our preconceptions that a home should have a front yard might be based on our own childhood homes but may not be what another person imagines. We must be conscious of our own space origins so that we do not impose them on clients or the public (at least without doing it knowingly!). The exercises—environmental autobiographies—enable designers to qualitatively and systematically explore their childhood memories and to look back in order to understand if/how they influence their design work today. The exercises can also be used to engage clients to think more deeply about what they want from a design.

The technique can focus on different environments—the home, parks, schoolgrounds, shopping districts, and so on. We first present a technique that explores childhood play spaces as a way to help designers recall the act of play rather than the objects of play. Second, the Fourth House delves into personal meanings of home and family. One of the early manifestations of this technique involved first reading cultural geographer J. B. Jackson's "Westward Moving House," which describes the landscapes of an American family over three generations (republished and available online at https://placesjournal.org/article/the-westward-moving-house/). The Fourth House asks the user to remember family stories embedded in the spatial details of certain places.

Instructions

Childhood Memories

1. Start with a small group of individuals in a comfortable and relaxed setting. Everyone should have something to draw on and draw with. Tell the group to get comfortable, close their eyes, and focus on their breathing. Then, slowly, talk them through the process of clearing their mind and relaxing. Get them breathing deeply.

2. Once you feel like you have them in a relaxed, quasi-hypnotized state, walk them through a set of prompts. Ask everyone to imagine a beloved childhood environment. When they have the image in their mind, quietly and slowly ask them to go through the following explorations—zoom in to see details, explore what it looks like, what it feels like, what time of year it is, who is there, what they are doing, and so forth.

3. Slowly talk them back into the present and instruct them to open their eyes when ready. Ask them not to speak but to draw what they just saw in their mind's eye.

4. When everyone is finished, show the drawings as a way to open discussion and share ideas.

The Fourth House

1. Ask each person to explore three generations of family homes: a grandparent's childhood home, a parent's childhood home, and one's own childhood home. While some people know their heritage and can do this exercise at any time, others will benefit from the opportunity to talk with relatives. It is not important if the person's memories are absolutely correct. It is expected that the process may give rise to questions that cannot be answered.

2. They should draw what they imagine or remember about these homes—a site plan of each home and its associated land, a floor plan of the rooms, and a front elevation. Each drawing should be shown in scale relative to the others and have a general sense of the size of various elements.

3. In order to explore their own expectations of the future (the fourth house), they need to imagine what home they will live in in 10 to 20 years (the number of years can be changed as appropriate). They should draw this as well.

4. Each person should fill out the worksheet "Home Comparative Analysis" to systematically analyze the homes using the same criteria.

5. After filling out the worksheet, they should go back and embellish their drawings, annotating as appropriate.

6. Pin up the drawings. What do they tell you about each person? How does this environmental history compare with the environments where they work today? Share and discuss these drawings with the others in the group.

Case Story

An early example of the childhood memories exercise is the Harvard Law Child Care Center project conducted by Randolph T. Hester Jr. While working with the parents, Hester heard their desire for a "top-of-the-line child care center" that would be similar to a newly built one in close proximity. But he also noticed that the center tended to invest more in staff than in physical improvements to their existing facilities. To understand this Hester walked the center staff and parents through a process of hypnosis, which yielded an entirely different set of aspirations associated with experiencing nature and finding wild remnants in the community. As a result, instead of a costly building rehab they planted a tree that was big enough to be immediately climbable and started to take kids on walks to play in "wild

	Grandparent home	Parent home	Your childhood home	Your future home
Who lived in the home?				
What did it look like?				
How did it feel?				
What did the landscape around the home look like?				
Do you have particular memories about the home? How do these relate to the space and people?				
What activities occurred in the home and where did they occur?				
List characteristics of the space.				

	Grandparent home	Parent home	Your childhood home	Your future home
How, if at all, was the space modified to meet family needs?				
What factors influenced how the home worked for the people living there?				
What image did the family want to convey inside their home and outside?				
Was the home influenced by external crises, such as war, natural disaster, etc.?				
What was the family's lifestyle, and how did the family make a living (doing what)?				
Are there other points to mention?				
Express your thoughts about how any of these homes influence your current work.				

natural remnants," such as streams with fish and frogs, using the nearby urban environment as its playground.

We both have conducted the Fourth House exercise with designers in the United States. In 2012 McNally tried it with design students in Taiwan. They noticed that each house in every generation had a "god room" or a place designated for ancestor worship; however, this was not present in the future home. They were also struck by the consistently strong rural roots. In the discussion they realized that this background stood in strong contrast to their studio assignments, all of which were for urban and suburban environments. Yet their most treasured environments were those of their youth, in particular, places like a grandparent's farm, where a few had grown up. As a result one student decided to take on the thesis topic of the impact of declining rural populations and the abandonment of rural elementary schools by proposing ways to repurpose the buildings for community use.

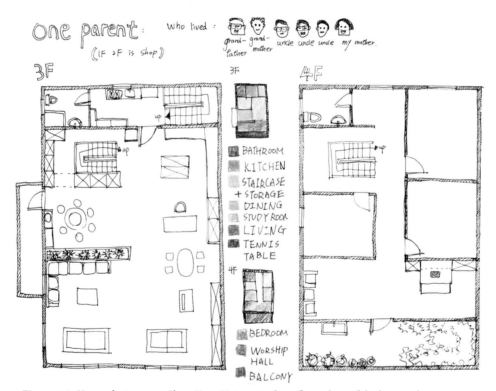

Figure 1-8: Young designers at Chun Yuan University drew floor plans of the house where a parent grew up. Most included a "god" or "worship" hall where the family could pay proper respect to deceased ancestors. These rooms typically contain a figure of a Taoist god and food offerings.

Figure 1-9: When envisioning their future home (10 years into the future) the designers did not make space for elder honoring. Instead they made space for a pet or friend.

Reflection

Each participant will experience the process differently. For this reason, the exercise should be performed with compassion and flexibility. The process can be calming, but it can also bring up painful memories. Group discussion can be revealing and dynamic, especially when members are sharing different cultural traditions or realizing shared experiences across cultures. However, some individuals may be very private about their responses. An individual can do this exercise many times and have different responses. It is a good exercise to do throughout your professional life.

Technique 1.5

FINDING YOURSELF IN THE CENSUS

Marcia J. McNally

In order to shed we first need to know what we are shedding. A straightforward way for designers to build self-awareness is to position themselves in the community they are entering. How does your demographic profile compare? Each of us embodies a quantifiable set of statistics—age, gender, income, ethnicity, household type, renter or property owner, and so on. In the United States, the American Fact Finder community profiles can be used to quickly work up a profile of the typical community member, the atypical community member, and where you would fit if you lived in that place. Taking things a step further, a designer can combine the profile with the physical reality of the community and compare it with design and planning standards for target amounts of open space, for example, to see how the profession would expect the place to measure up spatially versus what the community thinks it needs.

Instructions

1. Log on to American Fact Finder: http://factfinder.census.gov (other nations may have similar web-based census tools).

2. At the top of the page you will see "Community Facts." Enter the city/state where you live and hit "Go."

3. A list of data and tables you can look at will appear. Start with "General population and housing characteristics." Print it out. Do the same for the United States and for the state where you live.

4. Then go through steps 1–3 for the community where you are working.

5. Now answer the following questions:

   ■ If you had to describe your five most dominant demographic characteristics, what would they be?

   a.

   b.

   c.

   d.

   e.

   ■ Looking at the summaries for the community, state, and United States, what are the most interesting demographic "factoids" for the community? What story do they tell? Fill out the worksheet "Comparative Census Profile" to help put the characteristics in context.

Your Profile

Factoid	Community	State	US	Why interesting

The Community's Profile

Factoid	Community	State	US	Why interesting

6. Are there other things that you think would be important to take into consideration that cannot be found in this kind of data? If yes, list and indicate where you would find the missing information.

7. Now think about the place/landscape of the community. What are its important characteristics? How do they match up with best practice expectations of the "typical community"?

8. Merge the two—people and place. Do you think that given the "typical household profile" this community's place needs are well met? If there are a lot of young families, are there playgrounds where small children can play under the supervision of parents? If a large portion of the residents speak another language, are signs appropriately multilingual?

9. Bring your project into focus. If you were trying to use census data to design the perfect park in this community, for example, which pieces of information from these combined data would you use?

10. Bring your team together and discuss their answers.

Case Story

I have used this exercise when training community designers to formulate a hypothesis to shape their project. It was particularly useful at Smith College, an all-women's college located in Northampton, Massachusetts, in the context of a project to make proposals in the Ward 3 neighborhood. Census data helped the young designers see that Northampton differed from other communities in the state in terms of the high percentage of women residents and nonfamily households (in 2010 56.9 percent and 50.9 percent, respectively). How that played out in the ward, if at all, required further investigation.

Since the seventeenth century, Ward 3 has been an intricate mix of commerce and industry, varied housing types, farmland extending to the Connecticut River, two railroad tracks, creeks, woodlots, and several community and regional facilities. It is also gentrifying. As a result, residents are cautious about the City of Northampton's attempts to enact plans that embrace sustainable development principles because they unleash pressure to redevelop more densely and expensively, which challenges the ward's laid-back, funky style. Against this backdrop, the client, the City's Sustainability Committee, asked us to provide social-data-based proposals for the vacant lots that would meet the City's sustainability goals and fit the character of the place. Our team formulated design strategies about neighborhood open space needs versus desires and cross-checked with the City's sustainability goals and census data. Each team member chose an open space type, population, and geographic area and surveyed 100 percent of the housing units within their study area. Using the survey results and field data they made proposals for infill development that were sensitive to neighborhood needs.

Figure 1-10: At the studio review local members of the planning and design community questioned a team member's decision to minimize green space in her proposal. She had the data to show that residents of condominiums in the neighborhood felt adequately served.

One team member was interested in condominium households since they were atypical to Ward 3 but on the rise in Northampton at large. She was certain that the neighborhood would need more parks if it started to densify and this housing type was the one of the future. She learned from her survey that the typical condo household contained two people between 25 and 44 years old without children who moved to the neighborhood because of proximity to downtown. But different than her expectations and the norms for open space in medium-density neighborhoods, the occupants felt that the nearby bike trail satisfied their open space needs, they didn't need a park, and instead they wanted a place in the neighborhood to pick up daily necessities. Further, those surveyed felt strongly about new development staying in character with the old neighborhood form that had attracted them in the first place. She realized she had a park bias as a landscape student who grew up in a single-family neighborhood so she went back and looked at the spatial differences between the old, urban worker housing that was being condominiumized and the new and not-so-nice suburban condominiums being built. She joined forces with another team member, and together they proposed a mixed-use, spatial prototype that mimicked the neighborhood's historic ratio of greenspace to building on the site. Their proposal was endorsed and pursued by a local developer.

On the strength of this studio, the Landscape Studies Program at Smith was invited to keep working in Ward 3 and did so for three more years. The design students conducted a full-neighborhood survey about open space issues and developed a place-based open space hierarchy and strategy. One of the core participants was a city councilperson who used the team's work to initiate discussions about thorny planning issues as well as identify small open space interventions in the community. Another core participant was the principal of the elementary school. The data supported integrating the schoolyard with an adjacent pocket park and cemetery grounds for multiuse, multiage open space.

Reflection

The census technique can help designers (if they take the time to do the exercise) to match up residents and the community where they reside so as to find the gaps and think deeply about the idiosyncrasies of the place in comparison to the archetypal moves of design. In the case of the class, this systematic merging of population and place worked because we had an identifiable geography. It would not have worked if it were interest based, for example, if our client had been the local Sierra Club chapter. Further, application beyond the United States is unclear. From my own experience I know Taiwan has web-based census data (in English as well as in Chinese), but I haven't tried to access or use this type of data in other countries.

Chapter 1: Suiting Up to Shed   37

Technique 1.6

CONSUME, VEND, AND PRODUCE

Marcia J. McNally

Almost every project requires a designer to read space and people with reasoned and experienced objectivity. The goal of this technique is to stimulate the designer's thinking about space typology based simultaneously on both the designer's own daily life experiences and those of others. The focus here is on shopping spaces, but the technique can easily be applied to housing, parks, or other settings. It combines three different methods to produce a systematic and engaged way to look at built space and how people inhabit it—behavior observation, environmental autobiography, and the scored walk.

The technique is a two-step process. First the designer answers a series of questions about his or her shopping behavior. This can be done individually or as a team. The second part involves going on a shopping field trip together to look at different consuming environments to see if and how they vary, and whether they support the shopper, the seller, and the producer, and then to discuss the design and policy implications.

Instructions

1. Think about your "consuming" activities—activities to meet daily needs as well as leisure time—and fill in the worksheet "Consuming Profile" (page 39).
2. What things are important to you when you consume (check the five most important)?

    ___ convenience

    ___ price

    ___ quality

    ___ reputation of the business

    ___ I know the owner

    ___ atmosphere of the place

    ___ I can go with my friends

    ___ I can walk there

    ___ the products are locally produced (or organic or sustainable)

    ___ other (describe) _____

3. Consider your favorite places to shop and explain why you prefer these places.
4. Think back to your teenage years. What kinds of places did you go to for consuming when you were a young teenager? What were the characteristics? How do they differ from your current places?

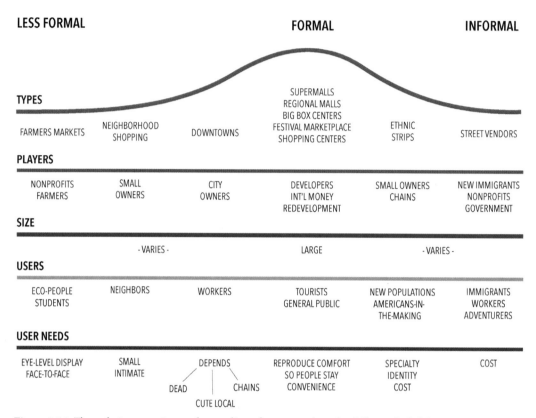

Figure 1-11: The technique requires understanding of space typology for different daily life activities, who makes space, and who uses it. This diagram introduces the concept.

5. Now consider the places listed in the worksheet "Consuming Venues" (page 40). Do you go to them? If so, why? If not, why not?

6. Prepare for the field trip. Select three to five different shopping area types from the list in the Consuming Venues worksheet. If you typically drive to consume, try to visit these places on foot or by using public transportation. In addition to your own habits, experiencing a range of settings is essential to getting the most out of this technique.

7. Create a field questionnaire so participants can document what people are doing, where they are doing it, and how the space supports or inhibits the activity; who the people are, what is being sold, and whether the place is formal or informal. Encourage analytical observation through sketches, cross sections, and measured drawings.

8. Be sure to eat a meal in one of these places, and take time to debrief with your team. Better yet, draw up rules of thumb or design implications for your commercial project.

"Consuming" activity	Time of day, day of week I do the activity	My needs at the time I am doing this activity	Place where I do this activity	Description of the place: spatial qualities, other people present, ambience, etc.
			s	

Venue	Do you shop here?		
	Yes/no	If yes, why?	If no, why not?
Convenience store			
Mall			
Grocery store			
Farmers' market			
Movie theater			
Online			
Flea market			
Downtown			
Student center			
"Superstore" (e.g., Target)			
Main Street			
Street vendors			
Restaurant			
Fast-food place			
Ethnic market			

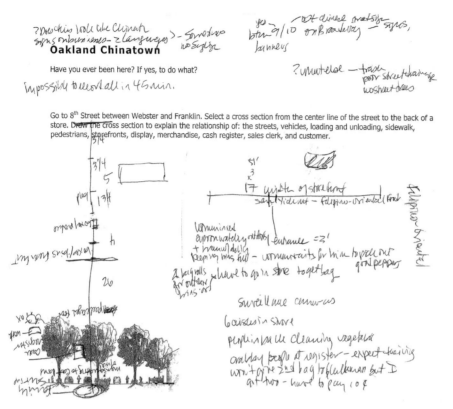

Figure 1-12: Field questionnaire and notes from a visit to Oakland Chinatown.

Case Story

I devised the technique when working with an organization of activist designers to write a book called *Blueprint for a Sustainable Bay Area*. As project manager my primary task was to create a process for participatory writing. After storyboarding the book with the group I organized "vision forums" for each of the chapters so that experts and members could discuss, debate, and experience the issues in real time. The chapter called "Old and Emerging Urban Centers" posed a particular challenge. In a region of 100 cities these districts were being repurposed and were reemerging as dynamic environments to which people were flocking for a host of reasons. To create new visions we needed to understand the range of centers— small town downtowns, "big box" retail malls, transit-oriented mixed-use nodes, and upcycled warehouse districts. In advance of the vision forum I found prototypes for each and then visited, taking notes, meeting with municipal planners, reading background material, and talking to friends who had worked on projects in the area. I contacted the local transit authority to help me figure out a schedule and route to link together the sites. I prepared a workbook for participants to fill out as we visited each site, and I prepared a script to lead the tour.

Vision forum participants loved the adventure of getting on the bus to see something in their backyard that was unknown. In situ we were able to evaluate what the real estate market was inclined to deliver and what it might take to intervene at the policy level. We then went on to identify more centers to profile in the book that exemplified the design and planning guidelines we wanted to promote—complex concentrations of space that support public life.

Reflection

I have found many applications for this technique over the years and used it in locations with different geographies and demographics. One use has been in a design course on social factors. A primary goal is to broaden the view of young designers about what constitutes recreation to include going out to eat and shop. Further, I want them to consider shopping districts as places where immigrant support networks can be found and identity is expressed. For example, close viewing of the shopping environments in different East Bay enclaves gave students at the University of California, Berkeley, a lot to think about because the places are home to dozens of different cultural groups. They visit Oakland's Chinatown,

Figure 1-13: Oakland Chinatown, a shopping district that spills out onto the sidewalk and street.

an organically evolved, traditional shopping street. It is a place where vegetables are sold along a cross section that starts inside the shop and extends out into the sidewalk all the way to the parking space in front, where vendors sell out of the back of a truck. They also go to Pacific East Mall in Richmond. The mall houses 99 Ranch Market, a big box grocery store featuring Asian food products, but it also includes restaurants, tax services, mobile phone services, travel agencies, boutiques, and beauty salons. The mall's website brags that it is "the best place for shopping, dining, and relaxing with families and friends." Both sites are lively, attracting consumers from all over the region and from many walks of life. They are both Chinatowns—just worlds apart in spatial form.

The technique requires that the leader have advanced knowledge of space types and local culture. It is an excellent way to learn about emerging populations in a region because they typically occupy unwanted space and convert it for their daily life needs. One key is preparation through self-analysis. The other is to create a tension between familiar behavior and analytic field experiences that yield discovery of the previously unconsidered. Looking at a range of types, or "containers" for familiar behaviors like consuming, provides training in objective space documentation because one has been prepared to look for what is expected and how the reality challenges expectations.

Figure 1-14: 99 Ranch Market in Richmond's Pacific East Mall.

2

Going to the People's Coming

Going to the people's coming is a way of thinking that invites us to get to know communities from within. It implores us to show up in the mundane places of everyday life so that we can experience them firsthand. In the process, we generate new knowledge by walking in other people's shoes, empathizing with their experiences, observing carefully, and sharing what we know and learn.

GOING AND COMING

Unlike the formal participation that requires citizens to show up for meetings and charrettes, going demands the direct participation of designers in the informal rhythms of community life. But going does not mean that we stop meeting; it is deliberately paired with people coming together in social settings. By going, we familiarize ourselves with people and place in context; by coming together, community members see those familiar places in a new light as they share their lived experiences with each other. As the techniques in this chapter demonstrate, the coupling of going and coming offers designers a way to begin a place-based design process with the greatest potential for discovery, collaboration, and empowerment.

THE POWER TO DICTATE PROCESS

As designers, we have an often-unacknowledged power to shape design processes. We know that, through our technical skills and positions within consultant teams, we make decisions that manifest themselves in the physical and social landscapes of communities. But when it comes to the design process itself, we also choose from differing approaches to community engagement, ranging from informative to radically empowering. The choices that we make shape our ability to understand the places where we work and the people who inhabit them. For example, we can start by gathering information about places by poring over maps and aerial photos, by reading demographic data, and by observing and documenting in person. Or we can learn about people by asking about their stories through focus groups, workshops, surveys, or informal conversations on the street. Both of these approaches are valid and can yield useful information, but if place and people are studied apart from each other, we can easily miss what makes them both tick. So how then do we start? We start by engaging people and place together, in context.

APPLYING ETHNOGRAPHY

The ethic that drives this approach for understanding culture and place is undeniably ethnographic, borrowing from long-established methods in anthropology. Ethnographers are often motivated by a sense of curiosity and respect; they pursue a kind of embedded knowledge derived from encountering a place, participating in its culture, and describing its internal dynamics and meanings. Designers who subscribe to this ethic start an engaged design process by seeking out firsthand experience, observing daily patterns, chatting with neighbors, walking together, drawing together, cooking together, and listening. As patterns and behaviors take on new meanings, designers add other dimensions by starting conversations about how places might change. Design is a tool that ethnographers rarely use, but as a form of participant observation, it deserves more consideration for its ability to open doors to new insights. The techniques here provide that consideration. By describing environmental conditions or introducing alternatives, designers provide stimulus that prompts reactions, evokes people's hopes and frustrations, and grounds narratives in place. By designing together, we learn together.

FUN AND GAMES, SERIOUSLY

As we see in the techniques that follow, the best outcomes are often realized by taking an oblique approach. Getting to know a community can involve creative scenarios that seem more like play than planning. Designers may set up games, provide food, or tempt passersby with music or spectacles, but more is happening than meets the eye. By actively and creatively engaging, designers interact with people who are normally missed by conventional outreach, but whose views are just as valuable. And by connecting through fun activities and everyday conversations, designers prepare themselves to approach difficult conversations and channel positive interactions into campaigns backed by local advocates that will sustain a project into the future. This is particularly important in places where community rapport is low or where relationships have been damaged from years of neglect or malfeasance.

TECHNIQUES FOR GOING, TECHNIQUES FOR COMING

Ethnography is often considered infeasible for practice because of the time required to undertake it. In anthropology this usually means a year or more of fieldwork alone. But many designers have succeeded in integrating its approaches in meaningful ways despite shorter time frames. In the first technique, Noah Billig admonishes designers to check their intentions and to "Start by Listening." In a similar vein, Hala Nassar and Paul Duggan introduce "Village Talk," which they observed in their fieldwork in Egypt, as a way to utilize the often-overlooked resource of informal conversations. Chelina Odbert and Joe Mulligan explain a technique they use with the Kounkuey Design Initiative that employs the "Community Camera," or *Piga Picha* as it is known in Nairobi, to learn about a community while simultaneously allowing locals to see and evaluate familiar places from a new perspective. Richard Alomar's "Sketching Together" adds a community dimension to the time-honored practice of drawing, as he challenges designers and community members, in this case homeless gardeners, to slow down, to see a place in person, and to reflect. "*El Carrito*," as explained by Javier Fraga Cadórniga and David de la Peña, subtly interrupts a community's everyday public spaces to provoke conversations and build rapport through the power of curiosity. Amanda Lovelee follows with a scaled-up motor vehicle for engagement—the "Pop Up Meeting" on wheels for the city of St. Paul, which literally brings the city meeting to the community and demonstrates how new voices can successfully be brought into public conversations with real outcomes. Taken together, these techniques help lay the groundwork for beginning a participatory design process that is embedded in local places and empathic with the people who are most affected by our work.

Technique 2.1

START BY LISTENING

Noah Billig

Transactive design often begins with a desire to help a community. As outsiders, we may perceive something to be missing or some way that our skills could be useful. However, if our efforts miss the larger picture of economic inequality, political power, and cultural practices, they can do more harm than good. This technique uses present, engaged listening to understand a community's needs and desires, providing a chance for participants to tell their stories without being prejudiced by a designer's assessments and intentions. By setting aside the designer's agenda, it creates space to understand a community's underlying values and to solicit direct, honest feedback. This knowledge, conscientiously interpreted, provides the designer with a framework to guide the next steps of action

Instructions

1. Write down your goals and objectives for the project. What potential outcomes do you envision for yourself, your collaborators, your client, project funders, and community participants?

2. Review the potential goals, objectives, and outcomes from step 1. Set these aside, acknowledging them, but do not let them drive the listening process.

3. Organize community meetings and locate them on people's own territory. Determine these locations through locals' recommendations and ask community members to help set up meetings if possible. Ideally these meetings are one-on-one, but cultural factors may require small groups.

4. Ask residents open-ended questions about issues directly related to their community as shown in the "Listening Questions" worksheet. Prepare questions ahead of the meeting, but allow for the likelihood that new questions will be generated on the spot as specific issues are discussed. Use input you have gathered from or about the community to formulate initial questions, and be careful to avoid leading questions that favor certain answers. Ask questions about the desirability of externally proposed projects only after exhausting open-ended queries.

5. Eliminate distractions that will prevent you and the participants from being totally in the moment. For example, turn off cell phones. If meetings are held in participants' territory (we strongly recommend this) then there may be a greater risk of being interrupted. Determine ahead of time what facilities and settings will be

---

WORKSHEET 2-1: LISTENING QUESTIONS

Sample questions to facilitate a general discussion about participants' community

What do you like about your community?

What do you think could be improved in your community?

Can you tell me stories or examples about what it means to be part of your community?

Sample questions to facilitate open dialogue with residents about a specific issue, in this case their open spaces

Are you satisfied with the amount and types of open spaces in your neighborhood?

Can you tell me any stories about the kinds of activities that occur in your neighborhood's open spaces?

What types of open spaces are you mostly satisfied with in your neighborhood?

What types of open spaces are you mostly unsatisfied with?

What would you like to see added to existing open spaces?

What types of open spaces would you like to see added?

Is there anything else you would like to talk about or think I should know?

---

used. If it is possible and culturally appropriate to meet in a quiet outdoor space or a quiet room, then suggest that as an option.

6. Remind yourself that this total presence is where authenticity is established, so make certain you have ample time. The amount of time will vary depending on context, but do not let time be your focus or a distraction.

7. Summarize your day's work on a daily basis. Evaluate the findings from the listening activities. It is helpful to organize the interview findings into common themes, including shared wants and needs of the community (for example, priorities for development and preferences for open space amenities).

8. Reevaluate the goals, objectives, and outcomes from the first steps. Has your agenda-free, present listening changed these outcomes? Although you likely had at least a general agenda of helping make a better place, remain open to the possible conclusion that your services might not be needed for the project intended.

9. Determine how to apply the results to the design project.

Case Story

I used this technique when I studied three informal settlements in Istanbul: Karanfilköy, Fatih Sultan Mehmet, and Pınar. My initial studies evaluated open space typologies and activities in order to understand the neighborhoods' open space needs. The studies revealed a rich sociocultural landscape, where the spaces on and near the street were used for a variety of social, domestic, and economic activities. After learning from these initial studies, I intended to design landscape interventions to help the communities address what I perceived as a lack of large open green spaces. However, before I designed anything I decided to ask residents about their specific neighborhood needs. This involved listening in residents' yards, in houses, on the streets, in shops, and in the mosque.

It became clear through my conversations with residents that the community did not necessarily need or want new open spaces. They wanted policy interventions to protect their neighborhoods, which are continually under threat of redevelopment that would displace their strong networks. I knew that policy interventions were beyond my expertise. However, I could help the community document the qualities of their neighborhood design and show why those arrangements and uses are valuable. My project subsequently changed from physical redesign to documenting the neighborhoods' existing spatial–social–cultural

Figure 2-1: Meeting neighborhood residents in their spaces and on their terms. This family was forthcoming about their relatively high satisfaction with their open spaces in the Fatih Sultan Mehmet community.

Figure 2-2: A neighborhood walking tour suggested and provided by a local family, which revealed nuanced uses and satisfaction of their open spaces in the Pınar community.

patterns and processes. This documentation of the community networks that are essential for everyday life became a new advocacy tool for the neighborhood and a learning tool for other designers and planners. This better addressed the communities' needs and desires than my initial, well-intentioned objectives for creating more open space, and it has hopefully helped the communities to preserve the qualities and patterns that sustain their everyday life.

Reflections

Community designers need to be open to the possibility that their intended services might not be needed or that other services are critical. This realization can be disheartening for designers committed to a community development outcome. It can also wreak havoc on design projects. This is one risk of the technique. However, knowing when to step away or where to step differently is a form of wisdom worth pursuing. To avoid design missteps, designers can start by listening and remaining open to opportunities that they had not imagined on their own.

Technique 2.2

VILLAGE TALK

Hala Nassar and Paul Duggan

Successful participatory design depends on effective communication, and public participation often involves dialogue between unequal and perhaps incompatible groups. Differences in education, vocabulary, social background, or goals can create tensions that undermine people's efforts to hear each other clearly. To bridge these differences, designers must study the ways people communicate and make strategies of participation that fit local conditions. Since residents themselves are a critical source of information, creative ideas, and design solutions, their input is essential. Fortunately, a type of verbal communication, village talk, already takes place in communities. It is a pattern of everyday life that speaks about things in ways that one never hears in formal meetings. It can be harnessed to improve the communication and thereby increase the effectiveness of participatory design.

By listening to village talk the designer learns different things from the community and can subsequently create a design that fits the local context. This method works best when designers utilize straightforward, ordinary, and everyday conversational styles with people. It requires that designers spend adequate time in the field gathering information and perspectives from local residents. Its goal is to enable designers to discover and understand the meaning of local experiences, histories, and critical contexts from an insider's perspective, and to identify unanticipated, and otherwise unknown, conditions. In other words, listening to village talk can enable designers to become participants in the ongoing community conversations.

Instructions

1. Familiarize yourself with basic ethnographic research methods. A good place to start would be works by anthropologists and sociologists like Clifford Geertz, James Clifford, Philippe Bourgois, or Galen Cranz.

2. Identify relevant neighborhoods and local groups that you will focus on.

3. Partner with reliable gatekeepers who can open doors to communicate with locals.

4. Make careful site observations through walking tours, activity mapping, memos, photos, and a review of relevant documents. Pay special attention to the casual conversations you encounter along the way. Keep a record of these observations and conversations in your field notes.

5. Build from the informal village conversations by identifying locals who are willing to talk more. Conduct face-to-face interviews that are semistructured or open-ended in order to allow locals to influence the topics being discussed, and take care

to select interview settings that are comfortable for the interviewees. People are more likely to open up when they are on their own turf or in a neutral place, such as a coffee shop or a quiet plaza. Ask for permission before you record interviews or take names.

6.   Review interviews and field notes through sorting, categorizing, coding, and analysis. Allow themes to emerge from the data you have collected.

7.   Craft relevant summaries and interpretations of the data. Use the knowledge you gained through village talk as a basis for design options and return to the community to test your conclusions and solutions.

Case Story

In the Egyptian village of El-Gourna, we used village talk to understand how people felt about the relocation of their town and to plan to meet their needs in the new village. The village was made up of world-class artisans and farmers. It had been settled 250 to 300 years earlier on the dry, sandy limestone ascent of the Theban Mountains, on the east bank of the Nile and opposite the ancient capital of Thebes (modern Luxor). The residences were built in an area known as the Tombs of the Nobles and consisted of about 3,000 families that inhabited 24 irregular building clusters, hamlets, and family compounds. Unfortunately, many of the structures were constructed atop tombs of priceless archaeological value. From 2005 to 2010, with resident approval, the village was relocated to a new site less than 4 kilometers (2.5 miles) away. We conducted interviews, held group meetings, studied documents, had casual conversations, made site observations, took photos, and participated in local village life to inform the move.

Figure 2-3: View of Old Gourna on the ascent to the mountains on the West Bank of the Nile.

Figure 2-4: Family gathers in the early evening in front of their new home.

As we gathered information, we perceived patterns of communication occurring at three levels that had their own communicative formats: administrative and executive meetings, public meetings, and informal communication between residents at various local venues. The last of these, which is village talk, emerged as respondents described how they received information and how they communicated with one another. It was a much richer source of local information than the other more standard and formal formats. As we involved ourselves in village talk, villagers told us about the unique environmental and cultural factors involved in new home design, the economic and cultural underpinnings of village life, the need for access to tourist venues and supplies for local crafts, and the personal, emotional impact of the relocation on families and their livelihoods.

In reality, village talk was the most active form of communication about everyday life patterns that were critical in designing the new village. It occurred whenever residents got together to share news or just to spend time together. It took place in the streets, at markets, in cafes and restaurants, at the mosques and *diwans* (town councils), and every night in front of peoples' homes with residents, relatives, neighbors, and guests seated on *mastaba* (stone) benches. It was especially useful because as people talked to us they could show us specific spatial patterns that were difficult to describe abstractly. All of these venues were

Figure 2-5: Design team engaging local residents in village talk.

easily accessed, and in fact villagers were eager to share their insights and experiences. The result was that we had access to a rich source of local information, all of which was essential for the preparation of a suitable village design.

Reflection

Whether at local or regional scales, planning issues often involve complicated problems at various levels of policy and communication that are intrinsically bound up with and influence each other in complex ways. Each level—administrative, public meetings, and informal village talk—serves important purposes. Socially suitable, successful design, however, almost always seems to depend on favorable outcomes at the most local level. The benefits of village talk as part of the design process and as a rich source of ideas and design solutions can be easily overlooked if participation is restricted to formal meetings and does not recognize informal gatherings and venues as sources of local knowledge.

Technique 2.3

COMMUNITY CAMERA: *PIGA PICHA*

Chelina Odbert and Joe Mulligan

Community Camera (or *Piga Picha*) is a photo activity used to help residents introduce their community to an outside project team, and in the process, to see familiar places through a new lens. It is most effective at the beginning of a project process. The activity works well in design-build, open space, and community planning initiatives because it allows a multidisciplinary team to quickly learn the physical, social, and political landscapes of a neighborhood.

The activity asks teams of residents and/or other stakeholders to work together to select and capture, in five photos, important places in their neighborhood. This activity's strength is in its simplicity. Fun, active, and low pressure, *Piga Picha* is not intended to comprehensively map or catalog a community; rather, it is meant to break the ice and initiate informal and semistructured conversations about multiple topics, such as priority needs of a community, presence/absence of public space, character and quality of existing spaces, materials preferences, and potential locations for a design or intervention.

Instructions

1. Provide one digital camera per group, a computer, a portable photo printer, a poster-sized map of the area, poster-sized paper, markers, and tape. If power is not available, the activity can be done with Polaroid cameras (yes, they still exist!).

2. Thoughtfully divide participants into groups (by age, gender, subneighborhood, or at random); different grouping methods will yield very different outcomes. The ideal group size is 4 to 6 and should not exceed 10. If there are enough project team members, one member should join each group as a neutral participant.

3. Give each group a camera and a sheet of paper on which is written the following prompt: Please take one photo of each of the following places in your community/neighborhood:

   - The most beautiful place (to understand materials preferences)

   - The place you go to be with friends (to understand character and quality of existing public spaces)

   - The place you go to celebrate (to identify public spaces)

   - The place most in need of improvement (to identify potential project sites)

   - The place you go to be alone (to acknowledge the presence/absence of intimate spaces)

4. Guidelines are intentionally kept flexible, but the following details should be explained for clarity and consistency among groups:

   ■ Groups are to set out on foot and return one hour later.

   ■ Groups must reach consensus on which location to photograph for each of the five places.

   ■ Groups can either share photography duties or select one photographer.

   ■ Photos will be presented to the larger group; thus photographers should capture enough of the place to be understood by the audience.

5. *Piga Picha*! Take photos!

6. Upon return, collect photo cards from each group and immediately print them on the portable printer, then have each group post their photos on the poster that corresponds to the place prompt. During the time it takes to process the pictures, groups can identify and map the location of their five photos on a poster-sized map of the area.

7. Have each group elect a spokesperson to present the group's photos and explain how and why each was selected. The facilitator and members of the other groups ask follow-up questions about each place. The facilitator looks for opportunities to open up discussions around issues of interest, where relevant. The facilitator also keeps a tally of the selections in each category to identify where there is overlap or consensus between groups.

8. Ask each group for observations about the activity and group dynamics, then explain how the activity will be used as the project develops.

Case Story

The Kounkuey Design Initiative team designed and used *Piga Picha* for the first time in 2006 in Kibera, a large urban slum in Nairobi, Kenya. We wanted to understand the community's priority needs, constraints, and opportunities for a public space project that we were developing together. We gathered in a family compound and divided roughly 30 participants into three groups—youth (mostly men under 30), women (primarily mothers, 30 and older), and men (from 30 to 80)—and gave each group a disposable camera. In 2006, cameras and smartphones were still rare in Kibera, and everyone wanted a turn to try. The simple act of trying to figure out the camera created a light, humorous mood and gave project team members an early peek into the group dynamics (e.g., who are the teachers, leaders, most vocal, etc.).

Project team members were invited into many unexpected places during the hour of exploration—places that we would not otherwise have thought to visit, nor have had the opportunity to visit until much later in the project process, including residents' homes,

Figure 2-6: Members of the *Piga Picha* women's group describe the place they go to be alone.
Source: Kounkuey Design Initiative.

polluted waterways, neighborhood schools, overgrown swamplands, and local pubs. We developed the disposable cameras overnight and reconvened the next day. When people had the opportunity to view the pictures they had taken, it was clear they were seeing very familiar sites from a new perspective—as spaces worthy of design consideration. The ensuing debate and discussion were so rich and animated that the conversations continued a long time after we'd finished the formal exercise.

For the project team, this activity was essential. We were so new to Kibera that, without this activity, we would have spent many more days with our misconceptions or limited understanding of how things worked. *Piga Picha* quickly introduced us to a range of different topics and helped residents become familiar and comfortable with us and our intentions. Though we would go on to do several other workshops to further define and refine needs and project location and size, it turned out that the final, community-selected project site was the site identified by a majority of the *Piga Picha* groups as "most in need of fixing."

Reflection

The beauty of Community Camera is in the informal interactions it creates—participants getting to know one another while walking together, the questions you ask that spark heated and productive conversation, the excitement people have when they take you to a particular place,

Figure 2-7: Residents assess the potential of a trash-filled site in Silanga, Kibera, in 2007 that later became Kibera Public Space Project 01. Source: Kounkuey Design Initiative.

Figure 2-8: Kibera Public Space Project 01 after design intervention. The site integrates physical remediation with social and economic functions to create a productive public space in the heart of Kibera. Source: Kounkuey Design Initiative.

the healthy debate that takes place when the group has to decide on just one place to photograph—these interactions set the stage for a more open, collaborative, and fun design process.

There is also something disarming about the activity that allows the designer, resident, and local official to swap roles for a minute and redistribute "authority." This reconfiguration of power provokes genuine exchanges, not based on pretense, which can set the tone for subsequent parts of the project process. *Piga Picha* seems to work well in different contexts—rural and urban, developing and developed.

Technique 2.4

SKETCHING TOGETHER

Richard Alomar

Sketching Together with a community is an activity that takes advantage of multiple modes of communication to document a group's attitudes and perceptions about the place and activities they share. Working with a small group of 10 to 20 people, the technique helps designers gather direct impressions about a proposed or ongoing project. Sketching Together promotes an informal mode of interaction that, over a few weeks' time, can create bonds of trust between designers and community members and provide information and insights not accessible through formal processes. Sketching combined with writing enables some people to describe things that are difficult for them to express in words alone. In addition the sketchbooks provide a valuable record of everyday thoughts and actions in a form that can help resolve conflicts and continue to inform a project's course.

Instructions

1. Give each participant a sketchbook and pen. Sketchbooks should be inexpensive and small, no larger than 4 by 6 inches, to avoid any semblance of an art sketchbook. Encourage participants to identify and personalize their own book as they wish and to bring in additional sketching tools, such as markers and colored pencils, if they want.

2. The designer should also maintain a sketchbook to become familiar with the process, to understand the benefits and constraints of group sketching, and to record impressions and participant conversations during the sketching sessions.

3. Direct participants to describe and record in their sketchbooks what they did that day, in words or images. Make sure the participants feel free to use whatever mode or form of expression suits them best. As a multimodal form of communication, this form of sketching in community is distinguished from a drawing or mapping exercise used to gather spatial information for a design.

4. Distribute the sketchbooks at the beginning of each session and collect them at the end of the day so the designer can scan the day's input. The work from each session is saved and tagged with the date and the participant's name.

5. Maintain close proximity between participants and designers during the sketching session, either around a table or sitting in a circle, side-by-side or face-to-face. The sessions should last 20 to 30 minutes to allow time to sketch, write, and talk. The designer can adjust the duration of the session. The goal is to provide enough time

to settle into the practice and allow for fluidity between sketchbook entries and conversation.

6. Be consistent. Trust, confidence, and fluidity grow over time, so it's important to schedule the sessions frequently, over a minimum of several months or until the group can continue on its own.

7. Lead discussions, asking participants to explain their drawings.

8. Review the sketchbooks and systematically record observations and expressions about the project or site. Scanned images or excerpts may be useful for further design stages, but make sure you have permission to share the participants' work.

9. You may use the scanned sketchbook sheets for a variety of purposes depending on your project. Evaluating the participants' preference for text or images, along with the content itself, can give insight into how they communicate ideas and feelings, which subjects they wrote about, and how they experienced an activity.

Case Story

Sketching Together was an important component of the Healthy Garden and Healthy Living project, a collaboration of Robert Wood Johnson Medical School; Elijah's Promise, a local organization that alleviates hunger through training, education, and social services; and the Rutgers University Department of Landscape Architecture. The project sought to understand the potential for community gardening to improve health of underserved individuals through gardening and food-related activities, with sketching and health screening as two key methods to assess impact. Participants were primarily homeless or previously homeless individuals who utilized Elijah's Promise soup kitchen and health services. They received modest stipends as an incentive for participation.

The sketchbook kept track of attendance, activities, and impressions. During the course of two to three weekly 30-minute sessions, over 16 weeks, the technique recorded the participants' attitudes toward work, gardening, the project, and each other. The loosely structured activity of "draw or write about what you did today" started with participants roaming the garden, looking for "things to draw," and evolved into them sitting in a common space to draw, write, talk, and discuss the day's work. In the sketchbook entries issues regarding pay and work were frequently raised. In one instance a participant who came late to the program started working on the compost pile. The person who had been working on the pile felt that the newcomer was taking credit for his work. Based on his sketchbook entries we made sure to publicly acknowledge his effort. The sketchbooks also provided valuable input with respect to our project management, most notably about our lack of clarity with respect to when participants would receive their stipends.

Figure 2-9: Gardeners gather for a sketching session at Elijah's Promise Garden.

The sketching technique in our project provided us with a measure of insight into the utility and shortcomings of the project that were not readily available through the project's existing evaluation structure. For example, the confusion over stipend payments was expressed only through sketching. This led to scheduled group update meetings and alternative sources of payment funding. We were also able to address the "who did what" issue to help improve the group dynamic.

Reflection

Sketchbooks and journals are often used by designers to document observations and impressions. Sketching Together takes this further and stimulates communication and reflection within the group. The informality of the technique's execution and its multiple modes of communication allow for an information-rich collection of participants and thoughts. It can be incorporated in multiple types of settings and with diverse groups.

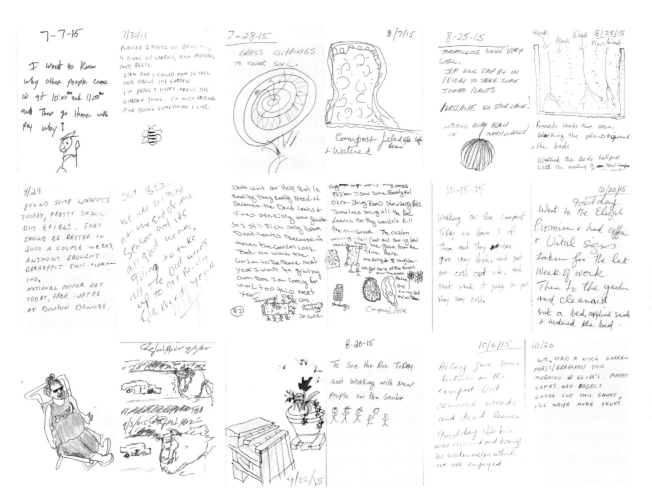

Figure 2-10: Writing and drawing examples can be analyzed to better understand participant views about the project, themselves, and others.

Technique 2.5

EL CARRITO: ROLLING OUT THE CART

Javier Fraga Cadórniga and David de la Peña

The *carrito* is a mobile interactive meeting point that catches people's attention as they move through public spaces. It is a versatile tool for passersby to participate and intervene in various design and planning projects, and it allows designers to get in touch with the people who actually use that public space. The word *carrito* is the Spanish translation of the French *charrette*, which is now associated with standardized design workshops. But in this Spanish iteration, the *carrito* takes participation out of the controlled meeting room and into the streets where the people are.

The *carrito's* power derives from the simple act of introducing a benign disturbance into everyday space. The object itself is a compelling art piece that attracts people because it is out of the ordinary. In a location that slightly disrupts but becomes part of the community's rhythms, on the edges of the flows of everyday life, it can be deployed on a temporary basis, or repeatedly. When carefully planned, it attracts more than the "usual suspects" that appear in most charrettes, reaching a larger and more diverse audience. Most importantly, the *carrito* flips the tables, taking experts out of their comfort zones, opening new ways for them to understand the communities they are acting within, and promoting new opportunities for exchange, reflection, and debate.

Instructions

1. Treat the design and construction of a *carrito* as a team-building exercise. The making of a *carrito* expresses one's attitude toward form-making, requiring some construction skills, but allowing every member of a design team to contribute.

2. Design the *carrito* to best meet the project's needs. Although there are many different possibilities, the most flexible *carrito* will be simple, light, sturdy, and easy to handle. It should be an attractive and unusual object so that it will not go unnoticed in a busy public space. It should also have a flat surface at a suitable height to be used as a table, and it should contain a space to store materials when it is not in use. Other possibilities, such as integrating screens or other gadgets, may be considered as the project demands.

3. Build a *carrito* with care and with an artisan's touch. Avoid making it too slick or polished. An imperfect object may be more approachable to passersby. Using recycled materials assembled in an understandable manner reinforces the notion that public space is created best with local resources. An inexpensive *carrito* can be

Figure 2-11: A used crate that once held a Joan Miró painting turns into a participatory device in Barcelona. This *carrito* was built in 2015 for the Miró Foundation to understand why residents of the neighborhood of Poble Sec felt disconnected from the nearby museum, and to propose new activities to foster openness. Source: Raons Públiques.

assembled in this way for very little money; otherwise a *carrito* can be built from new parts for no more than the price of a decent bicycle.

4. Prepare materials to accompany the *carrito*. Just as important as the device itself are the props that stimulate conversations, including maps, models of the project area, data sheets, surveys, flyers, or educational materials. If children will be present, include games or other activities so that their input can also be incorporated.

5. Plan a process for bringing the *carrito* into the neighborhood. Determine dates, schedules, locations, target audiences, and people in charge of each outing. Make sure everyone is familiar with the area and has walked around the site at different times of day. Previous knowledge of the study area will allow for more accurate planning, foreseeing the profiles of passersby (according to locations and times) and facilitating the design of the activities.

6. Enjoy the swirl of activity and conversations that ensue. You may find yourself in a square, pushing a strange object, full of questions, suggestions, and proposals to create and (probably) become the center of attention.

Case Story

We belong to a group of community urbanists in Barcelona called Raons Públiques. We are made up of environmental designers, anthropologists, sociologists, and educators dissatisfied with conventional opaque urban planning practices. We emphasize diagnosis and dialogue—getting to know a neighborhood in order to design its spaces transactively. For us, the *carrito* has been an innovative tool that empowers communities to make decisions about their own public spaces.

In our work, we often invite people to talk and reflect about their neighborhoods by using temporary interventions. We set up playgrounds, play street games drawn on the ground with chalk, distribute handouts where participants can suggest activities, help draw ideas, or set up outdoor cinemas. We first invented the *carrito* for an urban planning workshop in Sospel, a small town in the south of France; it was a way to connect villagers with workshop participants and to collect and display the artifacts we had created. The end result was a versatile, mobile, and striking element that toured the village for 15 days in search of residents' opinions. The *carrito* met this objective and more—it became a meeting point for neighbors and designers to exchange ideas and served as a support for a wide variety of discussions and celebrations.

We have since implemented a more mature version of this device in many different projects. A new version was used in 2014 in the project *Quina Gràcia?* (Whose Gràcia?), a participatory process to design public space in the District of Gràcia in Barcelona. In this case, the technique had three clear objectives: to provide information about the project and its proposed regulations, to call for participation in various meetings, and to collect information and viewpoints about the project. We conducted 13 outings in 11 different locations (five squares, two markets, and four metro stations), in which 130 people were reached and 29 of them registered into upcoming debates. In every outing, which lasted between one and a half to two hours, the *carrito* was guided by two people with a high degree of knowledge about the project and the regulation proposals. The *carrito* outings provided some key insights into how Gràcia residents perceived their public spaces. Through informal conversations, several themes emerged, were documented, and were put to use by local officials, including the negative impact of tourism on the daily life of the neighborhood, the loss of the connective tissue of small shops, the rising cost of housing, and the value of mutual respect and cultural diversity in the neighborhood's streets and plazas.

Reflection

After using this technique on several projects, it is clear that the *carrito* is a useful way of approaching a neighborhood and its citizens. By engaging the public in the context of its everyday public space, the *carrito* helps reach a much wider diversity of people and gathers more accurate and interesting information. The limitation comes about when we try to

Figure 2-12: In 2010, working with L'Atelier Sans Tabou, we took our first *carrito* to the streets of Sospel, France, for an urban development workshop, seeking out conversations with residents engaged in their daily routines.

Figure 2-13: Over time the *carrito* becomes a meeting place for daily dialogue. Source: Raons Públiques.

extrapolate this information to the city at large, considering that there is no statistical accuracy in the sample that could allow for a general conclusion to be produced. Although the data it collects cannot be said to be representative, neither is the alternative of the charrette. More importantly, the *carrito* creates more meaningful transactions between designers and members of the public. It brings designers into the everyday spaces of a neighborhood, and it also begins to transform those public spaces into stages for positive dialogue. As a testament to the usefulness of this technique, the city of Barcelona recently commissioned 10 *carritos* based on our model for its own use in its general plan update. We look forward to seeing how this inexpensive little tool continues to evolve, and how it sparks new thinking about participatory planning.

Technique 2.6

POP UP MEETING

Amanda Lovelee

Public meetings often draw few residents. They take place in multipurpose rooms, at City Hall, in the evenings. They assume everyone works a 9–5 job, has transportation, child care, and the desire to endure long meetings. Pop Up Meeting diversifies participation by going to the people with an artistically retrofitted vehicle, dynamically unfolding as the city's roaming front porch to engage communities with flexible civic encounters that appeal to residents and accommodate their needs. It goes where it is most useful—to shopping centers, libraries, or anywhere with space to park a van. As an added incentive, participants receive locally made treats from an accompanying, cheerful pushcart.

Pop Up Meeting demonstrates how the city values citizens by making participation fun, inclusive, quick, and productive. It is also demonstrably effective at expanding engagement from those who typically show up at meetings to those who are busy living life in the places that are being planned for.

Instructions

1. Prepare a vehicle. The design of a vehicle can be highly involved and costly, or it can also be simple and improvisational. Vehicle magnets and instant canopies can suffice in a pinch, but make sure the end result is colorful, fun, and attractive.

2. Prepare yourself. Involve neighborhood representatives to help you get to know the community and its issues.

3. Pick the right people to go. This includes a content expert or project manager, enthusiastic and outgoing staff members, a neighborhood representative, and translators if needed.

4. Design the props. Use visual aids (e.g., plans, photos, maps) to draw attention and explain the relevant project. Additional furnishings, a cart, tables, umbrellas, signs, or toys should be designed together to create a cohesive ambience of fun to draw in curious passersby.

5. Prepare your data-gathering tools. Remember that this information will be used to inform the planning of actual projects. Participants may fill out carefully considered surveys, or they may annotate maps, vote on different options, or just chat with organizers. Make sure these data are recorded and saved for later use.

6. Pick a place and go to the residents. Offer Pop Up Meetings at different times of day and in a variety of locations and event types to engage with different crowds.

Places of everyday activity work best to involve folks going about their business. Or, alternatively, take the meeting to the place being planned.

7. Interact with people. Instruct staff to make conversations personable and quick. The task can be as simple as asking passersby to stop and fill out a survey, answer questions, and continue on with their day.

8. Give something back. Offer something to people who stop and participate. A Popsicle does not cost money to the participant, but neither is it a free giveaway. An exchange happens between staff and participants, and the treat is a simple way of saying thank you. It is remarkable how well this generates goodwill.

9. Use the feedback you receive. Document who participates and prepare summaries of the outreach along with participant input on the project.

10. Continue to meet as normal. Pop Up Meeting is not meant to replace, but rather to augment, conventional planning tools. By offering more ways for people to engage, a broader range of opinions can be represented in the process.

Figure 2-14: Pop Up Meeting seeks to increase diversity and participation in Saint Paul's urban planning process. The meeting dynamically engages communities and customizes civic meetings based on place and stakeholder needs. Source: Tiffany Bolk.

Case Story

I developed Pop Up Meeting in 2013 as the City Artist for Public Art Saint Paul and have administered the program for major city initiatives, planning, and design projects. In the summer of 2015, we held 17 meetings at different scales in different neighborhoods for a variety of projects. We hosted one event at an intersection along a bike and pedestrian path at a dangerous intersection where new paths were being planned. In just two hours on one afternoon, we spoke with approximately 25 people who used the path daily and were able to explain the problems they encountered with more detail than would have been possible in a typical meeting. We also hosted a Pop Up at a busy neighborhood festival where we asked residents what they wanted to see in the mayor's budget. In under an hour, with the mayor and staff by our side, we collected about 250 questionnaires and gave away over 300 Popsicles. In this case we reached a demographic in the city that was underrepresented in our planning process. Whereas most city outreach events expend great effort at advertising events to attract people to come to them, we found that the element of surprise was our secret weapon; in fact, unpublicized events drew a crowd that might not otherwise participate.

During this first summer of Pop Up Meeting, we diligently collected data to evaluate the program's effectiveness, and the results were impressive. The Pop Up Meetings consistently attracted an average of 24 percent more participants than the city's conventional meetings. Of the people we engaged, 70 percent had never before been to a city meeting (compared with 25 percent at a typical meeting), and 71 percent felt the Pop Up was an easy way for them to engage. Those who engaged also came from diverse backgrounds. Whereas we noted that in our typical meetings most attendees were over age 50 (and hardly any under 25 or persons of color), Pop Up participants reflected the diverse neighborhood demographics of the event locations. Staff members documented racially mixed crowds, people on lunch breaks, professionals, younger families, dog walkers—a full range of citizens engaged in everyday life. These were the people we wanted to hear from but had been unable to involve in formal meetings.

Figure 2-15: The meeting visually and comprehensibly shares the ideas and responses of community members. In exchange for their thoughts and survey responses to the city, participants receive a locally made St. Pops ice pop. Source: Tiffany Bolk.

Reflection

Saint Paul's Pop Up Meeting has been a resounding success as an addition to the city's usual planning processes. Through experimentation and adaptation, we have refined our process to be as fruitful as possible. Overall we have found that the Pop Up technique still requires about as much time as conventional meetings, but with far more diverse results. Pop Up Meeting has been an important signal that the city cares about community voices, and it has shown that community members also care deeply about planning processes—we only need to find innovative ways to allow them to engage.

3

Experting: They Know, We Know, and Together We Know Better, Later

Every community has experts with primary knowledge of the social, cultural, political, and physical environment they live in. Yet people typically recognized as "the experts"—especially during design work—tend to be from outside the community. The knowledge these outside experts possess is usually based on secondary information and best practice norms. It is not generated within the community itself. Being aware that valuable knowledge lies with people *within* the community, and that these people can be great resources for designers, is critical to transactive and transformative design.

EXPERTS IN AND OUT

Experting gives equal value to and acknowledgment of the information and skills of all parties to ensure an authentic process that makes room for co-defining the problem and co-generating new information. It provides an approach that engages community members to use their knowledge and skills, enabling them to fully understand the implications of what they know about a landscape and how impactful that knowledge can be. In time this makes them more effective in problem solving because it shifts the focus from a onetime physical-solutions outcome to one that builds local capacity over the long term.

A Tradition of Devaluing Local Knowledge

This efficacy has been slow yet radical, particularly in acknowledging the wealth of expertise held by communities of color and other marginalized people. As Frederick Law Olmsted observed in his investigation of the southern states, African slaves were extremely knowledgeable about weather and seasonal patterns, plants, the land, the landscape, and building, which gave the slaves' toiling its specific value in the production process. Yet owners perpetuated the belief that their slaves were less than human creatures that knew nothing outside of what they were told to do. Brutality and punishment were the methods used to extract knowledge and skills, and the perpetual ritualizing of slavery as "forced labor" distorted who knew what about cotton, sugar, tobacco, and rice farming in the American landscape. The cultural remnants of slavery's belief system are as pervasive as ever, including in design practices that continue to devalue and usurp-sans-acknowledgment the environmental and placed-based knowledge of the many communities of color found in the United States today. Similarly colonialism and the acquisition and use of formal titles everywhere diminish the value of local wisdom.

Co-producing Local Knowledge for Higher-Quality Design

As professionals we often assume that community members can only contribute their personal perceptions and values, but resident knowledge of circumstances, events, relationships, and unique characteristics of place and their meaning almost always leads to higher-quality design. Often a community member is the leader of the collective creativity, producing the design itself with minimal professional help. Experting in community design recognizes and acknowledges local expertise, follows local guidance, and takes cues throughout the design process. Sustainable projects emerge with real partners because all can take credit for the knowledge base of collaborative work. The techniques are similar to the co-production model Jason Coburn put forth in *Street Science: Community Health and Environmental Health Justice*, which describes a process of environmental health research and decision making in Brooklyn, New York. After the community questioned the US Environmental Protection Agency's risk assessment framework, government representatives and the community worked together to design an investigation that combined professional research methods with the deep understanding of the daily life experience of residents. Local knowledge and professional expertise were given equal weight; local and professional knowledge were challenged and negotiated. The technical baseline changed, and political decisions about solutions changed.

How Far Is the Future? For Real?

The process of experting focuses more on discovery and knowledge exchange than other community design processes. Others are often organized according to structures of criticism of the existing condition followed by visions and ending with a plan for implementation. Depending on the community, the utilization of *existing* resources, emphasized in experting, rather than future visions that seem far-reaching for people focused on daily survival, can be essential for engagement. This expands inclusionary design so that it becomes truly transactional. Focusing on existing resources goes beyond the involvement of users in the design to include claiming ownership of the solution through the exchange of knowledge. This can be achieved with commitment if the skills and knowledge of the community are given value and considered essential to the process.

Transferring Expertise for the Long Term

Employing the variety and depth of skills that the community possesses can be beneficial to the short-term design but also creates stewards who are responsible for the project long after facilitators, consultants, and designers have gone. Another advantage of transactive design that transfers the title of *expert* to members of the community is that it provides the opportunity to develop empowering outcomes. When we as designers undertake an experting process in an underrepresented community, we too often aim simply to provide a solution to a physical problem that meets users' needs. But we might just as readily aim to build local human capacity so that future decisions regarding the built and natural environment can take place without a dependency on outside experts taking the lead.

Techniques for Experting

The techniques included in this chapter showcase methods to gain an understanding of a community and its history through the engagement of community experts. They also present ways to share design methods and expertise to increase the use of local knowledge in a manner that demonstrates mutual respect between community and designers. The techniques also include activities created to tap into expertise that citizens may not know they have. Or activities could reveal important expertise that citizens at first didn't value as contributing to the design or development process but that is key to developing resilient and sustainable solutions. The techniques lay out how to create a forum for citizens to share their skills, communicate their own ideas, and engage in the design process and problem solving with confidence. "Cellphone Diaries" from Kofi Boone is a technique that allows communities to celebrate and share their knowledge and points of view. Austin Allen's "Mining the Indigenous" technique shows how to cull expertise and knowledge within the community. Patsy Eubanks Owens's "Investigative Reporter" describes a way for designers to work with community teens as research and reporting partners. C. L. Bohannon and Terry Clements's "Reflect, Articulate, Project (R.A.P.) Method for Sharing Community Stories" is one of the many techniques employed by the Virginia Tech design team in its ongoing work in the Hurt Park neighborhood of Roanoke, Virginia. Yeun-Kum Kim's "Adults Designing Playgrounds by Becoming Children" provides a method to assist in developing a playful design program. Each of these techniques makes experting a shared experience. Each demonstrates that we can both develop concrete solutions and produce psychological empowerment of participants. This enhances how people think about themselves, builds an awareness of what it takes to achieve their goals, and internalizes the actions it takes to address their needs in their context. When experting is done with such acumen and sensitivity in a community, it enables citizens to control their own future.

Technique 3.1

CELLPHONE DIARIES: ASSET MAPPING WITH MOBILE TECHNOLOGY

Kofi Boone

Cellphone Diaries was developed so community members could document their place-based stories independently, on their own time, and in their own voices. Through the use of smartphones, community residents can create self-authored digital videos leveraging sound and motion to add nuance and context to their stories. Additionally, videos are geo-located and can be linked to online maps adding relevant spatial characteristics, increasing accessibility for community review and discussion. The documentation of community stories can assist in the discursive process of community planning.

Instructions

1. Focus. In the context of a design or planning process that will result in changes to the environment, what are the stories about the environment that help give cultural relevance to these places? Where do you want to document these stories? Local buildings? Parks or open spaces? A neighborhood area? Are these places publicly accessible? Are there any safety or safety-perception concerns that might impact the process?

2. Assess. Identify the technology access and skill level within the community. Do people have access to smartphones? Do people have access to laptop/desktop computers with Internet access? If not, consider contacting cellphone providers to receive donations of phones and service, as well as using public computer resources (libraries, local schools, etc.).

3. Recruit. Identify a core group of people who want to participate in the process. People should be willing to commit to a one-hour orientation workshop, as well as field study time (per your project needs).

4. Train. The process requires use of a smartphone with digital video capabilities, as well as GPS (Global Positioning System) built in to locate the videos. It also requires development and access of an online map to link videos to locations, as well as an intermediate step of uploading videos and linking them to the map. It is helpful to train a support person to assist with the process (someone who can help other community members if they get stuck, and can assist with linking videos to the map).

   - Teach people how to use smartphones to shoot digital videos. This includes holding the camera steady and speaking clearly. Teach people where the videos reside on the phone, and (if desired) how to find the "geotag" (showing the location where the video was recorded). Teach people how to upload their videos to an online storage location. Because of its compatibility with Google Maps, YouTube is strongly encouraged. Also, ask people to keep all videos recorded on their phone in case other mapping processes are desired.

■ Teach people how to create and modify an online map. For ease of use, Google Maps is strongly recommended. If people are comfortable reading maps, use pins on the map to mark video locations. If not, ask people to share their geo-tags with a support person.

5. Field study. Give a timetable for going on-site and recording videos. There is no limit assigned to video length. However, longer videos result in larger files and increase the time required in the next step (review and sort). If using donated mobile devices and service, require participation in the training workshop as a necessary step to using the devices. Provide contact information for support staff should people need help. Give clear deadlines for returning the devices (the case study required return of the devices after one week).

6. Review and sort. Review videos with community members and take notes. Are there key words, phrases, and ideas associated with the videos? Are there patterns? Analyze the entire collection of videos to determine if there are themes, commonalities, or differences in overall collection of videos. Discuss these themes with community residents.

7. Celebrate and share. Create an event that showcases the results. Gallery exhibitions, demonstrations at libraries, and other activities are impactful. Put the results in a form that can be used to access the information to influence community projects.

Case Story

Cellphone Diaries was useful in the inventory and analysis to complement ongoing community visioning and archival research processes for John Chavis Memorial Park in Raleigh. Chavis Park, a historically African American community, is in South Park East Raleigh and is a half mile southeast of Raleigh's downtown. Participants used digital videos to communicate the value of the park, which is the green heart of Raleigh's African American community, and to record stories of people, places, and events for which there is no longer any trace evidence. The process was facilitated by North Carolina State University College of Design's Downtown Studio and worked directly with members of the Raleigh Central Community Advisory Council as well the South Park East Raleigh Preservation and History

Figure 3-1: A resident begins the training process for Cellphone Diaries by reviewing a handbook created by the design team. The training was held in the Archive Room in John T. "Top" Greene Center, which contains memorabilia donated and curated by residents describing the history of the neighborhood.

Figure 3-2: Residents are excited that they mastered the technique and have successfully recorded a digital video for the first time. After training they are loaned the cellphones for one week to record as many digital videos on whatever topics they want. At the end of the week, they return the devices, and the team downloads, codes, and adds the digital videos to an online map.

Figure 3-3: Another resident is in John Chavis Memorial Park creating a digital video about the history of the Carousel. The image shows the on-site documentation process where residents point the phone at a topic of interest and narrate their stories describing the topic.

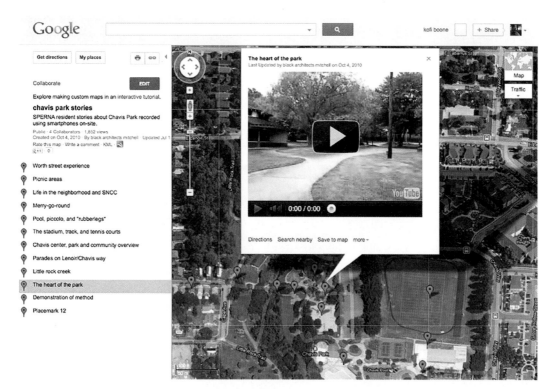

Figure 3-4: The Cellphone Diaries map and links to the videos. A free and online Google Map of the park was created by interns. Each video contained a GPS geotag showing the coordinates where the videos were recorded. Pins are placed in the Google Map to match the GPS locations of videos. The videos are uploaded to YouTube, producing a web link that has its respective pin, allowing anyone to go to the map, click on a pin, and view a cellphone diaries video.

Program. Although these groups included a range of people, the people who wanted to participate in the process and who had oral histories to share were all senior African American women.

The process produced 58 self-authored digital videos. The videos ranged from 30 seconds to seven minutes in length. The videos uncovered a range of previously undocumented park activities that gave the park meaning to local people. The most significant finding affecting park perception was the result of several residents identifying the historic main entry and programmatic heart of the park. A park that once allowed vehicular access and housed amusements, including an Olympic-sized pool and a miniature train ride, now has a pedestrian entry and plaza with no interpretive elements. This finding directly impacted the subsequent Chavis Community Conversation (led by Skeo Solutions) resulting in a master plan update for Chavis Park that aligned with community design values. The revitalization of the historic "heart of the park" is a key feature of the plan, and the park master plan was awarded a $12.5 million budget for first phase of implementation. Additionally, excerpted videos from the process were featured in local gallery exhibitions and were the subject of public radio broadcasts and a city educational program focused on cultural landscapes (see: https://goo.gl/J2HNwi).

Figure 3-5: The resulting redesign draws attention to no longer existing features that are important to older residents.

Reflection

The technique was successful in engaging the specific people involved—local African American seniors with an abundance of previously undocumented memories and local heritage. However, the technique could have been used with other groups in the community. In particular, young people, who generally have a higher level of experience and interest in mobile technology, could have provided different perspectives on the places documented. New neighbors who may not have local historic knowledge represent another important group. In future efforts, attracting and encouraging dialogue between different neighborhood groups could enable critical dialogue about the collective awareness of important people, places, and events defining community heritage and meaning. Engaging a range of people with varying views and attitudes of a place and using this technique to document and share different perceptions of the same place is a future direction for this work.

Technique 3.2

MINING THE INDIGENOUS

Austin Allen

Mining the Indigenous is an examination of the cultural struggle between the history and the codes of memory of a landscape, two often-opposing ways of identifying a place. Codes of memory are the visual or aural signs or physical forms, left by someone, to be read or experienced at a future point by other people, in order to reveal more about a place than what may be evident upon an initial experience in or around a place. Often the coding is a means to protect the memory from being erased by history, the official story. Thus history and memory are in a continuous contest to define a particular landscape, often two contradictory ways of understanding what happened in this time and place. History is where landscape architects traditionally settle in on defining a space over a designated time period. Certain facts are indisputable about a place. But the cultural aspects beyond the history of a landscape are less certain and are often found in the codes of memory shared by the indigenous—the "Cultural Keepers."

Mining the Indigenous starts with the premise that cultural aspects of a landscape are intertwined with codes of memory held by the Cultural Keepers of a place and time. Cultural Keepers are not necessarily the community leadership. Even if they are not official leaders, however, their neighbors recognize and respect their knowledge. As the name implies they are keepers of memory and interpreters of place.

Mining the Indigenous is a technique developed to accomplish at least two tasks: first, to empower an individual or a group of Cultural Keepers to fully realize the implications of what they know about a landscape (steps 1–4); and second, to assist in applying this knowledge to problem solving in a specific landscape (steps 5–7).

Instructions

1. Identify what is peculiar, missing, confusing, or conflicted in the known or official documentation of a specific landscape. What are those matters during charrettes, workshops, site inventories, and site analyses defying easy explanations or logic and often dismissed as fantasies, myths, or lies? List them; see where they overlap and, most importantly, start to identify the sources.

2. Identify those people who step forward or are known by others who have alternative interpretations to official accounts or thinking about a particular landscape. Who stands out in workshops, charrettes, and other gatherings with views that do not always align with historical documentation? These may be your Cultural

Keepers and should be seen as a potential valuable resource as you make sense of contrary or opposing points of view. You might even ask the individuals to self identify as Cultural Keepers: "Are you the Keeper of the Culture of this place?"

3.   Engage those people in informal discussion of what they know and how they began to understand this particular landscape with a different way of seeing and interpreting.

4.   Use techniques often employed through ethnographic and documentary filmmaking to record the stories explained by the Cultural Keepers as a means to examine how they see themselves and your role as one who can act on their narratives. Ultimately define and agree on the role of the Cultural Keeper in relation to the project at hand. This is particularly useful during disaster recovery efforts accompanied by a catastrophic disruption of place and the knowledge of the place.

5.   Be patient. Cultural Keepers are experts on their set of knowledge of place and its relationship to time and how and when to use this information. This is probably one of the most difficult steps to comprehend and embrace because of the expectation as outside experts that the transfer of knowledge will be shared in an orderly, predetermined pattern common to our field. This will not be the case. You will be told when it is time to tell you and in ways that may not be readily apparent.

6.   Interpret, ask for feedback from the Cultural Keepers and others, reinterpret, and begin to compose what you, the outside expert, have learned about a place. This step toward a greater collaborative trust in the process is driven by a critical awareness that Cultural Keepers exist in a world where the outside expert has been positioned as the primary source and the Cultural Keepers' knowledge base is considered secondary in terms of usefulness in problem solving. Cultural Keepers are aware that their knowing has value. But times of sharing this knowledge with whomever and for whatever reasons are critical moments. Will the secondary status be removed or will the Cultural Keeper be silenced in terms of usefulness? Each time codes of memory are revealed also holds in the balance the future survival of those memories and ultimately the survival of the keeper of those memories. Coded memories, by their very nature, have had to be protected knowledge! This knowledge reshapes the way that tradition and official stories are communicated; thus it is a disrupting knowledge, upsetting the norm. In return, many officials, professionals, or scholars invested in traditional or normative narratives have often suppressed or at least attempted to silence the Cultural Keeper's point of view. Thus Cultural Keepers often specialize in narratives, in coded and fragmented ways deemed as essential ways to eke out information without jeopardizing cultural preservation of practices, or the vernacular of the place.

7. Frame the problem to be solved along with the Cultural Keeper. This consists of revealing one's expertise to the Cultural Keeper in a manner that demonstrates mutual respect in assessing the value of information.

8. Keep the Keeper engaged as the project moves forward, asking for guidance as things become more concrete. This is an ongoing process in sharing knowledge and creating change.

Case Story

John Taylor is a Cultural Keeper. I have enlisted his expertise for 10 years in the disaster recovery phase of the Lower Ninth Ward and the adjacent Bayou Bienvenue Wetlands Triangle. He was born in the Lower Ninth Ward, centering his life in the culture of the Lower Ninth Ward and around the plants and animals and environment of the vanished cypress forest and now wetlands in the Triangle. Over time I have walked with him and conducted many interviews to begin to assemble his knowledge of the place into a transferable set of information to be used by all of those interested in rebuilding neighborhoods and restoring coastal areas and wetlands. He has lived in and photographed this landscape and regularly holds tours and educates people from around the world about how the flooding happened in 2005. He also explains to them the global-to-local impact of climate change today.

We met in 2006 when a group of us were climbing the levee wall at the site of what was to become the Bayou Bienvenue Wetlands Overlook. We had brought along a writer from the New Yorker Online who was writing a story about the need to prevent the development of a bridge that would isolate the Bayou Bienvenue Wetlands from the Lower Ninth Ward

Figure 3-6: John Taylor in the Bayou Bienvenue Wetlands Triangle, a self-portrait.
Source: © John W. Taylor.

Figure 3-7: Ghost cypress trees in the Bayou Bienvenue Wetlands Triangle. Source: © John W. Taylor.

Neighborhood. Taylor stopped me and asked what we were doing, having seen me walking with others in the wetlands over several months. When I told him, he was more than willing to fill in huge chapters of information and missing data. John knew where infrastructure lay (e.g., huge sewerage pipes that had been inaccurately located on official maps). He could explain ruins on a track of public land where no one lived. "At one time," he said, "people who had no money were allowed to live and build small houses on this track, as long as they kept it clean." Ultimately, with the help of John and many others, the bridge "to nowhere" was never built. John has become one of the Bayou Bienvenue Wetland Triangle's greatest protectors and Cultural Keepers.

Reflection

John Taylor's work in the wetlands and his ability to articulate another way of seeing this space has served as a catalyst and source for many artists, scientists, ecologists, planners, and designers. Journalists and scholars reference his words in publications, scientific papers, theses, and doctoral dissertations. His work encourages us to build a more extensive forum that legitimizes and encourages Cultural Keepers to become engaged in civic problem solving. Cultural Keepers can be authorized through a network of people to maintain codes of memory, even by communities who may not agree with the Keepers' stated memories. We benefit when we include Cultural Keepers on equal footing in analyzing a place, as co-investigators on grant proposals, in contentious problem-solving situations, and in strategic planning.

Technique 3.3

THE INVESTIGATIVE REPORTER

Patsy Eubanks Owens

The Investigative Reporter builds narratives to highlight important community issues. The community participants identify issues to be explored, formulate questions that will help them to learn more about these issues, and record interviews with other community members. After learning the basics of conducting an interview and how to operate a video recorder, participants practice and hone their new skills with one another. Community members to be interviewed are identified and investigative assignments undertaken. These reports are shared with one another, the design team, and the broader community.

These investigative reports may be used throughout a design process. For example, they can help to uncover community knowledge and sentiment early in the process, to inform design development, or to verify previous findings. This exercise can be implemented in stages. For example, steps 1–3 may be conducted during one community workshop, steps 4 and 5 at a second, and steps 6 and 7 at a third.

Instructions

1. The design team presents the overriding purpose of the effort (e.g., why were they hired, what issue were they asked to address, what are the objectives) and facilitates a discussion with workshop participants to identify the issues they think need to be addressed.

2. The design team asks the community participants to think about these issues and helps the group more fully understand the issue and identify related concerns. The design team should prepare for the meeting by identifying possible responses and developing discussion prompts.

3. Once the main issues have been identified and discussed, the group is divided into smaller groups of four to six participants plus a facilitator from the design team. The facilitator asks the groups to imagine they are producing a news story on this issue and to decide which questions need to be answered in order to be able to explain the issue to someone else. Their responses are discussed, refined, and developed into interview questions.

4. The participants are given a brief tutorial on filming. Afterward, they conduct practice interviews with one another, and, with assistance from the design team, refine their questions and filming technique.

Figure 3-8: Youth conducting practice interviews. This young woman was particularly concerned with schools and how they should become more welcoming to the students.

5.   Once the group is satisfied with their questions, the issue groups interview one another. For example, groups 1 and 2 interview each other.

6.   A member of the design team uploads the videos to a shared computer while another leads a discussion focused on what the participants learned about conducting interviews and what they learned about the issues. Participants are asked to recommend which of their videos should be viewed by the entire group, and these are watched. The number of videos to be watched should be determined by the time available.

7.   The design team leads a discussion on who should be interviewed to get the full story for each issue. The group develops a list of future interviewees, decides which of these interviews are most important, and determines who will conduct them.

Case Story

This technique was developed through our work with a group of young people, aged 12 to 18, on the Youth Voices for Change project in West Sacramento, California. Our youth partners had been collecting information for a few weeks about their favorite and least favorite places, and the places they would like to see changed. Although the youth had previously photographed these places around the community, it was difficult for them to express all the reasons they had for identifying the various places.

We conducted three 30-minute workshops over a three-week period. At first we divided the youth into small story circles. The purpose of these story circles was to flesh out the stories the youth had about their community, such as what places were important to them and why, and what places they wanted to see changed. The youth drew these stories out of each other. Using this input, we helped them develop their interview and paired them with other

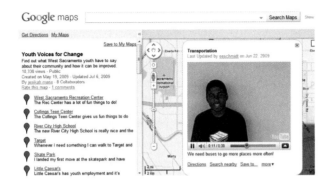

Figure 3-9: Youth videos posted to the Youth Voices for Change Google map. This video on transportation added to ongoing discussions about bus routes in the community.

participants. After practicing, the youth interviewed each other at these favorite and least favorite places, and the places they wanted to see changed.

The material gathered during these interviews was reviewed, summarized, and shared with the broader community. The youth developed a web-based map that linked their videos to the locations discussed. Over a 10-month period the videos were also presented, along with other findings produced by the youth, at a well-attended public project showcase. During this event, youth used their new skills and conducted additional investigative reports with adult community members, notably the city's mayor.

Reflections

The Investigative Reporter has four main positive characteristics. First, trust is developed between designer and community members by giving community members control over identifying the issues, questions, and collection of information. Second, novel information is obtained because of the diverse participant perspectives and the willingness of others to talk to them. Third, participant ownership of the process and the results grows through cumulative engagement opportunities. Finally, individual competency, contributions, and capacity are bolstered through guided inquiry, use of common technology, and modest training.

In particular, this process is ideal for engaging older youth and soliciting their opinions. They are naturally inquisitive and are comfortable with being behind the camera and on video. Potential hurdles to this technique include the availability of video-recording and editing equipment, adequate video-production training of the design team, and time. While recording participant impressions can be conducted during a shorter community meeting, the training of participants, the subsequent gathering of information from others, and the analysis of this information make up a longer process.

The Investigative Reporter technique is transactive in that it promotes the active engagement of participants. The design team helps the participants get the information out to others through this process. We also found that this effort was transformative. The videos produced by the youth and the process itself informed and transformed how city officials and adults view their community. The youth perspective on issues influenced city decisions. For example, parks and recreation officials immediately incorporated youth concerns into the recreation planning process and even recruited youth to assist in conducting a design workshop.

Figure 3-10: Youth Voices for Change project showcase. The city's mayor and community members listened intently while the young people shared their ideas.

Technique 3.4

REFLECT, ARTICULATE, PROJECT (R.A.P.) METHOD FOR SHARING COMMUNITY STORIES

C. L. Bohannon and Terry Clements

The process of Reflecting, Articulating, and Projecting (R.A.P.) provides community members an opportunity to actively participate in an oral history and a mapping process with designers that reflects on their core stories, and projects toward a future narrative of change and growth. This process advances the community physically and socially by building relationships between residents and designers. R.A.P. allows for active sharing of both individual and collective stories to facilitate archival documentation so community narratives become agents of change. Honest dialogue merges into transformative practices shifting ownership of the design process toward community members.

Stories convey complex practices that have shaped our lives. Stories articulate essential struggles, values, and hopes that we have. Stories shape historical understanding. These narratives have the potential to construct contemporary perspectives that run counter to dominant ideologies, and open a space for authentic dialogue about the future. Local accounts express opinions and views on issues that shape community identity and spatial realities. The R.A.P. method offers a safe space for communities to tell their stories, helps recognize and map shared aspirations, and honors local people as they address actions to meet needs.

Instructions

1. Prepare for the meeting. Work with neighborhood leaders to invite residents across boundaries such as age, gender, and ethnicity.
2. Make a toolbox for each table: a recent large-scale community aerial map with street names, note paper, sticky notes, markers, and colored pencils (sometimes a historic map will help too).
3. On the day of the meeting get there early to arrange the tables and chairs so six to eight community members can sit at a table.
4. Designate one facilitator, who can be a community member or design team member, per table to keep time, take notes, and ensure the storytelling process is open and inclusive.
5. Make sure all participants provide written consent if needed.
6. Make sure a recorder, which can be a community member or design team member, documents the stories.

7. Start the Reflection process, which will take between 25 and 30 minutes. Agree on ground rules and objectives so all parties can share stories without being interrupted.

8. Identify a community starting point, creating an open-ended dialogue between participants, for example, "What does this community mean to you, its history, and valued places?"

9. Have participants take turns telling stories while marking on maps the places where story events took place and what the story was.

10. Identify community strengths, weaknesses, and opportunities by a similar process of taking turns.

11. The next step is Articulate. Ask two members from each table to display their map and describe what they learned about the neighborhood. Take between 25 and 30 minutes for this step. Each team should take no more than 3–5 minutes to report to the larger group.

12. After all maps are shared; facilitators should invite comments from community members.

13. Develop a concept map of the community's strengths, weaknesses, and opportunities.

14. Refine and develop a set of goals and objectives that can be charted and explored.

15. Identify gaps in goals and objectives that need to be addressed.

16. The final step is Projection. It should also take between 25 and 30 minutes. Collectively, break community goals into manageable tasks that allow community members the space to express their hopes about a future story that can be used to shape community interventions.

17. Identify actors within the community and external partners that can make community goals achievable. Create an action plan positioning community stories as a catalyst for change.

18. Archive copies of voice recordings and maps so they are accessible to the community.

19. Keep the conversation fluid so that, as community needs shift, the R.A.P. process can continue.

20. Take action on projects that project a specific future.

Case Story

The Hurt Park Community Garden is the result of an ongoing relationship between Virginia Tech's Landscape Architecture program, the Hurt Park Neighborhood Alliance, the City of Roanoke, and the Roanoke Community Gardens Association. The project, started in 2009,

Figure 3-11: Hurt Park community member sharing ideas from the Articulation step of the R.A.P. method.

reflects the work of multiple community members, partners, and students. Critical parts of the process employed the R.A.P. method to understand the relationship between open space, local food (in)security, gardening practices, and community identity in Hurt Park.

An interdisciplinary university team facilitated the R.A.P. method during a community forum. Stories and three maps produced a design program and conceptual master plan. In particular, Reflection allowed residents to develop a critical understanding of community resources, including churches, schools, and other existing institutional assets. Articulation enabled community members to reenvision vacant land as a potential neighborhood asset. Projection yielded a mobilized populace who designed, developed, and implemented a new community garden and green space.

Since its completion, the community garden has transformed a half-acre vacant lot into a thriving neighborhood hub where low- and moderate-income residents have access to garden plots. The Hurt Park Community Garden has become a focal point of the neighborhood and serves, directly or indirectly, hundreds of Hurt Park residents.

Figure 3-12: Hurt Park residents planting vegetables at the opening of the Hurt Park community garden.

Reflection

The R.A.P. method offers a unique opportunity to realize the power of community through personal and shared histories. It builds and maintains trust with outside partners, but maybe more important, among community members with different priorities. R.A.P. can be difficult for community members who are not keen on sharing their personal stories or talking about difficult or taxing aspects of their lives. We continue to refine our process to overcome this.

Technique 3.5

ADULTS DESIGNING PLAYGROUNDS BY BECOMING CHILDREN

Yeun-Kum Kim

Adults Designing Playgrounds by Becoming Children encourages adults to think about design not from the perspective of guardians but from that of a child. This workshop method helps designers and other adults to develop and exchange ideas about play, and to incorporate creative childlike ideas into the design. It taps into expertise that resides in memories of childhood, not just the experience of parenthood, beginning with a familiar game modeled after Bingo, and progressing from there to a detailed design.

Instructions

1. Prepare for the workshop. The design team requires one main facilitator who leads the process, guides the group through all the activities, and encourages active communication among participants. Assistant facilitators, assigned to each group, help participants conduct activities at each step and record participant opinions about design ideas.

2. To enable effective idea sharing, limit the number of participants to less than 24 at any single workshop. Include residents of the area near the playground, kindergarten teachers, members of a local child-rearing community group, and playground management officials.

3. Choose a venue near or in the playground. The playground is a good place where participants can obtain a sense of realism; however, it may be so busy that participants are distracted. Prepare templates to play Bingo for breaking the ice, and forms for the persona technique activity with space to list activities and playground equipment. (See steps 7 and 8 for details.)

4. Prepare models of the empty playground site using Styrofoam or thick paper and diverse materials, such as colored paper or clay, for participants to create play areas. Provide sheets of paper to record results of discussions about questions asked by the facilitator. Set up activity tables according to the number of teams (four tables with six participants at each table). The tables should be big enough for model making but not so big as to hinder communication.

5. The main facilitator should take about five minutes to describe the playground to be designed, its location, and its present condition, and introduce the workshop's process, goals, and objectives. Explain the three activities and time to be spent on

each. During the first activity, participants will recall their own childhood play; in the second, they imagine who will play and how and what is needed for the games. The third activity is designing the playground.

6. Each team's assistant facilitator asks members to introduce themselves. Then participants recall and discuss how they played as children, and what settings and moments they remember as most interesting. This step should take 20 minutes.

7. If time allows (20 more minutes) participants can play Bingo using types of play they enjoyed as children. First, each team member writes down names of activities (tag, merry-go-round) on their Bingo card templates, and then takes a turn calling them out. This is a fun way to see which childhood activities were shared by the adults, and it establishes connections between people.

8. To generate concrete, lively results, use the persona technique. In 20 minutes each team member imagines one specific child; decides the child's age, gender, and character; and decides how the child wants to play. Then they describe the child's play on the sheet already prepared. After each person's character is detailed, they introduce their character to the other team members.

9. For the next 20 minutes participants are asked to imagine play, not play equipment, for each child. In our experience, when individuals without a design education design playgrounds, they tend to imagine familiar equipment like slides, swings, and seesaws, without considering diverse play activity. Therefore, we ask them to imagine how their hypothetical child might play, and then identify what settings best suit these activities. This activity sheet can be prepared as follows. The space on the right is for types of play, and the space on the left for play facilities. The left side can be hidden until the participants finish the right, allowing them to concentrate on thinking of play itself.

10. The final team activity is to create a playground model using the materials you provide (in 45 minutes). Before each team makes models, the facilitator informs the participants of the sizes of different objects, such as the height and length of the desk and the room, to create a sense of scale.

11. Once teams complete their models, they present their playgrounds to the audience, describing their imagined children, their intention, the activities, the play equipment, and the meaning obtained from the workshop. After each presentation, the facilitator summarizes the design character. Use only 15 minutes for this step.

12. With the remaining five minutes the main facilitator explains that, after the workshop, the designer will develop a design based on the workshop results and consult with the participants.

Figure 3-13: Participants working on park plans using childhood play memories to guide them.

Case Story

My company (Wul Landscape Architecture Company) has used this technique for over five years to design play areas in various Korean cities. Although we try something new each time, we follow the steps above, sometimes omitting Bingo if time is limited. In one Seoul playground design, an adult team decided to design for children's adventure play. Another chose to encourage youth to play with their friends, not with structures. One team imagined playgrounds for active girls, suggesting some structures that allowed girls to climb and jump. The final team discussed a playground that would allow young children to "play house." As adults recall their delightful childhood play settings and how they stimulated imagination, the play areas become more creative. In one case, adults decided to simply use existing trees in the site for youth who might enjoy a natural challenge. Still another team suggested a site for timid children to imagine their own world, such as a space hidden from view where a child feels protected.

Reflection

This technique encourages adults to imagine children's play rather than focusing on new play equipment. When designing playgrounds in Seoul, adults started out wanting a number of facilities. This is common in Korea. As the work progressed, they recalled that they had played with their friends, rather than with facilities.

Figure 3-14: This playground was built in Seoul in 2015 with the support of the nonprofit Save the Children. Responding to workshop design requests, the playground center was kept open for free play, with facilities around it.

The participants enjoyed recalling their childhood experiences, and they became less preoccupied with safety as the sole design determinant. This freed them to design more adventuresome play areas. They shifted their focus to inventive, interactive, entertaining, and often inexpensive games. In one case participants agreed what was needed was an empty space to play rather than the facility. As a result, we left the center wide open, placing the play equipment to one side of the playground so that the children could climb and slide.

In our park design projects we are able to integrate most of the adults' intentions, but care must be taken to tell participants that not every idea can be realized. We also need to inform participants this technique alone cannot establish consensus among diverse stakeholders. Therefore, other methods of communication must follow this workshop.

4

Calming and Evoking

Community designers are often asked to work in a place that is in a state of crisis due to powerful external forces. Sometimes we are asked to mediate among community members who are fighting over an issue that has reached an impasse. There are a lot of things the design team needs to do at this stage: listen to people, read, look at data, visit the site to observe, and make maps—maybe even a model. Rumors need to be sorted from the facts, and a whole picture knit together from the pieces each participant holds. By excavating and exhuming, ordering, and analyzing the information, designers and the community can articulate an agreed-upon situation. From this the community can determine goals for how to make change and give the design process direction.

ACCESS TO INFORMATION

As designers we assume the value of information and we assert our right to it—it is part of our currency. Yet fewer than 50 years ago in the United States neither designers nor the public had access to the information necessary to make good decisions or to prevent bad decisions from being implemented. Communities found out about neighborhood clearance only when the bulldozers arrived at their doorstep. The Freedom of Information Act (1967) and the National Environmental Policy Act (1970) changed all of this. Citizen awareness and control of "the facts" advanced during the 1960s and '70s, with environmental and civil rights activists in particular figuring out how to construct their own information to counter government or corporate misinformation and malfeasance. Today it is easier to determine the starting conditions in a community, both because of ready access to information and because there are techniques to co-create it with residents. As a result, the process of information gathering and analysis in design has evolved from extracting data and presenting it for citizens' reaction to a process that is educational, therapeutic, evocative, transactive, and transformative.

CALMING DOWN

Why go to the trouble? Because systematically inventorying the situation and establishing what is known and not known calms people down. Finding out the facts jointly can lead to agreement about what the facts really are. It is a process that can start simply with asking participants to list the things that are going right, then the things that are going wrong, and discussing the list. The list can come from interviews, a survey, a workshop. It points to what needs to be investigated to be better understood. Involving citizens in this step can also reduce costs and gain buy in. It is often the pivotal step in the process as reflected in the Chinese proverb, "Tell me, I forget; show me, I remember; involve me, I understand."

Data for data's sake has no place in community design; it needs to be presented to the community for validation. The community can be introduced to itself through a new lens in a workshop setting or more dynamically out in the landscape. On-site experiences provide more tangible opportunities for the designer to teach the community about some technical reality that must be understood, such as chronic erosion or flooding—constraints that need to be addressed before there can be a viable solution. In return citizens can point out important factors understood through daily life activities.

Collective information gathering is the hallmark of American conflict resolution methods and also the Japanese *machizukuri* movement. Early experiments in *machizukuri* entailed small walking-tour or "town-watching" activities, but as the movement has matured the techniques have become more complex, the goals more ambitious, and the boundaries of interests expanded. It has also been a significant form of engaging in society, first by strengthening social ties, second by tackling issues collectively. The physical environment may be changed as a result, and the community changes, too.

EVOKING DIRECTION

Community designers understand that data are not benign—they can evoke a powerful response because, ultimately, they are about place and people's relationship to it. Qualitative, experienced, sensory information needs to be captured in a design process so that the vocabulary of place becomes the language of the design. How we process and use what we gather is a wide-open opportunity for creative communication, analysis, and decision making that must evoke critical thinking.

Sometimes this action may be a rude awakening for community members because we are calling out what needs to be discussed in order for change to occur. Evoked or provoked, citizens should be primed to set goals at this point in a design process. For each experienced designer there is a different view as to when exactly to move toward goal setting. Some will tell you that setting goals first can inform the inventorying process. Others will say that a community cannot set goals without first understanding existing conditions. Either way, goals provide benchmarks for developing alternatives, evaluating plans, and monitoring after a project is complete. Combined with data, maps, and models, goals allow citizens to feel a level of comfort and readiness to take the next step toward their future.

TECHNIQUES TO CALM AND EVOKE

The techniques in this chapter provide a range of ways to gather and create new information that has allowed communities in three different cultures to take the next needed step. In "Mapping the Common Living Sphere" Kota Maruya used interview-based mapping to defuse growing conflict between potters in the historic village of Koishiwara, Japan, to find areas commonly valued that could serve as the framework for a tourist signage system. Sibyl Diver's "Visual Timeline" excavated the 100-year-plus history of US government decision making that robbed Northern California's Karuk Tribe of control over its land. The data were then combined with tribal oral history and place knowledge to create a larger-than-life timeline that shifted the dominant narrative. In his "Children's Exciting Neighborhood Exploration Event" Isami Kinoshita describes a walking activity that has grown over 17 years into a community development corporation in Kogane, Japan. Christian Dimmer and Yu Ohtani's "Community Innovation Forum" proposes a technique used in a declining Tokyo neighborhood to catalyze discussions about the possibility of change through exchange with activists from other neighborhoods who have already achieved success. Chao-Ching Yu's "Big Map" shows how using a Big Map, a Big Model, and a human body-scale demonstration floor plan in Hua-lien City, Taiwan, enabled citizens and designers together to untangle hidden property ownership issues that were preventing place-appropriate urban regeneration along an abandoned rail line. They were then able to create new opportunities for development.

Technique 4.1

MAPPING THE COMMON LIVING SPHERE

Kota Maruya

People tend to emphasize their human relationships and their own social standing relative to other people. However, we are not only a part of society but also a part of the environment. We own common spaces based on our daily life and its context. Mental mapping enables people to reach into their inner mind and express the relationship between the space and themselves. The expressed spaces that are important to individuals can make them notice the "common space," thereby solidifying the unity of the community.

This technique consists of nine steps. Steps 1 through 5 are done in interviews with individual participants. Steps 6 and 7 involve collating and analyzing the data from the individual interviews. In Steps 8 and 9 the results are presented to the whole community to discuss actions to be taken for managing the common space.

Instructions

1. In advance, create a topographical map of the target area to use when interviewing participants. Prepare questions to obtain participants' basic information (gender, age, work history, duration of residence, and so on).

2. Explain to each participant where the local landmarks and his or her house are on the map. Mark these so they can obtain an accurate understanding of the map.

3. Using the map, ask participants to indicate the area they recognize as their sphere of daily life, and then draw the boundary lines.

4. Confirm the boundary lines with the participant and correct any errors. Confirm whether the boundary lines cross any mountain ridges or surrounding local physical features to clarify the relationship between the participant's daily life geography and the topographical features.

5. Ask the participants to indicate the specific places they regard as important to themselves. Mark them on the map.

6. The next two steps take place back at your office. By hand or using GIS, draw all the boundary lines and places you identified in the interviews. Analyze the form and size of individual areas and compare them with the overall village or urban structure. Evaluate the space according to the degree to which individual areas overlap.

7. Analyze the relationship between the characteristics of the overlapping areas and the places indicated as individually important to find out the "common space and place" of the community.

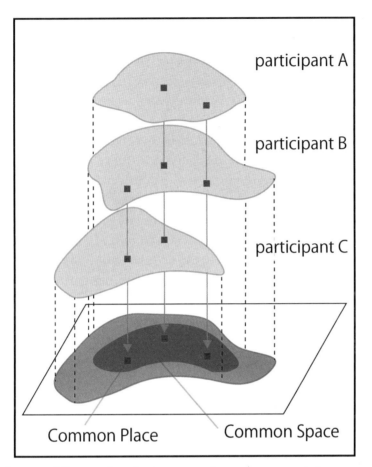

Figure 4-1: Conceptual diagram of overlapping areas and common space and place.

8. Hold a workshop to share the results of the mapping with the locals and discuss the management of their common space.

9. Construct the framework for community development based on the common space. Prioritize specific actions the group can undertake and achieve.

Case Story

The village of Koishiwara is located in a mountainous area of Japan. The village is well known for traditional pottery. In the nineteenth century, 10 households were involved in the local pottery industry. Potters often worked in cooperation, especially in using the kilns and distributing natural resources, such as water, wood, and clay. However, industrial and social modernization changed the nature of this cooperation. With the resultant increase in the demand for pottery starting in the late 1950s, disciples from different pottery households received increasing independence from their masters. The road was expanded to attract more tourists, and the landscape of the village changed, gathering new pottery households along the main road. Today, there are approximately 50 potting households in the area. Potters are making special efforts to increase the number of tourists and pottery sales. While the pottery community is motivated to change, competing priorities led to conflict despite their desire to work together.

I was invited by the potters of Sarayama, the birthplace of the pottery in Koishiwara village, to conduct a project that would help them collaborate among themselves to attract more tourists. I conducted mapping interviews with 36 potters in the village, out of a total of 43. I identified the perspectives of the different potters on the boundaries of the craft heritage area. Sarayama and the surrounding area were recognized by over 80 percent of the participants as the area where pottery in Koishiwara prospered. It was thus identified as the center of the pottery village. However the aforementioned areas and those along the main road were also recognized by over 60 percent of the participants, indicating that the road was considered an extension of the village—a newly recognized craft heritage area.

Figure 4-2: Sarayama potter.

Participants designated 31 places as being important, and they were classified into five types. Four of the place types—facilities, historical resources, raw material, and houses—are important bases for the potters living and working in the area, such as the creek where they collect water, common lands in the mountains for collecting clay, and kilns adjacent to their houses where they produce and sell pottery. The fifth place type was found in the center of Sarayama—places that have a strong connection with local gods (such as woods, temples, and lakes).

After sharing the map results and discussing local issues with the participants, we reached a consensus that the recovery of the local landscape was important for future tour-

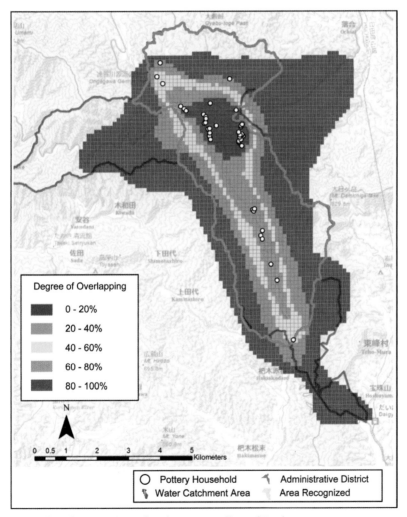

Figure 4-3: Overlay of area recognized as the pottery village of Koishiwara.

Figure 4-4: Potters set up a temporary signboard to work through what information is needed and what aesthetic is desired.

ism. From the perspective of simplicity of implementation, urgency, totality, and efficiency, we decided to make local information about the place consistent and improve the public and semipublic signboards. We set up temporary signboards and discussed the appropriateness of the information and how to make them harmonious with the landscape. Now we are creating the signboards, made of pottery, so they will be a landmark for tourists and customers.

Reflection

This technique helps visualize the common space and places that exist in the consciousness of people. It enables participants to decide which spaces to take action on and can be used as an evaluation tool after implementation occurs. It can be used depending on the objectives, such as to adopt visions that are based on the local people's lifestyles, by overlaying maps of land-use plans, vegetation, or ecosystems with the interview and map process used in this project. Analysis by GIS is useful for visualization and digitization of the maps; it can promote common recognition of problems to work together with local people on overlapping maps.

Technique 4.2

VISUAL TIMELINE

Sibyl Diver

The Visual Timeline technique uses a timeline format to reveal the history of why particular problems in a particular place came to be from a community perspective. This is an especially useful tool for shifting the dominant narrative in marginalized communities. Creating a Visual Timeline requires goal setting with community partners, analyzing data, and applying artistic design. The approach leverages community-engaged research to explain linkages between policy decisions, historical events, and community outcomes. Timeline creators pour rigorous and defensible information into a scaffold that organizes, validates, and presents community knowledge with beautiful design.

This technique was developed as part of a community-based participatory research project. Key goals included the following:

- Validating community knowledge and experience through structured inquiry
- Creating awareness about the structural causes of community problems
- Building positive momentum around community action

Instructions

1. Form a project team to include designers, researchers, and community members (e.g., a tribal leader, land manager, local school representative, public health official, local business owner, and so on). Agree on project goals—typically two or three as described above. Set mutually agreeable expectations about who participates in the project, accountability, time frame, permissions, data management, publications, and so forth.
2. Discuss community issues that require historical analysis and structural explanation. Determine questions for the inquiry (e.g., how have land-use policies affected community health?).
3. Create a shared project database. Collect relevant documents from community partners, libraries, and online.
4. Undertake a document review to identify themes and patterns that address your questions. You may use coding categories or information categories that help organize qualitative data (e.g., federal policy, water resources, community action).
5. Arrange relevant information in a database. To help identify causal explanations, use a spreadsheet to organize information about relevant policies (e.g., local,

state, or federal), actionable events (e.g., management actions, planning events, protests), and community outcomes (e.g., changes in socioeconomic conditions, community health, local environment). For each entry, record the date (or date range) and reference source.

6. Once your database is ready, reorder spreadsheet entries by date. Then group information into main categories: policies, events, outcomes.

7. Lay out timeline entries in a table format, where rows and columns provide "bins" for sorting information. Use rows for grouping policies, events, and outcomes. Use columns for marking segments of time. The time segments can vary by increment. They should represent logical eras in community history. Include images, such as historical photos or community artwork, and space for references.

8. Engage community members, teachers, and youth to generate additional artwork.

9. Print your draft Visual Timeline on large-format paper so that all text and images are visible.

10. Organize a community review session. Document all feedback. Create time for connecting with community members, such as sharing food, taking a walk, or going on a field trip.

11. Revise your Visual Timeline. Expand your inquiry or incorporate additional design elements, as needed.

12. Review your final draft and outreach plan with community partners.

13. Present the Visual Timeline findings to your target audience.

14. Leverage the Visual Timeline findings to build legitimacy for community actions and recruit new allies.

Case Story

The Karuk Tribe is the second-largest tribe in California and comes from the Klamath Mountains, near the border between California and Oregon (see www.karuk.us). The US Forest Service claims ownership over the majority of Karuk territory. However, because no valid treaty was signed to legally cede the territory to the US government, the tribe continues to dispute federal ownership.

In 2009, members of the Karuk–UC Berkeley Collaborative, an organization that supports Karuk eco-cultural revitalization initiatives, came together to understand barriers and opportunities to community participation in land management within Karuk Territory (see https://nature.berkeley.edu/karuk-collaborative). Over nine months the team, which included Karuk land managers and UC Berkeley landscape designers, compiled data from more than 100 sources on policies, land management actions, and environmental and

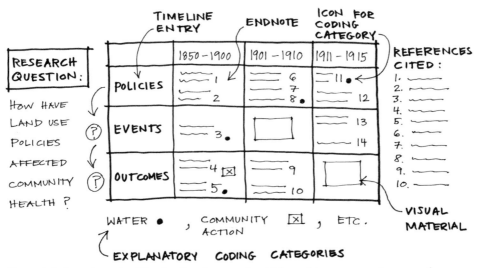

Figure 4-5: Core elements of the timeline framework, which combines community-engaged research and design.

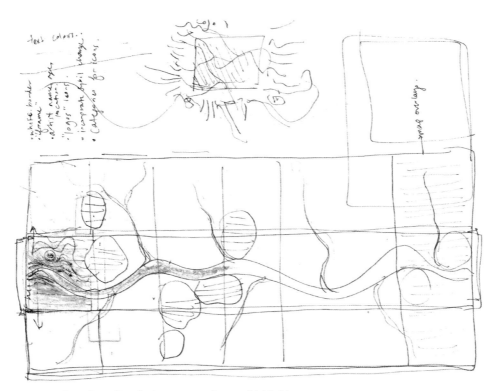

Figure 4-6: Initial timeline design concept. Source: Lichia Liu.

Figure 4-7: Sense-of-place student artwork contributed by Devon Tygart. Source: Karuk Lands Management Historical Timeline Project (CC BY-NC-SA 3.0).

Figure 4-8: The Karuk Lands Management Historical Timeline is a 15-foot artistic display that summarizes land-use policies, management practices, and environmental health conditions affecting Karuk people and landscapes from 1850 to 2010. Source: Karuk Lands Management Historical Timeline Project by Sibyl Diver, Lisa Liu, Naomi Canchela, Rafael Silberblatt, Sara Rose Tannenbaum, and Ron Reed. https://karuktimeline.wordpress.com, licensed by CC BY-NC-SA 3.0.

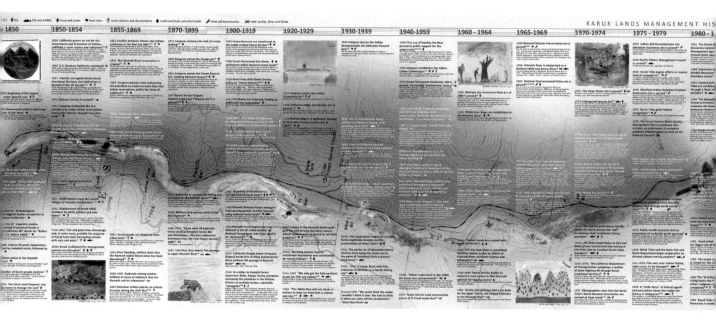

health conditions affecting Karuk people. Community members contributed oral histories. From this we developed the Visual Timeline technique as a tool for synthesizing our data and validating community knowledge.

Our process resulted in the Karuk Lands Management Historical Timeline (1850–2010)—a 15-foot artistic display that shows how land management history is linked to the social and environmental changes affecting Karuk people today. The Timeline documents how extractive industries (e.g., mining, logging, agriculture, hydropower, and industrial fishing) played a key role in displacing Karuk people and their land management practices. The resulting environmental and socioeconomic changes have led to significant community health impacts. For example, dam construction and other industrial developments have devastated Klamath fisheries, which has contributed to a major shift in the local diet for Karuk people and disproportionate levels of diet-related diseases, such as diabetes. However, recent shifts in environmental policy and the indigenous rights movement have enabled important Karuk eco-cultural revitalization initiatives, such as bringing back cultural burning practices to revive traditional food sources like acorns and salmon.

Tribal leaders have used the Timeline to educate agency representatives and academic partners about their long history in the Klamath Basin, their struggle for self-determination, and environmental justice issues. The Timeline has provided an important resource for educators in schools for teaching local history and reframing community struggles, as well as researchers working on land management and food security issues in collaboration with the Karuk Tribe.

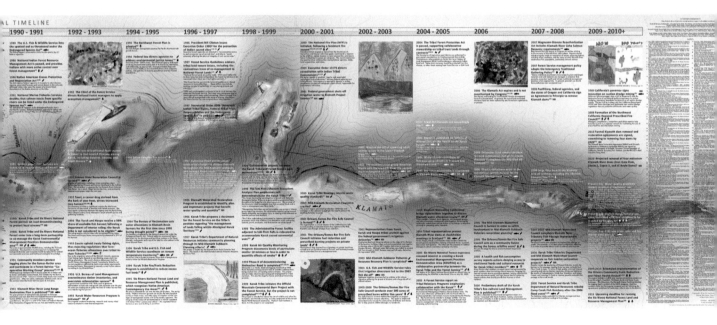

Reflection

Through the Karuk Timeline project, our team appreciated the importance of maintaining a strong connection to people and place, and we remain deeply grateful to the Karuk Tribe for the opportunity to learn from their experiences. For example, the most meaningful part of our community review was not the meeting itself, but rather the cultural resources training, salmon dinner, and forest walk organized by our Karuk colleagues. To acknowledge the ongoing relationships between Karuk people and the land, we organized the Klamath Art Contest, where local students submitted watercolors representing their connection to the river. By incorporating student artwork, our design team was able to reenvision the Karuk Timeline as a cultural riverscape.

Our community partners viewed the Karuk Timeline as a highly effective "scientific" format for presenting Karuk perspectives on land management. The Timeline also created a quick, visual communication tool that validated community experiences. In this way, the Timeline offers an important step toward reconciling a centuries-old dispute over land rights and responsibilities. The process placed isolated Karuk self-determination initiatives in a larger historical context. One tribal land manager told us, "I usually feel like I am beating my head against the wall, but now I feel like we're getting somewhere."

The Visual Timeline approach represents a tool for working with marginalized communities to shift control over dominant narratives. For example, the Karuk Timeline documents historical injustices and community actions to address them, thereby establishing the rationale for greater Karuk participation in land management decisions. By creating an enduring output for local people, the technique also avoided the problem of extractive research, where community knowledge is gathered solely for external use. The Timeline method was also an example of a respectful, place-based design process, which laid the groundwork for ongoing academic–community partnership through the Karuk–UC Berkeley Collaborative.

Technique 4.3

CHILDREN'S EXCITING NEIGHBORHOOD EXPLORATION EVENT

Isami Kinoshita

In this program children visit special places in the city, such as private gardens, the homes of craftspeople, and shops along the street, in order to investigate a theme that highlights community issues. The mission is created through collaboration between the owners of the places, or "spots," and the event organizers, who are neighborhood activists. By engaging with an exciting theme, children see their neighborhood from a new perspective, which stimulates their imagination and encourages further engagement with the place where they live. These events renew the communication between children and their community, in particular the elderly residents. These activities also help identify local resources and show them in a new light and can even lead to neighborhood improvements.

To prepare for an event, organizers (1) select the spots for the exploration event and (2) work with the owners to determine the theme. After the event the children debrief on what they have experienced and learned.

Instructions

1. The event organizers should first select the target area for the event and create a theme by identifying the local resources.

2. A preresearch workshop involving observation and interviews is recommended to develop the theme, such as "Edible Culinary Tour" or "Archeology Exploring Like Indiana Jones." Event organizers should be very creative in coming up with themes.

3. Once a theme is determined it is time to select the spots to visit. The number of places visited should be considered according to the number of participants and the time allotted. In general, six spots may be enough for one group of six children to visit in three hours. Reach out to shop owners, people in the neighborhood with knowledge of the local resources, and so forth.

4. Advertise the event by making a flyer that can be used to involve the stakeholders in the event and gain their assistance. If possible, obtain the administrative and financial support from local government, private firms, and local organizations. Distribute the flyer to the local press.

Figure 4-9: The owner explains to the students how he made the garden and how certain plants represent special events in his life, for example the birth of his children.

5. The exploration often involves creating activities at each spot to highlight issues. The site owner or tenant, local residents, and even the children should be involved in this step. It is the process of reconsidering the value of the resources of the spot. Site quizzes are popular, but children seem to get the most out of interacting with physical elements of the site.

6. Create a guidebook for participants. Include a map showing the spots and the valuable information collected during the preparation process—it may become a useful walking guide for the neighborhood at a later date. Draw the assignment instructions for each spot. The best instructions are those with more illustrations and fewer words. Other things to include are the program schedule and rules and an acknowledgment of the organizations and people who supported the activity.

7. If there are quizzes, hide them in the guidebook for later discovery—maybe in a secret pocket.

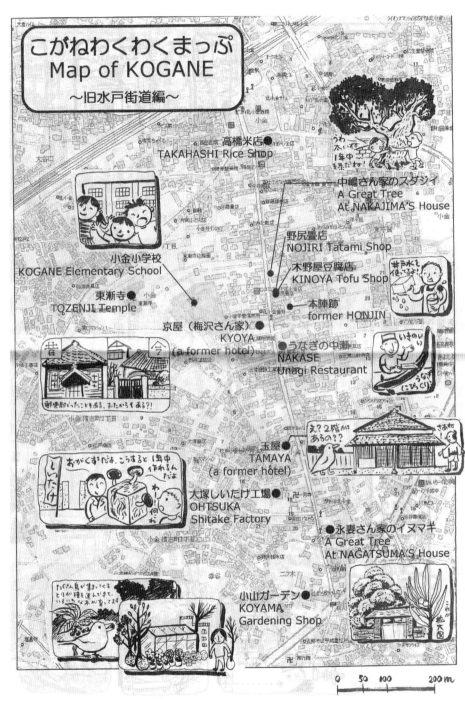

Figure 4-10: The guide map of the exploring tour.

8.   Create a script or scenario for the event and rehearse it in advance. Be sure the roles encourage collaboration between adults and children. Leaving room for improvisation is important too. Imagine the spot is like a theater necessitating roles for many people in the play.

9.   If you need permission from the police to stage the event, be sure to submit required documents with enough time to spare.

10.   Enlist volunteers and parents to unobtrusively supervise safety on the street.

11.   On the day of the event, gather at the starting point. Begin with an orientation of the mission, distribute the guidebook, and make introductions of guests who supported the event. A greeting speech might be needed if there are VIP guests, but it should be brief.

12.   After the event the children should gather to reflect upon the program and share their impressions. A short workshop may be useful where the students make a map or poster to express their thoughts.

Case Story

The neighborhood exploration program began in the Kogane District of Matsudo City, Japan, both a typical suburb and a historical post Edo-era town. The city is also facing the issue of an aging society, which is pervasive throughout Japan. The first event was held in 1999 with the goal of giving children the experience of picking *kaki* (persimmons) from private gardens. In the old times, children used to play a game by using bamboo sticks to steal persimmons. However, under modern societal rules these activities incurred offences if they happened without permission of the owner. Thus the theme was titled "Let's Steal Kaki."

In 2012, "exploration event" programs became part of the official school curricula, with a different theme each year. The 6th graders select the spots and plan the educational program. The participants are 4th and 5th graders. Over the 17 years this exploration has occurred, the spots are selected where the owners are eager to welcome children. One elderly homeowner went so far as to prepare 100 sets of juice and snacks, which delighted the children and gave the homeowner great satisfaction. It is an evocative moment when the owners, who are delighted by the visit, also recognize the value of the green environment and the history of their living environment, which they can share through the transactive engagement with the children.

This event is useful in encouraging property owners to open their homes, many of which are behind walls, to the neighborhood. These interactions bring to light the local history, landscape, and identity. In 2004, one of the members of the neighborhood

〇プロの記者になるための修業　その4

考え ✋ みよう！

〇本土寺参道の黒門屋、赤門屋

本土寺の手前に黒門屋、赤門屋というお店があります。な

ぜ黒門屋というのでしょうか？

いらっしゃい

ねえ
何を売って
いるの——？

千葉の
名産品が
あったよ

？

うーん
どっちが赤めやさんで
どっちが黒めやさん
だったかな？

12

Figure 4-11: A workbook page.

Figure 4-12: Mr. T offered his carport to make a park (before).

exploration group organized an open garden tour. After that he offered his carport to create a privately owned pocket park for the public to use. University students and children developed alternatives and worked with a carpenter friend of the owner to build the final design. The owner paid the construction fee himself.

After the event's fourth year the neighborhood organized a community development corporation with members of all ages. The organization has gone on to lead different community design projects to improve the townscape, such as putting flower planters along the street, providing night illumination in winter, reviving the market at the temple gateway, and holding regular concerts. After 10 years of consensus building, residents agreed to move overhead electrical wires underground, which, though common in Western countries, in Japan is quite difficult because private properties are involved.

Figure 4-13: The carport became a pocket park open to the public (after).

Reflection

Japan has changed as it has become more affluent and consumer oriented, causing a disconnect between people and leading to human isolation. However, Japanese society has learned the importance of neighborly communication from the great East Japan earthquake and tsunami disaster in 2011. By encouraging neighborhood exploration the Kogane program has broken down the social barriers that continue to exist in many other places and has connected the people to the greater community. Many more people in Kogane are now involved in public matters.

The neighborhood exploration event may also contribute to finding new methods to identify the valued characteristics of a community. Further, a child's feeling of place attachment increases. There might be barriers to gaining access to proposed visiting spots; however, through transactive exchange between children asking questions about the spots and the owners answering, resistance gradually turns to enthusiasm, and community pride surfaces. In Kogane, over time, it became an honor for the property owners, tenants, and residents to accept the children's visits and collaborate with them. Postevent surveys revealed that children developed a willingness to take part in community design processes and felt more attached to their neighborhoods, which fostered a commitment to live in the neighborhood as adults.

Technique 4.4

COMMUNITY INNOVATION FORUM

Christian Dimmer and Yu Ohtani

The Community Innovation Forum (CIF) is a mobile workshop and exhibition that initiates a visioning dialogue in and between local communities confronted with significant socioeconomic, demographic, or environmental problems. Where residents lack awareness and confidence and are skeptical of interacting with outside experts it serves to spark bottom-up development potentials, energize networks of neighbors already working on the ground, stimulate creativity, and increase local knowledge of community assets. These are important enablers for later, more systematic visioning processes.

The CIF is run by a design team, but the designers' role is one of enabler, working with local instigators to organize events and identify participants. Key elements of CIF are discussion forums where nonexpert but seasoned citizen innovators from nearby neighborhoods are invited to share their experiences that inspire and impel the host or "base" community to take action. These are followed by town walks that start in the base community and expand to other neighborhoods where revitalization has occurred. In community mapping sessions participants create an analogue exhibition that presents knowledge collected during the workshop. The co-learning process creates social capital, a more positive sense of self-efficacy, and shared problem awareness. In this way community innovators expand their network, while the dialogue creates new innovators, and together they have confidence to take on new collaborative projects.

Instructions

1. Make an agreement to work with a group in your base community—local people who have realized there are problems and want to do something about it. Within the group you will need to identify key participants or local organizations that can serve as intermediaries between the base community, innovators from other neighborhoods, and the design team. They are crucial to mobilizing the event but will also play a vital role in moving the dialogue forward after the CIF. At the same time begin to identify the human and place resources that can be knit together to create a cross-community dialogue about positive change.

2. Next select an appropriate workshop venue. It should have a strong meaning for residents in the base neighborhood and should not be monopolized by the corporate or government sectors. The space should be big enough to hold community discussions and to work in small groups. The space also needs to be big enough for a mapping exhibition that will become the record of what is learned. Community

members should be involved in preparing the workshop venue so as to showcase local identity.

3. Prepare maps for the base neighborhood and the other neighborhoods you will visit during the workshop. They need to be big enough to show street widths and building footprints.

4. Organize an introductory discussion forum to showcase grassroots innovations that emerged in response to similar problems. The forum speakers should feature nonexperts who "speak the same language" as the base neighborhood. They should have credibility and be good at engaging others—the guiding principle being that citizens teach and inspire other citizens. Generate a speaker list with your core group and use your own networks. Between four and six speakers is ideal.

5. After the forum mark the projects and initiatives presented on the exhibition map. This documentation is an iterative process that will occur throughout the workshop.

Figure 4-14: An introductory talk forum showcases community innovations so as to inspire citizens in other neighborhoods.

6. In the following days take participants on town walks. The initial walk should focus on the base neighborhood in order to construct a shared awareness about challenges and potentials. Then explore several other neighborhoods (usually three to encourage exchange). Local regeneration activists who are familiar with the urban history of the neighborhoods should guide the walks and connect participants to each other in situ. Strong participation of base residents should be safeguarded to make sure they will be prepared for subsequent community actions.

7. After each town walk the group should return to the workshop venue and collectively map the innovations they've discovered, along with challenges and the potential for regeneration. Mapping should be about the places participants have visited and the people of the places.

8. In addition to putting the information on the map, participants should record the information on "profile sheets" and add them to the exhibition. The profile sheet should include information about the who, what, and where—in other words a brief description of the people and place and why they are important, the location, and contact information for future use.

Figure 4-15: A series of town walks through different neighborhoods connect participants to each other in situ. Source: Kenichiro Egami.

Case Story

The first CIF took place in spring 2015 in a Northeast Tokyo neighborhood characterized by run-down local shopping streets, dilapidated and disaster-prone wooden buildings along narrow alleys next to large-scale housing estates, condominium towers, and expansive infrastructure installations. Deteriorated physical conditions were compounded by a high proportion of elderly residents. Few community regeneration activities had occurred here.

A recently closed public bathhouse—long an important informal community node—served as the workshop venue. The dressing room became the forum and workshop space while the connected bathing pool became the exhibition space. A nonprofit run by a local businessperson and arts-revitalization activist served as the intermediary, contacting the bathhouse owner and assembling the volunteers.

At the discussion forum the organizing group outlined neighborhood issues and established the framework for the CIF event. All invited speakers followed a rigid presentation template of 10 minutes and 10 slides, each addressing practical, shared issues, such as member motivation, resource mobilization, organizational sustainability, project funding, and problem-solving mechanisms. The forum was followed by four town walks and two more discussion forums—one featuring small, local innovations; the other showcasing area-wide regeneration projects. Town walks began in the base community and then moved on to three distinctly different Tokyo neighborhoods: one, a suburban setting, where a group of newcomer political activists revived a community together with elderly shopkeepers; another, a now-trendy district with historical buildings and a wealth of small boutiques, cafés, and galleries; and the third, an old working-class neighborhood with a history of 20 years of community design and socially engaged art activities.

The exhibition reflected the neighborhood character. Styrofoam boxes, obtained from a nearby fish market, were assembled to form a large Tokyo map, onto which the growing collection of community innovations was recorded. Every innovation identified on the walks, such as community cafés, intergenerational houses, recycling shops, and parent-run play facilities, was represented by a flag. Project profile sheets with short descriptions and contact details for community innovators they met were hung on laundry lines crisscrossing the bath. During the breaks, as well as before and after the forums, people experienced the exhibit, read and discussed the profiles, and contributed their own suggestions to the sheets.

The CIF forums, exhibition, and town walks were well attended, attracting visitors of all ages and walks of life. Physical changes have not yet occurred, but different community innovators from across the four neighborhoods have started to collaborate with one another. In May 2017 a 10-day pavilion was built for a food event that was held in one of the neighborhoods visited during the walks. The next CIF is planned for autumn in another of the neighborhoods.

Figure 4-16: An analogue exhibit grows out of the weeklong event, this one staged in the bath.

Reflection

The landscape of community activism is fragmented in Japan, and often emphasizes differences, not commonalities. The presentation template of the discussion forums helped to focus on common challenges and to facilitate communication between activists who wouldn't otherwise have met. Thus the event succeeded to connect fellow community innovators from across the city, creating links between Tokyo-wide known change leaders and local projects, as well as bridging social capital between innovators working on similar projects and scales. CIF also succeeded to initiate a dialogue among all participants, speakers, and audiences.

Yet each event was attended by different people, which hindered continuity in networking between guest speakers, base community members, and participants from the other neighborhoods. Also, the number of local residents from the base community was low; people are busy, and few were able to take part in activities lasting more than a few hours. This is a challenge for the next CIF.

Although similar network formats have since emerged in Tokyo, the CIF is unique in that it brings change makers together in a challenged community and promotes co-learning

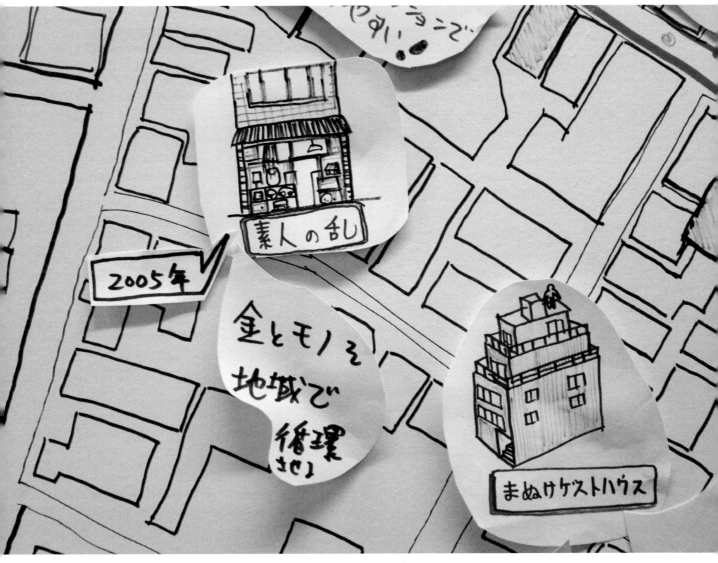

Figure 4-17: Participants map local resources (detail). Source: Kenichiro Egami.

and empowerment. Based on their experience from the first workshop, the design team is preparing for the next CIF by working more extensively with the base community members, the intermediaries, and local change makers in the other neighborhoods visited. The goal is to create a horizontal grassroots network of community innovators that expands but remains within reach of local citizens.

Technique 4.5

THE BIG MAP

Chao-Ching Yu

Large aerial photos and maps are powerful for connecting people to their environment during the participatory design process. These materials can unfold people's real life in the context of their place in the world. The Big Map can elicit memories of the past, awareness of the present, and imagination of the future for individuals, community groups, and government officials. It can also generate interaction, dialogue, discussion, and decisions collectively. It is indeed the "space" for a participatory design workshop.

The essence of this technique is preparing a larger-than-life map that can be used throughout the design process, from initial orientation through prioritizing a plan of action. This can be undertaken to foster long-term changes, shifting perceptions as the map is created, but ultimately the full impact may take several years.

Instructions

1. Make the map. Keep in mind that it will be the memory of discussions during your design process. The map should be large enough to occupy the main wall of the room or the center of the floor. When people enter the room they actually walk directly into the space that the Big Map unfolds. There should be no barrier preventing people from touching or walking onto it.

2. Gather accessories in advance. Some accessories and materials are necessary for discussion, such as stickers, labels, and tape in various colors and sizes; markers; and anything that will help to attach thoughts to the map.

3. Find home. Open by asking participants to locate their home so they can immediately relate themselves to the map. Starting at home, people can easily orient by tracing their daily paths. This is the threshold to bring people together; you will be surprised how quickly people can tune themselves in to a mood for discussion.

4. Walk through the map. The main job for the facilitator of a workshop is to get participants to visualize their past memories of the place, the present situation, and their future expectations by letting these local experts lead the "walk" through the map. Discussions of key events, everyday activities, and fond memories will arise. Record and post information on the map as the discussion unfolds.

5. Generate the issues. From the walk-through people will have a more integrated understanding of their home in the context of the community rather than a closed view from their personal experience. Urgent issues with public concerns will catch attention immediately and generate discussion. New information, observations,

and opinions are revealed. The places, paths, and boundaries of the issue that are the spatial focus of discussion need to be recorded.

6.   Pinpoint the projects. Over the course of a project detailed maps, drawings, and even scale models should be prepared for formulating specific projects. These can also be done at a "Big" scale. But the Big Map must continue to be updated so that it becomes the accumulated, collective, living archive of the process. By the end projects will be pinpointed on the map, accompanied by a list of prioritized action plans with distribution of responsibilities across different community groups to guide further professional and political efforts.

Case Story

There was an abandoned railway track corridor in the heart of Hua-lien City, Taiwan, waiting for reuse. I was asked by a friend whether my graduate design studio could work with the local residents on a bottom-up proposal of public uses for this "necklace of pearls" before the county government converted it into a new road and development corridor.

My friend knew where to find interested groups and communities that would form the backbone of the process. A three-by-nine-meter aerial photo, or Big Map, was prepared to kick off the community workshops. I needed to quickly identify some issues to focus on and, hopefully, a few public projects that my studio team could work on. The map did the trick. The participants were immediately drawn to places they knew and the issues they cared about.

In order to zoom in on specific issues we arranged workshops to invite different groups to the Big Map discussion. During separate workshops for neighborhood leaders and for local merchants, I discovered a crucial problem for regeneration. When the train was in operation a half century ago there was a section of the track with rows of shops on both sides fronting two streets, which were the main shopping area in the city. After the space of the track corridor was no longer in use, merchants expanded the rear of their shops to the center line of the track. The railroad company collected rent from them until county government proposed an urban renewal plan, which ignored the shop owners' right for continuing their business and precluded them from taking part in the redevelopment.

Because the problem was so challenging and intertwined with numerous factors, such as merchants' rights, zoning, and urban design, it was a good project for the design studio to engage in. After Big Map workshops, the studio team conducted other design workshops for all small shop owners in the project area to figure out an alternative plan for the county government to consider. Their proposal was accepted and adopted by the zoning department the following year.

After adoption we were invited by city government to help merchants work out a physical plan for a street market with an ownership distribution method, which reflected indi-

Figure 4-18: Neighborhood leaders use the Big Map for an early workshop discussion.

Figure 4-19: Shop owners are able to experience the actual space of their future store using a full-size mock-up.

vidual rights and shares while at the same time preserving the existing urban tissue. Again, large-size floor plans and sections were used for the owners to comprehend the complicated problems and solutions. During the process the design studio came up with alternative ways of sharing the public facilities and the easement equitably without sacrificing too much indi- vidual store area; but no one was satisfied. Surprisingly, the idea for the scheme ultimately agreed upon was proposed by a shop owner, by fax. A full-size mock-up of a typical store interior was built for the final discussion. Using the Big Floor Plan people were able to make decisions on the plan that had begun with the first Big Map discussion two years prior.

Figure 4-20: Shops on the revitalized street.

Reflection

Relating real experiences to two-dimensional, abstract technical graphics is difficult for most laypeople when they are not in the actual space. The Big Map is an effective way for participants to identify real places, especially when the size of the image is larger than our body size and exceeds the visual boundaries of our sight. Then we will be easily drawn into the space, body and mind.

The Map created a way to build the layers of information gathered from workshop to workshop so that the design team could fluidly consider the details of a single shopkeeper's issues and fold them into bigger, integrated design decisions. This was also the participants' experience—they could enter the discussion using their concerns as a tangible way to connect their lives to both the large domain of their living landscape and their sense of individual existence. In the case of Hua-lien City, large-scaled graphic tools with accurate dimensions, such as sections, site plans, and models, were equally effective as the Big Map in connecting people to design.

After any Big Map workshop, if there is a community space large enough to hang the map on the wall, then it will not only be a record of previous efforts but will also become a mirror that reflects the community's past, present, and future. People will still be able to interact with and learn from it. In short, the Big Map will bring the outside world to the room and keep connecting people to their dynamic environment, their story, and will continuously unfold their imagination and reveal the unknown.

5

"Yeah! That's What We Should Do"

Hindsight may be 20/20, but the vision that inspires place-based community design often gains clarity only through the iterative process of engagement. One may begin with "near" vision, for instance a sighting that zooms in on an immediate problem or proposes a solution based on what a community lacks when compared with others. This near vision is often guided by a scope of work—the design team is hired to design a new plaza so it is open space that we focus on. However, as more information is collected, the clarity we may have started with begins to cloud. Yes, a new plaza would be very good for the community, but is it enough to address some of the other issues that people are beginning to discuss?

As people contextualize why things are the way they are, "far" or distant visions of what is possible may appear. The moment of clarity can be very tangible, such as when, at a community meeting, an older gentleman in the back of the room tells a story about something that happened during a bygone era, but the sting of failure is still fresh. Others add to it, and that story turns the conversation in a new direction. New examples of the age-old problem bring the audience back to the present, but someone has an idea, and soon everyone is nodding, saying "yeah, that's what we should do." Or, the true issue might remain unspoken, bound in uncomfortable discussions of deep-seated, structural inequalities that require conscientious work to exhume.

With this far vision we realize what we should strive for. But it can be difficult for participants to openly discuss their hopes for the community. This is especially true when community members aren't used to being asked their opinion, let alone to find the common ground required to make change. How do we create a process that is both open to dreams and grounded in the practicalities of getting things done?

SETTING PRIORITIES

After collecting information and working with a community to identify a range of issues, it is critical to shift from what is known to what needs to be done. In other words, to set priorities and develop a plan of action. While there are various techniques to choose from, the one employed must establish a fair forum for all community members to state their concerns and interests. A classic approach is the Nominal Group Technique, first developed by André Delbecq and Andrew Van de Ven, which allows every participant to generate his or her own list of ideas first, and then the group discusses and ranks all the ideas. Such methods avoid domination by the most vocal participants and prevent overlooking the more reserved. With all voices heard, we are able to set priorities and identify next steps. It is also possible to identify who will be responsible for furthering the work.

CAPTURING THE ESSENCE

When it becomes obvious that a community is saying one thing but working toward another, it is essential to change gears and call up synthetic or responsive techniques that evoke qualitative results. Reorienting the discussion away from a list of wicked problems or compromise solutions that no one is happy with and toward solutions that showcase what makes the community special liberates creativity and allows transformative, place-based visions to emerge. Such tactics remind us what the deeper goals are and push us to restructure the project toward helping us reach that destination.

BREAKING THE RULES AND CHANGING THE BOUNDARIES

There are projects in which the scope and the solution don't match. When consensus is elusive and the long-term goal is unclear it may be important to identify small actions that move the community forward, one step at a time. Or it can be an issue of scale—we realize we are working on stopgap measures that are too small to achieve a sustainable outcome. This may require crossing boundaries into new territory that is beyond the immediate project and exploring ideas that initially seem unrealistic or remote to the needs of the community. At such times we need to create opportunities for thinking outside the box in order to better understand what we may be able to achieve. Changing the boundaries may also suggest the need to engage others and partner across communities with like issues.

TECHNIQUES THAT GET TO "YEAH"

This chapter includes techniques that shift the view and bring to light underlying issues in ways that catalyze new visions and solutions. Maren King's "Prioritizing Decisions" starts with a technique designed to facilitate community decision making by providing a forum for each participant to state his or her concerns and interests. In "Community Voting, Local Committees" Sago Network from Papua New Guinea explains a technique that identifies community concerns as internally or externally driven in order to clarify what the group is able to do and what requires additional resources. It also charges local committees with the responsibility to work toward solutions. Randolph T. Hester Jr., in "Getting a Gestalt," provides a technique for extracting salient issues that are raised in community discussions and then organizing the information in a way that expresses the essence of the situation. Similarly, Marcia J. McNally's "In-House Aha!" allows the design team to explore nascent ideas that may or may not be appropriate to share with the community in the beginning and may require a redefined process to discuss. Working from time-tested *machizukuri* techniques of neighborhood community building, Yoko Tsuchiya and Masato Dohi in "*Renkei* Method: Scaling Up by Connecting Scenes," describe a *Renkei* process whereby a group of neighborhoods share their ideas and activities to scale up to a new lens of possibility for the region.

Technique 5.1

PRIORITIZING DECISIONS

Maren King

Community design processes often result in multiple possibilities, desires, and needs (e.g., different land uses, program elements, activity settings, or specific features). The Prioritizing Decisions activity allows a group to distill this list and progress toward agreement by setting priorities that they will use to frame the next stage of the process. It is a version of the Nominal Group Technique that engages participants in discussion through graphic and verbal cues to allow assimilation of new knowledge, promote understanding, and provide a foundation for discussion.

Instructions

1. Prepare an image-rich presentation and poster(s) to describe and illustrate the possibilities that have been determined thus far in the community design process. Possibilities may refer to activities in a park, land uses in a downtown area, or housing choices. Select images that show distinguishing characteristics. Provide space around each possibility for placement of dots. Make sure what is shown in the presentation is the same or similar to what appears on the poster(s).

2. Gather materials, including dots, markers, a flip chart, and notepads.

3. Present the possibilities to the entire group. Provide a basic description of each and allow for clarifying questions.

4. Divide into groups of 5 to 10. Each group should have a facilitator and the poster(s) of possibilities. The facilitator is typically someone from the design team but could also be a community member who has been coached to facilitate. Review the possibilities and add other ideas to the poster as suggested by the group.

5. Define the number of possibilities that each participant can choose and distribute that number of dots to each participant.

6. Individual participants decide on the possibilities they believe are most appropriate and mark each selection with a dot.

7. By counting the number of dots assigned to each possibility, identify the top priorities. There may be clear top priorities or a mix of them.

8. Engage in a group discussion of the choices each person made. Start with the top priorities and go around the group one by one for their responses. Document responses on a flip chart and have a member of the design team or a community member take detailed notes for later analysis and synthesis with other groups. During this process, other group members can ask for clarification but cannot criticize the responses. If agreed to by the group, modifications can be proposed.

Figure 5-1: Participants in the Onondaga Park play area design process used dots to identify their top five priority behavior settings on a poster with 15 choices.

9. After the discussion the priority list may need to be further narrowed or the discussion may have yielded a modified list, and another dot selection may be needed.

10. At this point, depending on the type of decision being made, the group may use the priorities they agreed on to immediately move to a next step, such as creating a site design, neighborhood diagram, or model, or they may come back together with the larger group to present the results that will be used for next steps by other members of the planning or design team.

Case Story

The Prioritizing Planning and Design Decisions technique has been used by the State University of New York College of Environmental Science and Forestry's Center for Community Design Research in several community design projects, including the design of a natural play area in Syracuse's Onondaga Park. The process was organized by a working group of community members, parks department staff, and landscape architecture students and faculty in a thematic community design studio. Approximately 60 residents from the surrounding neighborhoods participated in a series of three workshops that progressed from exploration of values to review of conceptual design models.

The Prioritizing Decisions technique was used during the second workshop to select program elements for a play area. After a presentation of natural play principles and examples of possible activity settings (active water play, gathering spaces, flower and vegetable gardens, moveable play parts, etc.), participants divided into three smaller groups to review and prioritize possible activity settings shown on a large poster. There were a total of 15 activity settings illustrated, and each participant placed dots on their top five priority activity settings. There was significant deliberation in making selections but also lots of talking and laughter. In all of the groups most priorities were clear from the dot distribution. Discussion was framed by several questions, including "Why were these settings selected as priorities?" and "What activities could occur in each of the settings?" Discussion confirmed their group's basic selections and led to decisions that were then used to create basic designs.

Once priorities had been articulated, the next step was to figure out how the activity settings would relate to each other when placed on the site. Large aerial views of the two-acre site and context were the basis for these designs. Participants used color-coded squares of different sizes to represent activity settings, such as gathering spaces, pathways, water or sand play areas, planting areas, play structures, and others. Each group tried various layouts, took digital photos, and ultimately created "final designs." Team representatives presented their designs, followed by comments and questions. The working group then outlined common ideas and features. Design team members presented models of conceptual design alternatives at the third workshop. The final design of the play area emerged from the results of this process.

The first phase of play area construction was completed in spring 2016. One of the first elements completed was a splash pad. All of the workshop groups had identified an active water play feature as a top priority and sited it in the same area on their diagrams—in the vicinity of Star Lake, which was filled in the 1970s. Images and memories of the lake strongly influenced community members' desire for a water feature in the same location.

Figure 5-2: Before coming up with a final design diagram the small groups used color-coded paper to explore layout and relationship ideas.

Reflection

This technique has been used successfully to facilitate design decisions at a site or neighborhood scale, including green infrastructure for stormwater management, community gardens, small plazas, and parks and open space planning. The technique provides a clear structure to help ensure that all participants have the opportunity to individually express their desires or preferences. The physical placement of dots is an action enjoyed by participants of all ages. In addition to making selections immediately visible, it provides an opening for people who might not know each other to talk and interact. It was used to initiate discussions for a memorial garden design with Vietnamese community members who had limited English language skills, helping to establish a shared understanding between the design team and community members beyond that facilitated by the translator.

While the dots provide a basic representation, facilitated discussion is necessary to understand different perspectives and develop new ideas. It is a useful technique to explore disparate ideas or viewpoints, identify areas of disagreement, and find common ground.

Take great care in selecting the information and presentation examples because they will serve as the frame for discussion. Consider having community members submit photos or examples to include in the presentation, and always consult and review your choices in advance with community members of your team.

Technique 5.2

COMMUNITY VOTING, LOCAL COMMITTEES

Sago Network

Community Voting, Local Committees are democratic planning tools deployed at the outset of a participatory design process to ensure a project's relevance to the community while also building community ownership and empowerment. Community Voting lets communities voice their needs and values and then determine their own priorities, whereas Local Committees facilitates the leadership of proactive community members who need to take care of important decisions throughout a project's design and delivery and into its ongoing future use. Local Committees, formed from a representative cross section of the community, often prove to be a key vehicle for advancing a mutually agreed upon project. As local champions they become community spokespeople, facilitators of further decisions, and local organizers of action.

Instructions

1. Identify a facilitator equipped to convene an inclusive workshop with the objective to prioritize the issues that community members want addressed. The facilitator should be sensitive to the quieter voices of less represented community members and should document the discussion in large format in front of the crowd by whatever means is most convenient, such as large-format paper or a whiteboard.

2. Having arrived at a list of issues facing the community, categorize issues as either internal or external based on whether the community is able to address the challenge solely by proactive internal self-organization or the community requires the assistance of external collaborators.

3. Ask community members to vote on both the internal and external issues that have the most importance to them. Ten voting tokens are provided to each community member to apportion to the list of identified issues, with the sole caveat that five tokens are to be directed to internal and external issues, respectively. It is possible to allocate more than one token to an issue. The resulting list of community-determined development priorities provides a design team with insight into genuine community sentiment and often either confirms or contradicts original assumptions about the most relevant community project.

4. The workshop concludes with a call to action for proactive, vocal, and engaged community members to serve on Local Committees to address each development challenge and serve as the key driving energy for addressing each issue and any potential project that might be the result.

Figure 5-3: Women from the village of Laukanu cast their vote with tokens to decide the development priorities for their community.

5. The first meeting of each Local Committee aims to formulate a strategy by which the development challenge should be addressed. Central to this task is "connecting the dots" between priorities and the internal and external skills sets needed to achieve the desired change. Where an external issue is to be addressed, Local Committee members become the key intermediaries between the professional collaborators and the community, soliciting the opinion of community members and forming key decisions that shape the project's direction.

6. With an agreed-upon strategy in place and project collaborators identified, the Local Committee is next charged with the responsibility of forming a Project Partner Agreement that clearly notes all parties' agreed-upon roles. This is often a multilingual and graphically illustrated agreement that clearly identifies the key contributions toward the proposed project, formalizing these commitments into a document that is signed by the Local Committee, community leaders, and all project partners.

7. As the iterative design process unfolds, Local Committees convene regular presentations and consultation sessions to keep community members informed of progress, field questions, and secure continued input. The frequency varies depending on the nature of the design process—a rapid process may require presentations every two days, whereas a larger and more complex project might require presentations once a month or once every two months. With a Local Committee genuinely engaged in the project process and collaborating with the design team, it is a powerfully effective gesture to have the community members from the committee deliver or contribute to key design presentations to fellow community members.

8. As important decisions arise throughout the project process, the technique of Community Voting often warrants repeating to secure open, transparent, and community-wide decision making. For instance, further Community Voting can be undertaken to decide between design options developed by the design team and the Local Committee.

9. The Local Committee's leadership role should be acknowledged and celebrated when the completed project is unveiled to the broader community. For them, the work is not over; the Local Committee's role and sense of ownership often remain beyond project completion, transitioning to ongoing project stewardship where monitoring, maintenance, or further program rollout is the longer-term test of a project's success.

Case Story

The techniques of Community Voting, Local Committees are crucial to each community development project undertaken by Sago Network in Papua New Guinea and have helped to establish a long-term and continuing collaboration with the community of Laukanu. This remote and largely subsistence-based village was suffering significant health issues stemming from a lack of access to potable drinking water and safe sanitation facilities. During multiple early community visits, Sago Network's team of architects and community development professionals were careful not to presume the community's commitment to addressing their water and sanitation challenges, nor the type of project response that might be appropriate, nor any promises about what professional capabilities they could bring. Rather, a professional community development officer within the Sago Network team facilitated a two-day workshop to let the community identify their development priorities and commitments. Full community meetings facilitated open community-wide debate and were complemented by smaller and more focused discussion groups. These discussion groups were, at different times, formed around either common concerns, such as people with shared regard for the lack of formal sanitation facilities, or along age and gender lines to let often-muted voices, such as those of senior women or young men, give voice to their particular issues; overcoming social mores and taboos.

Figure 5-4: Led by a professional community development officer Laukanu villagers debate their development priorities.

Figure 5-5: Using a process that engenders a sense of ownership in the program being delivered and a capacity for ongoing maintenance of the soon-to-be-completed water pumps, a representative from the Laukanu Village Water Committee assembles a pump, surrounded by other committee members and interested villagers.

The workshop identified a raft of issues that community members were eager to address and revealed important local knowledge about a land dispute with a neighboring tribe that, unbeknownst to the government who had formulated their own water supply proposal, would have rendered their intended project futile had it proceeded. It also provided a supportive forum in which social mores and taboos were successfully overcome to discuss important issues surrounding existing sanitation practices throughout the village.

The workshop culminated with Community Voting in which all community members were allocated five stones to apportion to internal issues that the community could proactively address themselves and five stones to apportion to external issues that required expertise from beyond the village. Water and sanitation were identified and confirmed as key community concerns, but, crucially, it was a transparent and democratic process that enabled community members to collectively discuss and determine these things themselves.

The process also gave rise to a committed and diverse group of men and women who formed local water and sanitation committees and became the key leaders and instigators of grassroots change by facilitating community discussions, leading presentation sessions, and, ultimately, determining key decisions that guided the project. This group of proactive and proud community leaders continued to maintain the water and sanitation facilities that they had played an active role in realizing.

Reflection

As part of a community workshop, Community Voting, Local Committees provide approaches for discussion and prioritization as well as sharing responsibility and leadership. In some cases, it may be most appropriate to conduct the community voting process in a manner that lets community members cast their votes without oversight by others and without the knowledge of how others are voting, as opposed to the open community meeting setting employed at Laukanu. Equally as important is the value of engaging a professionally qualified and culturally conversant facilitator when the design team is working in a cross-cultural context. This facilitator often becomes a key linguistic and cultural translator and also enables the design team to remain in the background while a forum is convened in which community members feel open and comfortable to address their most critical development challenges.

Technique 5.3

GETTING A GESTALT

Randolph T. Hester Jr.

A gestalt is a simple structure of natural, cultural, and psychological phenomena that expresses the essence of a community issue and a direction for explicit transformative actions. This structure is integrated with properties not derivable from the mere sum of its parts.

There usually comes a time when a design appears to meet community needs, but the result is a lifeless compromise satisfying no one. The parts address symptoms without creating a more perfect union. The community must reflect deeply to develop a distinctive organizing principle. This process is "getting a gestalt." A good gestalt gets at the heart of the matter by being simple yet comprehensive. It sees the forest *and* the trees. It provides a "coat rack" upon which disparate needs may be hung. A good gestalt makes the community smile because it so captures what they are pursuing and provides clear direction for making design decisions.

A gestalt can be expressed in many forms: words, a sketch, a performance, or poetic prose. A gestalt is more than a concept that expresses emotionless function; more than a "valentine," expressing emotion without practical means of function. A gestalt captures both effective and affective qualities as one.

Instructions

1. In preparation, be sure the community has done the background work. A gestalt typically can be articulated only after a lot of searching for answers to local problems has been completed.

2. With your design team, develop a short list of key conclusions from each of the previous steps in your process. This might include recurring points learned from listening; the most consciously and unconsciously deeply held values; how historic and future issues and resources intersect; key points from inventories that may have been ignored; things that are unsaid; how people respond to various alternative plans; and what most touches your heart here. Summarize these into a wall presentation and handouts for community members.

3. Decide on the best forum for the community to work together on the search for the gestalt. Usually an open forum in your usual meeting place is fine. Or you might decide participants will be more creative in a new setting, often on-site, exposed to the sensual pleasures of the place. In some communities there is a building associated with poetic or artistic activities that might evoke inventiveness; we sometimes will move the gestalt workshop there. In any case be sure it is an accessible setting

Figure 5-6: One citizen-generated collage showed front porches where Manteo residents could share their dreams. The past is underfoot, and the future, where unemployed boat builders are back at work, floats above. This collage approximated the gestalt, "Come sit on our front porch, let us tell you of the dreams we keep."

for people who have participated throughout the process, and personally invite them. You need participants who have absorbed the previous findings and have been thinking deeply about the project.

4. Make a script that outlines how the forum will proceed in order to reach agreement. This step is critical in getting a gestalt because participants are not accustomed to this kind of activity. Prepare design staff to lead the process at tables

of five to six people. The script should begin with explanations of each of steps 6 through 12 so that participants know what they will be doing, why, and what the likely outcomes will be. Be brief but check to be sure people understand how this is different than other processes. Pause to explain words like *essence*. Warn participants that they will need to use their left and right brains, thinking in both complex and playful terms simultaneously. Explain the importance of shaking the sillies out at some point.

5.   Arrange tables and materials to write, draw, paint, make models, collages, and the like.

6.   Introduce the whole group to the exact task at hand. A gestalt takes some explaining and may require multiple examples. Using the case story described here is helpful because the Manteo gestalt led to distinctive design solutions. Then go over the prepared summary (created in step 2), slowly, encouraging clarification and elaboration.

7.   Tell each person to read the summary handout and to carefully note the important things that immediately come to mind. Have everyone close their eyes and sit quietly, mulling the information for a few minutes. Then instruct them to write or draw what came to mind as the essence of the community situation and a positive, encompassing outcome.

8.   Let them work quietly for 5 to 10 minutes then ask everyone to pause. Do something unexpected to distract them momentarily from their left brain effort. Play musical chairs or shake the sillies out for a few minutes.

9.   Have everyone return to their tables to review individual gestalts, then use whatever media they feel are most appropriate to express their ideas.

10.   Take turns sharing with others at the table. Tell participants to listen intently to each other without comment, making mental connections between all the gestalts, searching for commonality. Be sure to collect all the individual gestalts for later reference.

11.   Instruct each table to combine their ideas into a single gestalt. Be prepared for groans. Each of these steps is taxing. The staff at each table may need to offer leadership after everyone has presented; be ready to suggest several organizing schemas if no one speaks up. Be sure everyone contributes to the effort. Capture the resulting gestalt (gestalts if people insist on multiples) in a simple form; get someone to present to the whole group.

12.   Reconvene as a whole group and take turns presenting the gestalts from each table. Take a straw vote to see if there is one gestalt that people feel best expresses the essence. If there is, lead wild applause.

13. If not, acknowledge that "we are close but we do not have the compelling gestalt yet." Ask for a committee to complete the process. Ask all the participants to continue thinking about the gestalt and to bring ideas to the committee within the next few days. Help the committee develop a proposed gestalt to present at the next forum.

14. Present the gestalt at that forum. Have a means for feedback and/or adoption. Use the gestalt to make decisions.

Case Story

In Manteo, North Carolina, the gestalt process revealed the importance of recovering from 22 percent unemployment by revitalizing the town's waterfront as the center of boat building without disrupting daily life. A forum produced insightful collages, two of which were strongly preferred. One emphasized the lofty aspirations of the colonists who first settled the area in the 1580s and then disappeared. The other showed the many uses of front porches, central to the sacred structure. These two collages were satisfactory but did not "hit the nail on the head." A few days later, the mayor asked me to repeat all the keywords from the collages: *unemployed boatwrights*, *porches*, *Elizabethan history*, *dreams of freedom and*

Figure 5-7: The gestalt inspired the design of the waterfront, now miles long, as a community front porch with each building and civic landscape incorporating places to linger. The economic revival of Manteo, grounded in its distinctive boat-building history, reduced local unemployment from 22 percent to single digits.

Figure 5-8: Each building provides a variation of the indoor-outdoor front porch.

responsibility. Suddenly he blurted out, "Come sit on our front porch; let us tell you of the dreams we keep." He combined the practical aspects expressed through the collages with poetic lines from *The Lost Colony* outdoor drama that most local people knew by heart. This conveyed what the community was trying to achieve. It commanded inspired action grounded in cherished values unique to this place and people. When the mayor's imperative invitation was repeated, everyone nodded; many spontaneously clapped their hands in agreement. That was when we knew exactly what to do. The gestalt "Come sit on our front

Figure 5-9: Many public buildings invite visitors to linger, contemplating the dreams Manteo keeps.

porch; let us tell you of the dreams we keep" inspired the design of the entire waterfront, now miles long, as a "community front porch" that has won local devotion and international acclaim as a model for grassroots economic development and hands-on learning of a noble craft and values.

Reflection

Thinking about a problem comprehensively, deeply, and freshly is essential in community design because the issues are wicked, the resources limited, and rubber stamp solutions tempting. With so many superficial images to copy it is not easy to express a community's essence. And the community may have trouble understanding why it is important to seek something so poorly understood as a gestalt. However, results in other contexts convinced us years ago of the value of this technique. "She's a Hollywood Natural, wild and urbane" inspired a unique park in Hollywood. "Keep the Country Country" and "No Rush Rush" transformed a plan for the North Shore of Oahu. Getting a gestalt is central to "problem-seeking," a deeply creative approach to community change.

Technique 5.5

IN-HOUSE AHA!

Marcia J. McNally

The process of design is typically fluid, yet in community design it is expected to be articulated, step by step, and that the big ideas will transparently, automatically emerge through community engagement. However, the idea that participation excuses the designer from seeking the essence of the problem is antithetical to our practice. Participatory design demands deeper, not superficial, exploration by the professional. Some of the most essential discoveries are made by the designer in the office or studio—activities that can yield important "aha" moments. The In-House Aha! technique can produce those moments. The process is an opportunity to nail down what is known and what it means, to commune with the site and each other, and to establish a draft "place narrative." It is similar to a charrette, an activity familiar to community designers.

Instructions

1. Schedule a time when all team members can work together for at least four hours without interruption.
2. Prepare base maps and tools for hand drawing—tracing paper, pencils, tape, and so forth. One set for each team member.
3. Each team member is assigned with giving a 10-minute summary of what he or she has learned to date from listening, mapping, documenting, and other relevant sources. This part of the exercise should be done in advance of the meeting so that everyone is prepared and presentations are thoughtful.
4. Start the charrette with presentations of this information. Spend up to 90 minutes presenting and discussing.
5. Break into one-person "teams" to develop a first-take plan or design using this information. Be sure to define the assignment and the final product—clarify if each team is to articulate goals, list relevant analysis, develop alternatives, work at a certain scale, and so on. Take no more than 15 minutes to sort this out.
6. Work on individual plans for about an hour. Start by taping a piece of tracing paper over your base map. List the key information, goals, rules to adhere to or break, muses to satisfy, and so on that shape your approach to the plan. Give your plan/design all you can think of, as if it had to go public tomorrow.
7. Ask each team member to present his or her plan, followed by discussion. Each should take about 15 minutes.

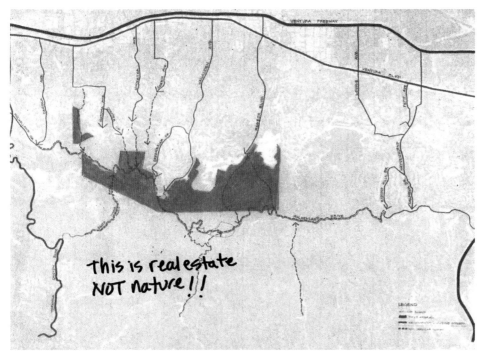

Figure 5-10: While my teammates were busy drawing at the site scale, I sat looking at the base map for Mulholland Gateway Park. It looked like what it was. Four beat-up parcels without ecological integrity that were to be the San Fernando Valley gateway to the Santa Monica Mountains.

8. Collectively summarize what you've learned. Discuss the political ramifications.
9. Identify next steps and follow-up.
10. As needed, plot the strategy to introduce your ideas to your client or to build community support, to determine if you need to change direction, or focus on a certain aspect of the project.

Case Story

In my office, Community Development by Design, we worked in Los Angeles (LA) on parks and open space plans for 25 years. Our primary client was the Santa Monica Mountains Conservancy (the Conservancy), a state agency charged with acquiring lands in the LA region for open space and ecosystem preservation. Starting in 1989 we began work on Mulholland Gateway Park, consisting of four noncontiguous parcels totaling 1,081 acres of land in the mountains. As is often the case in LA, the politics were a mess. The developer at the northern edge of the park was required to build a road up to Dirt Mulholland, an extension of Reseda Boulevard that had once been envisioned as the "Reseda-to-the-Sea" highway.

Environmentalists had already chained themselves to bulldozers; fistfights over traffic had broken out at community meetings. The project had become a battle between cars and mountain lions, roads and wildlife corridors rather than public access to urban wilderness.

An In-House Aha! provided an opportunity to process all the information that had been gathered from listening to people with multiple interests and from data collected about

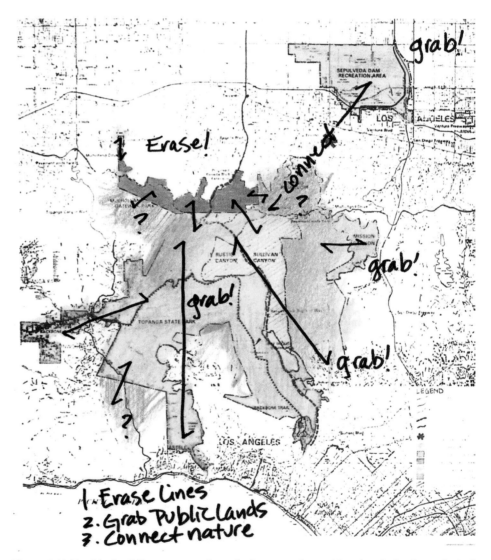

Figure 5-11: I grabbed a different map, at the scale that seemed more like what the landscape looked like when one was in it—real chaparral in every direction. I outlined all public lands close by and colored them yellow. Then it hit me—it was a big green that was supporting large mammals while offering an unparalleled urban wilderness experience. All we needed to do was erase the lines.

the site and larger context. As I approached my individual plan, I started by outlining the site and the large properties that were adjacent to the site but far beyond the scope of the project. Then I stopped. It dawned on me that I could erase the lines, because most of the parcels were publicly owned; they were just owned by different agencies. I realized I was looking at the proper scale of analysis from a habitat perspective. It was just 20 times bigger than that which we had contracted to work on.

A REGIONAL EVALUATION OF SITES IN THE PACIFIC PALISADES FOR THE SANTA MONICA MOUNTAINS CONSERVANCY

BIG WILD
ACCESS

Figure 5-12: The design team eventually proposed Big Wild, approximately 20,000 acres with vehicle-free, undisturbed core habitat and a series of gateway parks at the edge that were accessible by all transportation modes.

I presented my plan to my teammates, and we agreed to expand our focus to an area of 20,000 acres and to use a landscape-based strategy. To convince our client, we made a map with a big green in the center that showed the contiguous open-space areas. The Conservancy loved it—as Joe Edmiston, the executive director said, "Heaven forbid you tell a land acquisition agency to buy more land!" This big green quickly became "Big Wild," a concept that we then introduced to the public through tours and other activities. For instance, we

Figure 5-13: View from Big Wild across the San Fernando Valley to the Santa Susana Mountains.

arranged for school buses and one weekend drove 253 people to seven pre-scripted stops. Participants were given a "score sheet" survey to fill out at each stop, and asked to reflect on things like, "What is your most memorable wildlife experience in LA?" and "Do you ever drive through this neighborhood to take a short cut?" The impact was overwhelming—people were excited. During the weekend we heard comments like, "I've lived here all my life and I never knew this existed," and "It's like I'm a million miles from LA—this is fantastic!"

We pressed on with our ever-evolving process. We presented a draft plan to the Conservancy board, and the *Los Angeles Times* ran a lengthy article announcing "'Big Wild' Access Plan Unveiled." We were asked to meet with the city councilperson for the district, Marvin Braude. We brought a 20-foot-long pastel rendering that we had drawn to express overarching ideas of the plan, not knowing we had embodied his vision for LA when he first ran for council in the 1960s. He was impressed but felt that we had overemphasized the importance of preserving the area for biodiversity. "You need to serve the broad public interest," he admonished. Still, he was so taken with Big Wild that he was willing to reverse the developer's requirement to extend Reseda Boulevard to Dirt Mulholland. Ultimately the road extension was abandoned, the lands preserved, and gateway parks created. One of these parks is named for Councilman Braude.

Reflection

For me, being forced to use what little I knew at the time to quickly come up with a big idea opened up the black box of creativity. As such the In-House Aha! is a good process to use within a team to formulate ideas while also demystifying the design process and getting everyone to think big and "outside the box." Further, this project was an early experience in working with others from different disciplines—a traffic engineer, a lawyer, and a group of wildlife scientists—in order to make a defensible case for preserving urban wildlife habitat. Asking participants to mix the expertise and important factors from other fields with spatial thinking allows them to understand the complexity of design decision making.

Technique 5.5

RENKEI METHOD: SCALING UP BY CONNECTING SCENES

Yoko Tsuchiya and Masato Dohi

Community work and stewardship prevail at a relatively small scale within one's daily life. *Machizukuri*, or community-building work, is typically a localized process that engages residents in planning to improve their neighborhood while forming partnerships with local government. *Renkei* means "connection" in Japanese, so the *renkei* technique expands small *machizukuri* activities to larger scales of work without losing richness in its specificity and particularity. It can originate with a small group and grow to a neighborhood, a neighborhood to a community, then to an entire city or watershed basin. The core activity is to exchange the knowledge and resources of each community to reveal the inherent but not necessarily obvious connections between communities. The technique makes possible the opportunity for social and physical engagement between people and places that previously did not exist.

The goal of the *renkei* technique is for participants to develop a view that situates them in the larger region by mapping and connecting experiences and everyday life scenes that neighborhoods have in common. The first steps are taken by an individual *machizukuri* group in advance of the *renkei* meeting. On the day of the event groups take the next steps in pairs, and then ultimately all participating groups convene.

Instructions

1. The first series of steps require a *machizukuri* group to develop maps that reflect the neighborhood or geographic area that is the focus of their project. Provide one large map that can be located in a place that allows group members to gather around it.

2. On the map locate the activities that have been done by the group by placing photographs, sketches, and dialogues or key quotes to visually explain the experiences and information gained.

3. Once the maps are done, the group should confirm that each activity is shown and that the map establishes a representative image of the whole neighborhood.

4. The team should then evaluate the condition of the neighborhood by indicating the problems, resources, and characteristics on the map.

5. Once satisfied with the map, form a team with another *machizukuri* group that is working within the same neighborhood, whether you are familiar with the group or not. Present your maps to each other. Your presentation should include basic information about the neighborhood but also your evaluation of the issues and opportunities in the neighborhood.

6. Then take your collective neighborhood map and share it with a group from a completely different neighborhood. Ask them for feedback and record it on the map. Reciprocate by providing feedback to that group's map.

7. Act as consultant stewards for each other's work by recording mutual problems, solutions, and resources. Identify how your groups could be of reciprocal help to each other.

8. Collect the maps from all of the teams and create an overall map of the region. Each pair of groups should cluster their maps to summarize the neighborhood's characteristics, resources, and problems and the ideas raised about how the two groups could work together to yield a fruitful outcome.

Case Story

The Setagaya ward of Tokyo consists of 800,000 people in a land of 60 square kilometers (23 square miles). The ward is recognized for its high-quality residential areas, shopping arcades, and remnant urban farmland. The Setagaya Machizukuri Fund is a fiscal and oversight unit that administers funding to support local *machizukuri* activities. In its 20-year history it has funded over 300 groups with small grants up to 500,000 yen (roughly $US5,000). Fund recipients are required to attend two meetings annually, during which groups present their work. In 2013 the Fund's governing board initiated the opportunity to scale up the discussion to include not only neighborhood activities but also shared regional characteristics, resources, and problems. Approximately 140 people from 40 different *machizukuri* groups were assembled in a large classroom on October 26. The groups represented 13 of Setagaya's 17 neighborhoods.

For the *renkei* activity, the 40 groups were divided into 14 teams of two groups each (one neighborhood had two teams). In teams each group presented their activities to the other group using photographs. The activities and issues varied greatly: "There is no place for children to drop by after school," "We're making a course for bicycles to run through the city," "We make a safe and bright environment by cooperating with every shop in the arcade," "We make furniture and tableware out of neighborhood trees that were struck down," "The *ayu* fish returned to our river, now we wish for the children to be able to play in the river again," "The historic waterway in our area should be restored." Participants started to converse about each other's activities, pointing out what they had in common: "The park is what is valuable in our neighborhood," "We live alongside nature in a quiet residential area," "There aren't enough shops," "The farmland existing to this day is our treasure," "The neighborhood is full of energy with youth taking up most of our population," "We admire the good, old atmosphere we have."

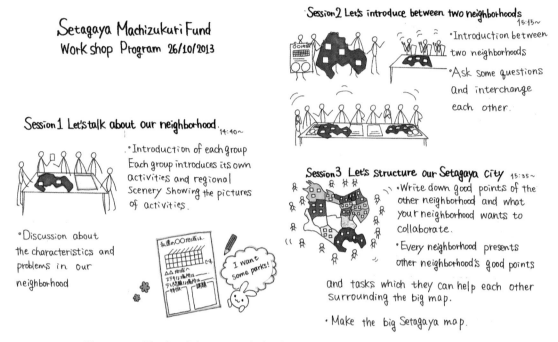

Setagaya Machizukuri Fund
Workshop Program 26/10/2013

Session 1 Let's talk about our neighborhood. 14:40~

• Introduction of each group
Each group introduces its own
activities and regional
scenery showing the pictures
of activities.

• Discussion about
the characteristics and
problems in our
neighborhood

I want
some parks!

Session 2 Let's introduce between two neighborhoods 15:15~

• Introduction between
two neighborhoods
• Ask some questions
and interchange
each other.

Session 3 Let's structure our Setagaya city 15:35~

• Write down good points of the
other neighborhood and what
your neighborhood wants to
collaborate.
• Every neighborhood presents
other neighborhood's good points
and tasks which they can help each other
surrounding the big map.
• Make the big Setagaya map.

Figure 5-14: This hand-drawn agenda for the Setagaya Machizukuri Fund workshop was distributed to the participants in order to give them an idea of scaling up.

It was up to the participants to lead the conversation and introduce their work to the other group. Participants were nervous yet excited to talk to people from other groups in their neighborhood even though they had little prior knowledge of each other's experience. While sharing their activities participants began to nod in acknowledgment, bringing the conversation to a new level. "Although the streets are narrow, the park is loved by everyone," "Problems like drunken people and too much traffic must be tough in a downtown area," "A ward with steep hills creates beautiful scenery."

While the discussions were rich, it took determination to distill and identify the resources and challenges that were revealed through the process. Were there opportunities to be worked on together? To do this, the teams created a joint map, sharing descriptions and colorful notations of activities. This inspired the teams, and the discussion snowballed. One group would say, "Let's act on saving nature within residential areas," or "We could support each other on our lack of shopping malls." The other group would continue: "We could act together to address our shopping problems," "We have some knowledge on conserving nature," "How about selling the vegetables produced on our farmland in your shopping arcade?"

Figure 5-15: Stewards of the base neighborhood meet another neighborhood's stewards and share their scenes with each other.

Reflection

The *renkei* technique relies on a simple principle—to deliver, express, and act for a broader sense of community. The incentives for participation include sharing one's knowledge and experiences with others, building and expanding a human network that helps with problem solving, and gaining a sense of political or ecological identity as a citizen. Physical and social barriers can restrain the use of this technique, but participants more often become

Figure 5-16: Groups brought their neighborhood maps together to make up the entire Setagaya map. Setagaya, as a region that is stewarded by 40 groups of 140 stewards, has emerged.

aware of the fact that their everyday life activities serve their own neighborhood while simultaneously contributing to the health of a larger region. In the Setagaya *machizukuri* case, the exchange allowed the teams to identify common interests and possible joint activities. By scaling up, the local stewards ultimately transformed into a stewardship consultant to the whole region. By the end of the meeting they were in a position to "think regionally while acting in community."

A new grant program based on the idea of stewardship was launched within the Setagaya Machizukuri Fund in 2014. In this program, groups receiving the grant are helped by mentors, and both the groups and the mentors work as stewards of the entire Setagaya region (we call this the ecosystem of *Machizukuri*). Currently, there are seven groups receiving a total of 11 million yen (almost $US100,000), supported by 30 mentors.

6

Co-generating

Co-generating is the process by which community members and various stakeholders generate designs through active collaboration and critical exchanges. Everyone
brings their ideas, knowledge, and skills to the table, and, rather than simply soliciting inputs to inform a design, co-generation guides the community and designers through the negotiation of form alternatives and solutions that embody multiple
perspectives and values. At this stage in participatory design, social learning and
shared exploration intensify. The process suggests that participatory design is most
powerful if participants are engaged in meaningful ways as creative partners rather
than as passive recipients. When truly shared, co-generating simultaneously builds
and reinforces community as one outcome and defines environmental interventions
as another.

THE PATH TO SHALLOW DESIGN

Despite the best intentions, participatory design often limits engagement at the most
essential times. Input from participants is limited to written or verbal feedback while
the professionals proceed to the drawing board or desktop to develop the actual
design. The process follows a linear, unidirectional progression of design decision
making, with professionals maintaining their role as experts. With no meaningful
interactions or exchanges, participants remain consumers rather than partners.

This results in a lack of focused dialogue, minimal debate about spatial alternatives, and lost opportunities for co-learning. The limited exchange results in shallow design solutions that often fail to fit the community or address fundamental issues it faces. At the same time, superficial acts of engagement do little to enhance the democratic capacity of the participants or raise the level of community understanding, problem-solving, environmental intervention, and local design works independent of professionals.

Participatory designers search deeply and inventively for ways to truly co-design. They do this in at least five ways: leveling the field, informing imagination, shaping common ground and differences, "going shares," and empowering to sustain.

LEVELING THE FIELD SO COMMUNITY MEMBERS REALLY DESIGN

Co-generating goes beyond a recognition that community stakeholders possess unique perspectives and knowledge to contribute. It levels the "field" of design so that participants become partners in the creative process. With some effort community members can be, must be, and are assertive co-designers, expected to be involved in shaping not only concepts but also detailed design proposals. When they become informed co-creators the design outcomes suit their distinct needs, unique to their social milieu and place. This doesn't just happen; it takes effort. The designers must shed professional arrogance and share their essential expertise with community participants in ways that avoid condescension, in forms that make common sense, and by means that activate critical shaping.

INFORMING IMAGINATION

As everyone at the table becomes more skilled in the fundamentals of design decision making and the nuance of the place, confidence allows more participants to contribute explicit ideas about spatial arrangements to accommodate distinctive cultural patterns or precedents from everyday life, or even a memorable, once-in-a-lifetime experience. An informed imagination infects the group, freeing reason and fantasy to intermingle within the group. This collective genius is almost always wiser and more creative than what the designer can come up with alone.

SHAPING COMMON GROUND AND DIFFERENCES

Co-generating as a form of transactive design requires negotiation and sometimes creative compromise. To the extent that common values and wide-ranging perspectives exist in the community, co-generation maximizes the potentials of

Figure 6-1: Drawing upside down emboldened residents to take the sketchbook from the designer to illustrate their own ideas. A resident measured, then drew the *zócalo* 18 paces wide without a water feature in the middle to better accommodate festivals. An arcade allowed everyday uses in cool shadow.

Figure 6-2: Each construction detail was a creative collaboration, with drawings emerging from many hands. A fence drawing, rejected in Spanish for a design that could be easily fabricated in metal, resulted in hummingbirds.

Figure 6-3: The design also included natural flourishes like the arroyo rocks that children rearrange daily.

Reflection

The first question is almost always, How do you get people to draw/design with you? People will draw if certain conditions are met. If you start drawing upside down for one-on-one listening, each step in the progression builds a stronger working relationship and a common pictorial language. In our experience, after months of working together with sketches, almost everyone will draw as needed to communicate, enabling people to freely offer ideas, argue with the expert, and expect the expert to argue back, all with pictures. The technique overcomes language barriers and provides marginal, less vocal participants a "pictorial voice."

The technique works best in a group of fewer than 20 people. With a larger audience, an alternative is to work in small groups, then report to each other via a modified nominal group process. This requires several people to draw upside down. Often participants are interested in different aspects of the plan and divide into small groups. The design team needs to then budget for repetition. Drawing upside down taxes the designer who must learn to draw to communicate instead of impress, then facilitate, engage the reluctant, evaluate, criticize, elaborate, interject site and budget realities, call up precedents, imagine additional choices, and design, all at once. To do all of these simultaneously requires extensive practice or a partner to share tasks.

Technique 6.2

GREEN RUBBER STAMP

ChenYu Lien

Green Rubber Stamp is a simple and easy-to-do technique for residents to generate their own designs of places in the community on postcards using prearranged stamps that represent features, such as trees, hedges, and planters. The method allows for quick and direct designs from the participants themselves. Everyone can design realistic spaces with the appropriate stamps on postcards, which in turn facilitate specific conversations and exchanges between the participants and professionals. The exercise enables identification of the existing uses in a space as well as desired outcomes from design changes.

Instructions

1. Before the workshop analyze potential sites for design in the community and classify them into categories, such as streets, alleyways, and so forth.
2. Choose a prototypical picture for each spatial category and print it onto 4-by-6-inch postcards.
3. Select several popular plant types, such as arbor vines, bushes, flowers, grass, and vegetables, and make easily recognized stamps for them.
4. During the workshop, each participant picks one postcard at a time.
5. Each participant may choose different stamps to pictorially assemble and build up the spaces on the postcards. Encourage residents to use a variety of stamps to represent their wishes.
6. Talk to participants and confirm their ideas of improving the community environment. Write down participants' words carefully.
7. Display the postcards so they can be viewed and discussed by all participants.
8. After the workshop categorize ideas from the postcards to understand patterns and trends of the participants' ideas.
9. Use these ideas as prototypes for developing design alternatives.

Case Story

The Big Tree Classroom is an annual service-learning program of the Department of Landscape Architecture at Chung Yuan Christian University in Taiwan. In 2015, the program brought 30 aspiring designers to the Gongxueshe Community in Taoyuan City to practice the participatory design process. As part of the program, students had to initiate new techniques for interacting with local people.

Figure 6-4: Green Rubber Stamps allow for quick rendering of impressions and ideas by community participants. In addition to the stamps, participants can also draw their impressions and ideas.

Gongxueshe is a residential community established in 1979, consisting of mostly apartment buildings with front yards. Over time, some residents added covers to form a parking space in the front yard. Other front yards remain as open space with plants, and still others have shutters facing the street. One household even has chickens in the semicovered front yard. Through the participatory process, public aesthetics in the neighborhood alleyways, where it's customary for people in Taiwan and Japan to enter their houses and apartment buildings, were identified as a major issue. But how can we better understand community intentions and get residents to design their own solutions?

Instead of conventional interviews and surveys, we developed Green Rubber Stamp as a technique to show different possibilities for remodeling the front yards, walls, balconies, street corners, and even rooftops in the community. People who came to the workshop first picked from postcards representing different neighborhood spaces, such as alleyways and front yards. Then they used rubber stamps representing different planting elements and printed them on the postcards to create a design.

The postcards and rubber stamps allowed the participants to easily show their ideas for improving the neighborhood spaces. There was something about the stamps that seemed to encourage spontaneous artistry. One resident got creative with the technique, reversing flower stamps to show plants hanging down from the balconies. After the workshop, we carefully categorized the ideas participants expressed on the postcards. We better understood the residents' desires about how to green the alleyway and were ready to lend our professional design skills. In the meantime, some residents began rearranging planters, adding flowers and greenery to their blocks on their own.

The workshop helped bring participants closer together, collecting necessary information for design, analyzing community issues, and generating principles for design proposals. The technique encouraged both older and younger people, including children, to show their ideas and express their imaginations. In the beginning, elderly residents said they were not professionals and didn't know how to design their own front yards or façades. After trying the rubber stamps on the postcards, they became interested and engaged, and even invited other neighbors to join our workshop.

Figure 6-5: Display of postcards created by community members showing a range of ideas and allowing for conversation between neighbors.

Figure 6-6: The design team has begun to co-design murals with residents.

Over the last few years we have worked with the community on improvements, some of which flow from the tree-stamp workshop. The results include decorative woodwork outside the community meeting center, wall painting, and mosaic collage. Through the establishment of trust and as residents see each transformation, more people are willing to release the wall space for artworks.

Reflection

The Green Rubber Stamp technique has been an easy tool for people of any age, but especially children and elders, to show their wishes. For residents without any design training, it is much easier and quicker to present their thoughts by stamping on postcards than creating a drawing on paper. The postcards and standardized stamps allow for easy organization and categorization of ideas. On the other hand, the postcard size and predetermined stamps also presented limitations. Specifically, participants could choose from a limited number of stamps representing only a few different types of trees or plants that were decided before the workshop. Although neighbors were allowed to draw some extra elements with colored pencils or crayons, it stopped some people who were afraid of drawing. Another predicament was that the background pictures on the postcards were in perspective. Without many different sizes of stamps, the final image on the postcards always looked a little deformed or unrealistic. It is also clear that we cannot use Green Rubber Stamp independently without interacting with participants. Workshop staff members have to gather information at the same time as participants choose stamps and create their designs. It would be a missed opportunity to only collect the postcards without interacting with the residents and engage them in further conversation and discussion.

To expand upon the Green Rubber Stamp technique, one may print perspective pictures showing many kinds of public and semipublic spaces on paper or card stock larger than typical postcards. Preparing stamps of different sizes for each design element would be better on top of perspective background images. The larger size would enable participants to represent their ideas with enough stamp choices and to write keywords on the side. If possible, one could prepare a digital camera and printer, invite participants to take pictures of actual neighborhood spaces and print them out immediately at the workshop. They could then use the stamps to design spaces on pictures of a real site instead of a preselected space. Furthermore, the technique can be adapted for different project contexts. For example, workshop hosts can change the theme of stamps into other aspects of the urban or rural environment, such as "street furniture stamps" for urban designs, "playground equipment stamps" for park designs, or even "farm equipment stamps" for community garden designs.

Technique 6.3

DESIGN BUFFET

Jeffrey Hou

In Design Buffet, the designer invokes the familiar setting of a buffet meal to invite community stakeholders to design a project. During the game, participants collect "food" (design ingredients) from the trays and create a design using those ingredients. When finished with their designs, participants share with each other and learn from the different designs that reflect multiple perspectives in the community. For the participants, the familiar arrangement eliminates possible discomfort or a sense of alienation in joining a design workshop. Using a culturally understood metaphor makes it clear that everyone can design. It makes the design process easy to understand for an audience without prior training. The format enables participants to share with each other their ideas and to exchange multiple perspectives about important design elements.

Instructions

1. Plan. Talk with community organizers about the choice and appropriateness of the game; determine the buffet style and arrangement that is most familiar and appropriate to the community. Study the design problem to determine the appropriate "food" or game pieces; design the game pieces (food) and the site base (plate). Estimate the number of participants and the number of pieces and sets necessary for the game.

2. Prepare. Fabricate the game pieces and site bases, with volunteers or by using laser cutters. Advertise the event, allowing enough time for the word to spread. Create an agenda and set up the design game. Leave enough room for participants to queue and pick up the pieces along the buffet table.

3. Begin. Welcome the participants and organize them around (dining) tables before the game starts. Explain the context and objectives, and provide instructions to the audience (keep them simple): grab a site model (plate), select the game pieces (food) they want, and then return to the table and begin making the design (provide the design problem) (20 minutes).

4. Facilitate. As the game unfolds, monitor the situation and provide assistance when necessary, pay attention to the conversation at the table and take notes, and give people sufficient time to complete the design. For those who have already finished, you may chat with them about their design while waiting for others to finish (30–40 minutes).

5. Share. Once participants around the same table complete the design, have them take turns introducing their designs to each other and encourage all to ask questions. Have someone record the presentation and discussion (20 minutes).

6. Wrap-up. When the presentation is done, have participants put their name, age, gender, and other relevant information on the model for documentation and analysis. Make sure all the pieces are securely attached to the base. To close, congratulate and express gratitude to all participants, and announce the next event or any follow-up steps (10 minutes).

Case Story

The Donnie Chin International Children's Park is a small neighborhood park located in Seattle's Chinatown-International District. Built in 1980, the park once served as a much-welcomed open space in the district. As it later fell into disrepair and became underused, a community effort was initiated to renovate the park. To engage the predominantly immigrant residents in the district in redesigning the park, a Design Buffet was organized with about 30 residents. They were joined by about an equal number of bilingual high school students who were members of a youth leadership program.

The design game required little explanation to the local audience. As soon as it was announced that the workshop would be in buffet style, the audience immediately queued up. With "plates" (site base) in hands, the participants selected park design elements (cutouts) from aluminum trays on what looked like a buffet table. The trays had bilingual labels to ensure people understood what the elements were. Each person was asked to generate a design for the park. To spark interactions between the different age groups, we assigned high school students to sit next to the elderly. This way the students could also help the elders with the design. In concluding the game, each person was asked to share and explain his or her design to others around the table.

The outcomes of the workshops were analyzed and synthesized into a list of program and design preferences for the park renovation. Based on the findings, five teams of students each produced a design alternative and presented them at a community open house. At the open house, the workshop participants returned to examine the design proposals that were developed with their inputs. The outcomes of the workshop were incorporated into the redesign of the park. Construction for the project was completed in 2012 following additional rounds of meetings and community inputs, which affirmed the earlier outcomes.

Figure 6-7: Design Buffet used in an intergenerational workshop to engage teens and older adults who created individual designs with each other's help.

Figure 6-8: Completed park with design based on inputs from the early workshops focusing on creating a green common for flexible use and an enlarged play area for children as well as seating areas for teens and older adults.

Reflection

Despite benevolent intentions, participatory design can be an alienating experience for community members, particularly in immigrant communities where language and culture present challenges for communication and engagement. Design Buffet is meant to build on knowledge and skills that community members already possess and the settings they are accustomed to. As a game, Design Buffet has a sense of novelty yet familiarity that can alleviate the distress or discomfort some community members may feel in typical public meetings, especially for immigrant community members.

In the case of International Children's Park, even though the process was planned to engage people in their own comfort zone, it was still surprising how quickly and almost effortlessly the participants were able to go through the exercise. Informal conversations at the tables also reinforced the design game as an extension of everyday activities. These conversations can provide invaluable information to the designers on aspects of daily life in the community as well as the efficacy of the game itself. Taking notes of the conversation and debriefing at the end of the process are therefore essential, and so are collecting, documenting, and analyzing each design that participants created. Follow-up interviews may be necessary to fully capture the inputs from the participants.

In the Chinatown community the Design Buffet was an appropriate metaphor for design. A luau in Hawaii or a pig-pickin' in the American South should work in a similar way. But it doesn't have to be food. Comparing design to preparing for a special, local festival or everyday work, like auto or boat repair, could also work in the right community.

Technique 6.4

PLACE IT WORKSHOP

James Rojas

The Place It workshop makes the creative process of urban planning accessible to residents through animated visioning activities. Rather than asking people simply what they want or need, participants build solutions using found objects, based on their own on-the-ground knowledge and imagination. Through material designs made by participants themselves, this method improves communication, inquiry, reflection, collaboration, ownership of the process, and idea generation in a playful manner. The outcomes can be used to articulate common values and significant differences. They also create a metric to measure development of urban plans or policies.

Instructions

1. Identify the players. The facilitator explains the process, outlines the objectives, guides the group through the activities, and helps synthesize their findings. He or she encourages participants to talk, smile, laugh, move, nod, make eye contact, and communicate through body language. The recorder documents the activities and findings for everyone to see. The number of participants can range from 5 to 30. Larger groups require more time for each activity.

2. Set up. Choose a time and venue for optimal attendance and create a safe space for people to listen to themselves and each other. The activity can be performed outdoors or indoors, in a classroom or a park. The materials should consist of everyday, nonrepresentational, vibrant, and interesting objects, such as colorful beads, painted blocks, hair rollers, pipe cleaners, buttons, plastic flowers, and other nonarchitectural objects.

3. Introduce. The facilitator introduces the workshop goals and objectives, the reason for the activities, and why urban planning matters. The first activity, Childhood Memory, helps participants reflect on place and how it impacts our lives. The second activity, Collaboration, teaches participants that city planning is not competitive but collaborative, where ideas are generated, vetted, and shared to achieve consensus and values (5 minutes).

4. Reflect. Ask participants to build their favorite childhood memory (as related to place), choosing from the simple objects provided and building it on a sheet of construction paper (10–15 minutes). Once the time is up, ask participants to give their name and explain their memory to the group (1 minute each). The recorder

should write each memory down and photograph the accompanying model for everyone to see. After each participant has presented, summarize the presentation to the larger audience, and acknowledge the accomplishment with applause. To close the activity, ask participants to identify three words or themes to describe settings, places, relationships, or details that were consistent throughout the exercise to achieve consensus (5–8 minutes).

5.   Collaborate. Now that the participants have bonded by sharing a few place values, they can collaborate. Place participants in teams of five to eight, and ensure that each team is diverse by age, sex, profession, ethnicity, race, and interests (3–5 minutes). Ask each team to solve a community problem by building the solution together. Have team members choose from the objects they used previously. They can start building from scratch or incorporate previous model sections. Encourage visual, verbal, and spatial negotiations to allow new ideas to emerge from existing ones with the help of others (15 minutes). Once the time is up, have each team introduce the team members and present their solutions using the model. Afterward, synthesize the information to the larger audience (10–15 minutes). Acknowledge the team with applause. At the end of this activity, have each participant identify three words or themes, ideas, and solutions that were consistent throughout. Once it is over, ask the participants if they enjoyed working together and what they learned (5 minutes).

6.   Synthesize. To wrap up, discuss what the groups learned about themselves, others, and the goals and objectives of the workshop. This allows people to reflect on the process and consider what impacts the workshop may have on their lives, place, and the broader urban planning process. Write down the findings and share with co-sponsors and participants (5–8 minutes).

7.   Next. Depending on the objectives and goals of the workshop the next steps can vary. The workshop can be used as a one-time learning experience, to help collect data, or to kick off a long-term plan, policy, or development.

Case Story

I have facilitated Place It workshops for a variety of projects and plans, ranging from long-term, complicated projects like high-speed rail in Bakersfield to a "parklet" in San Bernardino. In San Bernardino, I facilitated a Place It workshop with a fellow artist and urban planner to have community members use their imagination to establish community values. Youth, adults, and seniors—the workshop participants—imagined their ideal city using found objects. The workshop inspired the adults and seniors, and they wanted to imple-

Figure 6-9: A team member presents the project to the entire group.

ment their community values. San Bernardino is bankrupt and has no money for such projects, however. With the help of the artist and planner, community members decided to implement what they imagined by making some quick changes on a street. Building on the creative energy from the Place It workshop, the artist facilitating the next phase of the process asked the participants to each bring an object they would like to see in a public space. They brought blankets, pillows, buckets, and other objects to create two parklets. From this experience, the participants wanted to scale it up and do it again. This was a collaboration where people had ownership of the process and the product because it was their work. The power of the imagination helped transform people and places.

Reflection

The Place It workshop is low in cost, requires few preparations, and is spatially flexible. The looseness of the method encourages participants with disparate experiences to join in the small-group activities. It also works across projects of dramatically different type and scales. By tapping into people's memories and imagination, it generates creative solutions, and people learn how to solve problems themselves.

Technique 6.5

PICTURE COLLAGE GAME

Hideaki Shimura, Kousuke Masuo, and Shigeru Satoh

Picture Collage Game is a simple means for everybody to imagine and visualize an improvement of a place by collaborating with others. Through the game, residents get a chance to design public spaces with their own hands. By jointly making a collage as they move through the game, participants are prompted to discuss issues facing their community or a site, engage in role-playing, and recognize community assets and values. Once it is done, they make a presentation of the finished work, and confer on the future of the community with each other. Through the game, participants can feel the joy and satisfaction of shared work.

Instructions

1. Hold walking tours with a community organization, residents, and local authority with the goal of making them aware of the community assets, about which panels are to be created as the basis of the game.

2. Prepare "life scene cards" and "goal image cards" after discussing with the community board. The life scene cards are the residents' future image of their life activity, such as watching their kids play in a park, and the goal image cards are the residents' future image of their own town or neighborhood, such as different development or preservation scenarios (more mixed-use buildings, or a greenway network, for example).

3. Take photos of places where the community organization and local authority want to make improvements. Study those places, and clarify what would be the appropriate elements for the places. Make photo cutouts of the appropriate elements.

4. Have the community board advertise the workshop to residents. About 20 participants would be a good number for the workshop.

5. Set up the Picture Collage Game: prepare posters of community assets and photo cutouts.

6. Welcome the participants and explain the purpose and methods of the workshop.

7. Describe community assets using the posters, and have a discussion among participants about the community assets and goal images of the community. After the discussion divide the participants into groups of three to four people.

8. The picture collage begins. The facilitator with each group provides assistance when necessary. The groups develop and visualize their future life activities with life scenario cards, and decide on goal images using the goal image cards. The groups then put photo cutouts together to create a rough image of their future life activities.

Figure 6-10: A picture collage made by residents with premade labels and photo cutouts.

9. Have each group present its work to all participants at the end of the activity. Afterward, have participants deliver remarks, analyze issues, exchange ideas, and share views on their picture collages.

10. Congratulate and express gratitude to all participants, and announce the next meeting, workshop, or any follow-up steps.

Case Story

We used the Picture Collage Game and other simulation games to revitalize Takeda-Nezaki, a district of Nihonmatsu City in Fukushima Prefecture, Japan. Nihonmatsu was a castle town during the Edo period in Japan, and Takeda-Nezaki was once a merchants' district. The local economy declined, along with a decrease in population in recent years, yet a relatively large number of historic warehouses remain in the district. In 1993, when a plan to widen the main street was introduced, the community began a campaign to revitalize the local economy, attract visitors and residents, and improve the townscape. In 1997, the residents established the Takeda-Nezaki Community Board and started community design projects. We began to assist with their efforts in 1998 with support from the Fukushima Prefecture government and the Nihonmatsu city government.

The Community Board held walking tours and map-making workshops, and practiced the Picture Collage Game, targeting the district's main street. Through the game, participants proposed integration and leveling of vehicular lanes and sidewalks on the main street so that people could feel closer to drum floats at the festival time. They also proposed to give the townscape a traditional Japanese touch to strengthen its identity as a historical castle town and to attract visitors.

The Picture Collage Game was carried out as part of a series of simulation games through which the Community Board and local authority designed the main street in 2001. A townscape agreement was reached in 2002. In order to implement the agreement, a Community Townscape Board was organized, with members including residents, architects, and a professor who had participated in the simulation games. Altogether, the Board held 114 meetings with building owners to examine the design of 57 buildings along the main street to improve the townscape. The construction was delayed because of the financial difficulty of the prefecture and the triple disasters in 2011. But the implementation was completed in 2014. Meanwhile, two more nonprofit organizations were established and started community actions in this district. With the successful outcomes of the project, the Community Board received prizes from the City Planning Institute of Japan and the Ministry of Land, Infrastructure, Transport, and Tourism in 2015.

Figure 6-11: The renovated street in Takeda-Nezaki after completion.

Figure 6-12: Drum festival at night.

Reflection

The Picture Collage Game can be a good starter for each resident to participate in the design of public spaces in the community. As a sequence of community design workshops, it is hoped that those who participate in the game are those who have also participated in the town-watching and map-making workshops. The Picture Collage Game can benefit from recognition of community assets and discussion of future life activities. The outcomes of the game can provide an important foundation for subsequent steps, including the design simulation games using physical models. Through collaboration, the game provides opportunities for sharing and exchanges of values and supports negotiation and consensus building. By developing these design games step-by-step in cooperation with local residents and stakeholders, residents are provided with meaningful opportunities to design and make improvements to their own community.

Technique 6.6

DESIGNING LIFE

Shin Aiba, Jing Jin, Akihiro Soga, and Hirotaka Ikeda

Designing Life is a board game for envisioning "life scenarios" using everyday resources in a community. During a workshop, participants learn about assets and stories in the community and use them to find a solution to a problem facing the community. Through the game, they discover the importance of collaboration and gain awareness of urban design and planning issues in their community. The game was inspired by Game of Life, a board game created by Milton Bradley Company in 1963.

Instructions

1. Collect data for the game. Start by interviewing the people living in the target area to ask the following questions: (1) How do they typically spend their life in the region? What are the major changes and turning points in their family, place of living, and occupation? (2) What is a priceless resource (material, human, or knowledge) in building their lives? This step can be performed by designers or workshop participants.

2. Construct "community tasks" that could be undertaken through collaboration of residents. These tasks should be simple yet realistic, such as planning an event in a festival, founding a new industry, recovering from a disaster, and so forth.

3. Design the game kit using information obtained from steps 1 and 2. The kit comprises a game board, resource cards, and crossroad cards. Three typical life scenarios are indicated in the game board in chronologically organized cells, each showing a life event. In addition, three "crossroad cells" and three "community task cells" are included on the game board.

4. Play the game. Invite five participants to join the game. Take turns to play, and roll the dice to advance. Once a participant stops at a cell, an instruction on the life event and the resource from the event are indicated in the cell, and the participant gets a "resource card." For example, the card may say, "You get an NGO (nongovernmental organization) member as a friend by supporting the NGO project."

5. Every participant must stop at a crossroad cell (at ages 18, 25, and 49, for example) and draw a crossroad card. A turning point and choices of life scenarios are indicated on the card. The card may say, "Your elderly mother needs nursing care. Do you wish to live with her? Or stay at your present home and have a private service to provide care for her?" The participant may choose a life scenario by asking for advice from others.

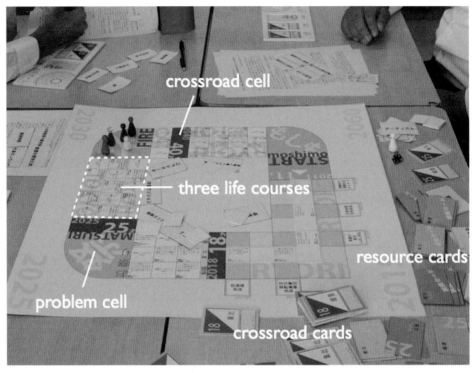

Figure 6-13: The game board showing how the different cells are organized.

6. Every participant must stop at the community problem cell (at ages 25, 35, and 60, for example) and wait for others. The cell could say, "Your hometown was on fire and half of the village was burned down. What can you do to recover by using your resources?" All participants then propose solutions for the task by using resource cards that they collect in the game. After discussing and examining the proposals put forth by all participants, the best idea is chosen, and the proposer gets a title, such as "master of reconstruction," as a reward.

7. Take turns until all participants experience three crossroads over their life span and face three community tasks in the course of the game.

8. At the end of the game, report on the results and ask the participants to reflect.

Case Story

The Designing Life board game was developed in a class called "Recovering from the Tsunami" for junior high school students in the Ryori village of Ofunato City in Japan from 2014 to 2016. Ryori had been struck by a large tsunami in 2011. The village was also destroyed by tsunamis in 1896 and 1933. The residents of Ryori village believe that the next tsunami will occur in a few decades. A workshop was organized in Ryori to provide youngsters with an opportunity to prepare for the future tsunami.

Ryori's main industry is its fishery. As the industry does not provide enough employment for local people, many young adults seek jobs in other towns. The three major life scenarios in the game include life in the village, life in neighboring cities, and life in a metropolis, such as Tokyo. The authors designed the first version of resource cards and

Figure 6-14: Junior high school students in Ryori playing a game.

crossroad cards by interviewing local people and schoolteachers. Three community tasks were selected: (1) planning an event at Ryori's annual festival at age 25; (2) recovering from a fire or starting a new business in Ryori at age 35; and (3) recovering from the next tsunami at age 60. The time frame was designed for junior high school students who were born in 1999 to 2001 and were 11 to 13 years old when the last tsunami destroyed the village. The first cell of the game board was set for year 2011 so that students could recall their experience of the tsunami. Many good ideas arose from playing the game. One team recommended, "Supply candy as emergency food."

The workshop was conducted in a class of 20 students on two separate days in July and September. In July, students first played the board game to familiarize themselves with it. They then collected stories about their elders' lives as homework during the summer vacation. The second workshop was held in September when the students returned to school and had a chance to analyze the stories, then design and play the game. Based on questionnaires collected from the students after the program, it seemed that many participants found small clues for building their life.

Reflection

The success of the game seemed to depend on two conditions. First, the game was put to practice in a local society that had together faced a large-scale recent disaster, in this case a tsunami. As such, it was easy for the participants to focus on a common challenge. However, not every community may have such a challenge. To replicate the game elsewhere, one needs to identify a common challenge relevant to the local context. Second, the game was practiced in a small, isolated village with a population of only 3,000. There were not many variations in people's life courses, resources, or common events. Therefore, it was easy to develop the game kit. Designing a game kit for a more complex locality will require more thoughtful preparation.

7

Engaging the Making

Making is deliciously engaging. There is really nothing like it. When something is being created in public, it invites attention—a spectacle, minor or supersized, that passersby cannot resist. It doesn't matter whether the construction is a skateboard park or volunteer-built housing, protest murals or pallet furniture. They observe the energy and joy of the builders; the bold invite themselves to join in. Others may need a "Hey, do you want to help out?" Soon the workforce is doubled, reinforced with participants who might never have attended a planning meeting or a public hearing. Grassroots democracy has expanded its active membership. And many become active in other community projects.

BC²—Building Community Squared

Engaging the making is all this and more. Yes, there is the irrepressible joy of making something. And yes, it draws people in who might not have been involved before. There is also the undeniable benefit of "building community squared." Through actual construction a sense of community is created, one brick and one friendship at a time. Community improvements that would never otherwise have been undertaken are built in record time. Unimagined social exchanges break cultural and generational boundaries. Sometimes these are personal. Colleagues of ours met when she nailed his work boots to a two-by-six at a Habitat workday. They now have eight-year-old twins.

BUILD LOCAL

Engaging the making enables participants to contribute time, previously unknown skills, and untapped resources that already exist in the community. These range from knowledge of site histories, local building techniques, and traditional arts to secret stashes of materials, access to equipment, and networks of individuals and organizations critical to the project. Through a hands-on approach, participants contribute their skills and acquire new ones. This creates places that are distinctly locally made, expressing unique identities with beauty shared by insiders. And we gain new respect for the many capacities that exist in our community. This is a bonus not to be taken lightly.

BUILDING OWNERSHIP AND PRIDE

The tangible products of co-construction imbue a sense of accomplishment, pride, and ownership like nothing else can. Sweat, blood, and sore muscles create a more visceral connection than other forms of participation. Co-construction awakens passion. It is transformative. We become long-term stewards of the project and others in our community.

PROTOTYPING

Making is often the only way to test something new. We make prototypes to evaluate something unknown. The prototype might fail or turn out to be a wondrous invention, or a serendipitous discovery might be made during construction that never revealed itself on the drawing board. Prototypes are low cost and low risk. Often mock-ups are necessary to convince skeptics that something is worth trying. Showing a full-scale model of an imaginable future allows participants and funders to picture it, experience it, and possibly even pursue that future. It may even overcome bureaucratic inertia and attract public support and investment.

BUILDING TO OCCUPY A CRISIS

Making is fundamental to nonviolent protest or response to a catastrophe or crisis. From informal settlements to temporary housing after a tornado, from Arab Spring to Hong Kong's Umbrella Revolution, each occupies public space in ways unexpected with grassroots community-made structures. The occupation can be desperate and politically passive as when homeless people inhabit abandoned places or neighbors occupy a vacant lot for a community garden. Yet, making something new may save lives, disrupt normalcy, or call attention to an unacknowledged injustice that must be addressed. Additionally, these makings engage the public conscience; sometimes igniting dramatic change.

BUILD NOW

Making something spontaneously is seldom the final stage of a project. Rather it serves as a tool to achieve a longer-term goal. It is a bridge between now and the future because fabrication produces immediate results and demonstrates the potential for more change in the community. Building some small thing instills a sense of tangible accomplishment, which is especially important in communities facing prolonged struggles. Often self-help projects, like barn raisings from generations ago, are the only way to meet a need for which there is no funding. The immediateness of a positive change promises more, and we begin to believe we can achieve transformations, even amid desperate times.

These "quick and dirty" improvements are increasingly important in places where government-sponsored participation in planning occurs years before a project is expected to be implemented. In these cases, we must heed Alinsky's warning, "A tactic [transpose 'project'] that drags on too long becomes a drag." Part of this is due to the need for greater public involvement in long-range and large-scale planning, but much of it is the slow progress of public works. In all these cases small projects bridge the gap between final plan adoption and construction. Making alleviates frustration, anger, and apathy from process without products, replacing these with confidence, joy, and intensive and continued involvement.

TECHNIQUES THAT ENGAGE THE MAKING

We present techniques in this chapter that highlight the multiple benefits of making. In "Start with Building" Alex Gilliam of Public Workshop shows how a job site is arranged to draw people in. His construction projects consciously invite diverse participants who in turn create new skills and facilities that would not be built without their efforts. In "Early Success through Banner Making" Milenko Matanovic of the Pomegranate Center describes a technique that allows participants to take part in a collective project to make utilitarian art amid a bigger project, the progress of which can be painfully slow. Similarly, in "Pallet Furniture" Lauren Elder discusses how shipping pallets provide inexpensive (usually free), versatile, and commonly available materials to community members, who learn to make simple furniture that can quickly activate vacant spaces.

Making and engaging can be applied in other more specific project or community contexts. In *"La Maqueta,"* Andrés Martínez de la Riva Díaz presents a technique that makes it possible for participants to discover the parts of a site, study its present, and create its future using a scaled, interactive model. They are nurturing a generation of city makers who as schoolchildren design their own scenarios for the future of Barcelona. Kofi Boone's "Cross-Cultural Prototyping" technique allows outsider designers to learn from and interact with community members through hands-on craft making to test prototypes that can be reproduced quickly to meet open space needs in rapidly growing urban cities. Finally, in "Design/Build Service Learning Studio" Daniel Winterbottom discusses a successful model of design/build that creates sensitive and beautiful places for underserved communities with limited resources. The projects create gathering and healing places for neglected people by systematically mobilizing university, hospital, and community resources.

Technique 7.1

START WITH BUILDING

Alex Gilliam

For participatory design/build projects, "Start with Building" sets the stage for broader and deeper engagement. The seemingly mundane needs of a job site represent powerful tools for drawing in a diverse group of stakeholders and growing a real sense of teamwork among participants. Participants collectively learn more about the site and challenges at hand. Hidden skills within the community are discovered, and participants realize they can do significant things.

Instructions

1. Meet with your community client to discuss the primary need and overall goal for the project.

2. Determine the essential tools for the team to work effectively together on-site and meaningfully engage others. Items may include workbenches, signage, weather protection, tool and material storage, as well as a community message board. Additional items may be needed as the project evolves.

3. Determine the design/build schedule and optimal time(s) for building. Is it a one-day or two-week project? When are the heavy traffic times of the day and week? Are there regular events nearby? It is important that this work be highly visible.

4. Determine, order, and schedule delivery of materials, hand and power tools, as well as hardware to the site. Use reclaimed wood materials only if they require minimal amounts of preparation. You don't want to burn your team out right at the beginning by having them spend 75 percent of their time pulling nails, milling, and sanding.

5. If time is limited, predesign the essential items. Consider precutting all or most of the materials. It is important to create at least one thing that is awesome; this establishes expectations for what is possible from a spatial, aesthetic, and fabrication standpoint. Build a prototype for participants to copy.

6. Divide your group into teams of three to four people. Set a reasonable time schedule for the teams to copy the prototype with the given tools and materials. Ensure that all participants are properly trained for safety; include the use of safety glasses while using power tools. Use the building process to teach tool use, but don't ask your team to learn about too many tools and methods at once. This process may be challenging, but it is incredibly empowering and forces peer learning and collaboration, while allowing hidden experts to emerge.

Figure 7-1: Team members and additional passersby are designing and building a shade canopy, community message board, and rain screen for the mini-park.

7.   If multiple teams are building the same thing, do not hesitate to turn it into a playful challenge. Competition can be a useful and powerful tool for stimulating team building, positive risk taking, and an acceptance of failure. Something always goes wrong in design/build projects, and it is important that everyone understands this from the outset.

8. Building piques curiosity, and passersby will want to talk and even get involved. Assign at least one person to say hello to passersby, disseminate a flier with regular building hours, and gather ideas. Document the ideas. Encourage people who want to get involved to leave their contact information. Invite people to pick up a drill or hammer—it is addictive and will entice them to come back.

9. Celebrate! Test out what you've built—climb, jump, have a meal, and toast what you have just built.

10. At the end of each day or building session, have everyone reflect on what they've learned by sharing one moment of pride and one thing that they would like to do better or learn next. Assess the feedback from passersby. Document and share this information meticulously; it is essential to growing an effective team.

Case Story

As soon as I saw it, I wanted to participate.
—Will S., age 23.

Two summers ago, Will, Tiffany, Joseph, Brian, and others got involved in the design and building of a pop-up skate park and playground in Camden, New Jersey. They were drawn to and ultimately became the key leaders of the project. Trust is a huge issue in their struggling neighborhood, and they had become conditioned to neglect, empty promises, and lack of action from past experience. The public fabrication of picnic tables and other initial improvements to the site as well as immediate invitations to participate instantly communicated to Will and his friends that their efforts would amount to something this time. They worked with friends and other participants, which allowed them to feel connected; it also helped grow the core team necessary to accomplish more difficult design-build work later in the summer. Some passersby were inspired to get involved; others—including friends and neighbors—stopped to talk and give them a thumbs-up or high five. Several hundred people with varied skills and expertise participated in the design/build process. Some built one time for 30 minutes, whereas others devoted four to six weeks. It is estimated that the combined effort logged 1,500 hours.

The participation in construction expanded the contracted scope for the project, which was a direct result of the leadership, initiative, and ownership of the young adults who ultimately helped lead the project on the ground. The nature of the public work became a tool for advertising and building community around the project. Over the summer, through their own initiative, Will, Tiffany, and others conducted user research with everyone who visited the site. They made sure the site was taken care of on a daily basis, and they began advocating for other skateboarding interventions in the neighborhood.

Figure 7-2: Testing the newly built skateboard ramp.

Reflection

The client for this project was Cooper's Ferry Partnership but we have also deployed this method in places such as Chicago, Flint, Cleveland, Philadelphia, and rural Virginia. More complex versions of this approach involve a larger degree of co-design and full-scale rapid prototyping. They require more experience and run the risk of participants burning out if too much commitment is required from the outset. In the process one can identify and help grow a powerful team of formerly invisible local leaders who care deeply about their neighborhood. They simply need a different form of engagement to show how they can make a difference.

Technique 7.2

EARLY SUCCESS THROUGH BANNER MAKING

Milenko Matanovic

The period between design and construction is traditionally the most dormant phase of a project, during which a community's engagement can significantly diminish. At the Pomegranate Center, a Seattle-based nonprofit organization, we find repeatedly that people are eager to spring into action and suffer "visioning fatigue" if something concrete doesn't happen soon after a plan is completed.

To keep a project's momentum going, we typically incorporate into our process an "Early Success." An Early Success can involve a small artistic project, lasting a few hours or a day, during which we invite community members to create elements that will be integrated into the final project. Community members who until this time participated only with their ideas now participate by making things.

By finding the right balance between artistic vision and volunteer participation, volunteers can create cohesive artworks that will be incorporated into the final project, ensuring community ownership is generated throughout the process. Banner Making is often used because the materials are inexpensive, almost anyone can participate, and they add a celebratory element to a project. We typically employ a pointillism approach, using nylon fabric and acrylic colors in small dot-creating bottles. The bottles allow people of all abilities to participate and to work without spilling the paint.

Instructions

1. Generate a design theme and/or collection of artistic shapes derived from ideas generated at a community meeting.
2. Trace the shapes onto sticky contact paper.
3. Volunteers cut out these shapes with scissors.
4. The lead artist arranges the shapes onto the nylon fabric of the banners.
5. The cutout shapes create negative white spaces around which the color dots will be painted.
6. The lead artist directs the color scheme and the basic pattern of the artwork. Volunteers, under the direction of the artist, begin to paint dots around the shapes.
7. Start with a solid line of painted dots along the edges of the contact paper and then disperse them outward, leaving increasingly larger spaces between dots.
8. The net result is a coherent artwork composed of hundreds of small individual contributions—a symbol of the community's larger placemaking efforts.

Case Story

In 2011, Tuscaloosa, Alabama, was ravaged by a tornado that cut through the heart of the city. A year later, the city was still working to rebuild in the wake of the storm. Using the debris from the tornado, Pomegranate Center helped the community to design and build a gathering place that brought neighbors from all walks of life together. An expansive amphitheater featuring colorful canvas for shade, made with volunteer labor and donated or salvaged materials, now anchors one end of a greenbelt pathway planned to help revitalize Tuscaloosa as it has been rebuilding.

As with all our projects, we assembled a Convening Group of community and government leaders who identified five possible sites. They helped organize a meeting where representatives from the five neighborhoods were introduced to our model, and they presented the pros and cons of each site. The site in the Alberta neighborhood was chosen because it met the greatest need for people around the park. Then we organized a meeting in Alberta Park where community members told us which needs our project could meet: a place that was colorful and safe for children, where families could have picnics, and that could also serve for outdoor gatherings.

Figure 7-3: Banners were created to bridge the time gap between project conception and implementation. Source: © Tim Matsui/timmatsui.com.

During a design workshop, we developed a plan for a small circular seating area with a central stage accompanied by two smaller picnic areas. The project, the Alberta Gathering Place, was built a few months later over 10 days with volunteer labor and technical assistance from the parks agency. It features a seating circle made from salvaged concrete pads, columns made from salvaged metal, and old logs from the trees that came down in the disaster, and colorful canvas for shade.

An important part of this project was banner making. Seven banners were suggested to bring more color and add festive atmosphere during events. Tuscaloosa is referred to as the Druid City due to the many oak trees that grow there. Oak trees in different stages of growth became a theme that was used for both the banners and for other artistic elements throughout the project. Local artist Kimberly Conway, who involved many volunteers, led the banners project. She used the primary colors of the rainbow as a reminder that just after the tornado's unimaginable devastation, many witnessed a rainbow in the sky. This event felt celebratory because it signaled that the amphitheater project would happen.

Figure 7-4: Projects allow for volunteers of any age or skill level to participate. Source: © Tim Matsui/timmatsui.com.

Reflection

It is not unusual that new participants show up for these Early Success sessions. Hands-on work is often more attractive to some than meetings. The additional benefit of an Early Success is that these new participants become engaged and will be more likely to participate in the final build.

Our approach at the Pomegranate Center is to ensure that anyone who wants to work has the opportunity. We have developed techniques that allow skilled professionals to work alongside nonskilled people, including children. A lead artist oversees the overall thematic and design direction of the piece, and provides a framework within which volunteers can apply the technique. Without a lead artist, the final artwork may lack compositional finesse and thematic consistency, reducing its overall aesthetic impact.

One issue in this approach is that banners can tear in high winds. We prepare community members for such a possibility. In Tuscaloosa banners are attached to poles that can be placed strategically for different purposes—guiding people to the site, or a backdrop to the stage. Afterward, banners and poles need to be stored, and for future programs, someone needs to place them in new locations. Sometimes this does not happen because organizers, already busy with putting on an event, run out of time. Now we make sure that communities budget time for this additional task.

Figure 7-5: To help revitalize Tuscaloosa as it was rebuilding following the 2011 tornado devastation, Pomegranate Center built an expansive amphitheater featuring colorful canvas for shade. Source: © Tim Matsui/timmatsui.com.

Technique 7.3

PALLET FURNITURE

Lauren Elder

Artists, designers, and do-it-yourselfers can generate attractive and serviceable furniture and architectural elements by repurposing the ubiquitous wood shipping pallet. Pallets are a free, universally available resource. They are easy to collect, easy to work with, and have a wide range of outdoor applications. This technique involves cutting one pallet in such a way that it yields all the elements for a single folding garden chair. The work can be accomplished with a handsaw, a battery-powered screwdriver, measuring tools, and simple hinges. The technique can be adapted as a community engagement tool that teaches basic design and carpentry skills to community members, especially teenagers. Two teens working together, for example, can complete a chair in three to five hours.

Instructions

1. Begin the process by determining the group's capabilities. Find out who has used the tools required and who has built things before. Then explain what pallets are, how they are traditionally used, and why they were chosen for this project. Show a sample pallet and discuss its features. Ask again if participants have done something like this.

2. Have the participants noticed stockpiles of pallets in their neighborhood? Conduct a mapping exercise to determine number, quality, and accessibility. Get them to identify places the furniture would create an important place to sit in their community. Make a plan for collecting and storing the pallets. Collect pallets that are uniform in size and shape. Inspect the pallets for codes. Look for pallets stamped with "HT" (heat treated), which means they haven't been exposed to chemicals (at least not in the treating process). Avoid unmarked pallets or those marked with "MB" for methyl bromide. The possibility of chemical coatings makes them unsuitable for use indoors or with edible plants.

3. Examine the structure of the pallets. Have the participants measure the different sizes of the component pieces and note the quantity of each.

4. Show participants a pallet furniture sample for style reference. This could be a chair, bench, or table. Depending on the group's skills, start simple and then encourage more complex projects after the initial success.

5. If participants are eager to design or were inspired by the furniture samples, supply graph paper or lightweight cardboard and encourage them to create their own configuration.

6. Assess the practicability of their designs. How many useful cuts can they derive from each pallet? If any participants have experience with dressmaking, you can reference the need to lay out pattern pieces for maximum use of the cloth.

7. Demonstrate proper use of each hand tool and when it will be used in the process. If there are participants in the group, get them to show their peers how to use the tools. Participants can take turns with different tools, switching off after they complete a task or when they want to try something else. Use masks and gloves while cutting and sanding as the pallets may be coated with preservatives and insecticides (be sure you use a mask in demonstrating).

8. Have the participants work in pairs to start. They can support each other through the process. Provide a pallet and necessary tools to each group.

9. Instruct them to measure and mark all the cut lines on their pallet following your example. Let them practice on some scrap wood first. Move the participants who have made all their cuts on to the next step—drilling and screwing, joining the sections, and so on.

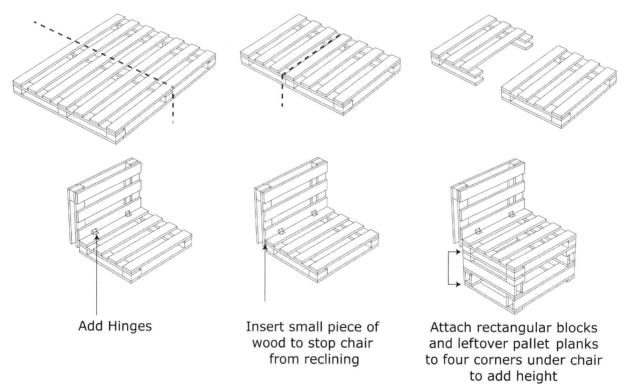

Add Hinges

Insert small piece of
wood to stop chair
from reclining

Attach rectangular blocks
and leftover pallet planks
to four corners under chair
to add height

Figure 7-6: Pallet chair sequence. Source: Lisette DeVore.

10. Evaluate. Does the piece hold your weight? Is it well balanced and well proportioned? Are all the joints firm? Do you need glue or extra screws for some joints? Complete by sanding the pieces carefully to avoid splinters.

11. Optional decoration: Finish the furniture with a colored penetrating sealer or primer plus exterior acrylic paint.

12. Place the chairs where they will improve the community. Document and enjoy!

Case Story

Adam Rogers Park Community Garden is one of 35 city-owned sites managed by San Francisco's Recreation and Parks Department. The land is available to community members to grow edibles and ornamentals on a hilltop site adjacent to public housing. The garden is part of a city park that affords magnificent views and ample space on a sunny, south-facing site measuring over 6,000 square feet. It offers a variety of amenities and opportunities for engaging local youth. The garden program is managed by Hunters Point Family (HPF),

Figure 7-7: California College of the Arts mentor Jasmine Ho demonstrates the use of a cordless drill.

which offers programs targeting specific youth development needs and academic gaps. HPF partners with 200 youths (ages 10 to 22) and their families each year in programs that comprehensively support and serve each young person's social, educational, recreational, and home needs. Recognizing the multidimensional needs of our youth and their families, HPF began its youth outreach with a single program, GIRLS 2000.

GIRLS 2000 develops and leads activities based on the HPF philosophy that our youth can transform their current reality if they gain awareness of their capabilities, develop the courage and ability to make life-affirming decisions, and have access to necessary resources and support. A key component of the program's success is its gender-specific programming, targeting the healthy development and empowerment of girls and young women. The Pallet Furniture Project challenged GIRLS 2000 in the following ways: (1) to look critically and creatively at their neighborhood, where small industries leave pallets on many street corners and the waste can be transformed into a resource; (2) to learn tool use—fearlessly—for this project and for future needs; and (3) to create an enduring piece that supports their presence in the garden. With the help of student mentors from California College of the Arts, pairs of teens completed the pallet chairs in three to five hours.

Reflection

The GIRLS project succeeded because the college mentors clearly defined it in a way that was appropriate for the skill level of the group. Community volunteers provided an additional level of expertise and teaching support. The young women were eager to participate and demonstrated a great degree of focus, perseverance, and satisfaction. The teens learned to use new tools and to transform waste from their neighborhood into useful and attractive objects. They also benefited from having other young women of color as mentors. This activity can be successfully extended to the creation of other needed site furnishings, such as work tables, as time allows.

Technique 7.4

LA MAQUETA: INTERACTIVE MODEL FOR STUDYING AND IMAGINING THE CITY

Andrés Martínez de la Riva Díaz

La Maqueta (the model) is an interactive version of a tool commonly used in architecture and urban planning to design and showcase projects. Adding to its intrinsic virtues (such as three-dimensionality and ease of understanding by anyone), we offer these three innovations: creating it alongside community participants, making it portable, and above all designing it to be modifiable. *La Maqueta's* life does not begin when it is displayed, but in its making—it is essential that the users of the model participate in its design and construction. Doing so diversifies its use and amplifies its potential in collaborative design.

Instructions

1. Interview members of the community or public who will use the model, so that it meets their specific needs.

2. Build a base model. A 4-by-5-foot (1.2-by-1.5-meter) model is portable and works well in almost any space. Pick a fixed scale, such as 1:1000 or 1:500, so that city blocks can fit into your hand. We use wood to create a sturdy foundation, but you may also use cardboard, chipboard, foam board, or a combination. Consider building the model piece by piece so that it can be assembled like a puzzle, with separate groups contributing their parts. Make an instruction card to guide participants in the building process.

3. Work with community groups to organize workshops for interactive games using the model. The workshops may be open and inclusive, or they may be used with a more limited group.

4. Use the model to help connect participants to the past (memory and layers), the present (mapping routes and places), and the future (building the city). Take advantage of the model's versatility and didactic potential. Use the following three games as a template:

    ■ Game One: City Memory. The model reveals that the city in which we live was not always as it is today. There is history below, in layers. Together, build pieces that fit into the model that show layers of historical maps printed on translucent paper. When the current layout is lifted, participants can discover why streets are straight or crooked, or how a shift from rural to urban occurred. Allow time for discussing the discoveries.

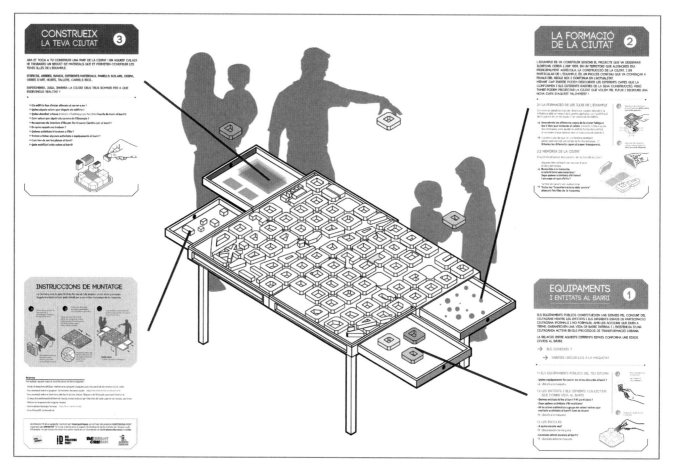

Figure 7-8: Instruction cards explain the design games to participants: mapping neighborhood spaces, learning about city growth, building your own city, and instructions for assembling the model. Source: Raons Públiques.

- Game Two: City Mapping. Ask participants to locate the neighborhood's most important places using stickers or other props. Using colorful thread or wire, add common itineraries, such as routes to school, work, or between locations. Discuss the reasons that these routes and locations were selected.

- Game Three: City Building. What if the city were a blank page? Provide a new packet of templates with blank city blocks and various building materials, and ask each participant to imagine what the city could be. For example, what if there were parks instead of buildings, and vice versa? Save time to share the results with the group.

5. Thoroughly document and preserve the memory of the workshop so that it can be shared with the beneficiaries and used for design and planning.

Case Story

Our team at Raons Públiques used this technique in 2014 at three schools in the *Eixample* district of Barcelona. We named the model Germaqueta, after the Germanetes convent that once occupied this part of the city. The workshop took place on the site under consideration, on which a neighborhood association (Recreant Cruïlles) had lobbied for new green spaces in this dense area. One of our main objectives was to introduce the project to schoolchildren (ages 10–12) and solicit their ideas.

We conducted three separate workshops, one for each school, with groups of approximately 50 children each. The workshops were moderated by four people (two from our team; two from Recreant Cruïlles). Given so many participants, we divided them into two groups—one working directly on the model and one engaged in related activities, such as building new blocks or touring the space itself. In this case, the activities focused on their pedagogical value, especially the city memory game.

The technique was successful in raising students' awareness of the Recreant Cruïlles space, and hopefully enlisting them to transmit their knowledge of the space to their families. Additionally, students gained interest and insight into how the city is built. Through the technique, we reinforced the idea of city as a living organism. Why not imagine a city without cars, or with more parks? The model allowed us to visualize these changes and compare them with what exists now, which empowered participants to know that they too can bring change to the city. This technique also helped to advance grassroots efforts to reclaim the abandoned space where the workshop was held, and to put forward a winning proposal to use it for the community's benefit. The new space, called Espai Germanetes, includes a community garden and a covered gathering area, and serves as a success story for the city's vacant lots project, called Pla BUITS.

Reflection

In over two years of employing this technique, we have seen many positive outcomes, as well as areas for improvement. Promisingly, the technique can be applied to very broad and diverse contexts. We have found that it is essential to involve project beneficiaries in the early stages of designing the workshops. When you do this, participants easily take ownership of the model and thereby have very positive experiences. Being part of the building process is key.

Some of the games, such as the memory layers and place mapping, work well with little facilitation. Others, such as mapping routes and city building, require more time and explanation. It is essential to have two people who know the tool and can facilitate in an agile manner. Additionally, some tools are more difficult for participants to use. Route mapping, for example, can become complicated and messy. We recommend starting with one or two games and then adding more as needed.

Figure 7-9: Participants debate and create their emerging city by uncovering layers of memory in the urban fabric and by proposing new uses and forms. Source: Raons Públiques.

The success of applying *La Maqueta* to other contexts depends on several factors. First, users must express interest in having such a tool, and a small group must be capable of facilitating its use. Second, model building requires some technical skill and willingness to work together. At the same time, the fun and pedagogical nature also give it great potential for youth involvement. In any case, the act of building models together is a useful first step for learning how to build cities together, better.

Technique 7.5

CROSS-CULTURAL PROTOTYPING

Kofi Boone

Cross-Cultural Prototyping enables designers from different cultural backgrounds—insiders and outsiders—to collaborate through the process of making and testing full-scale, working models of design solutions. The process requires careful study of the design context and local traditions of art, craft, and making. The creation of physical prototypes can overcome barriers to understanding text and drawings; this refines the design through use, testing, and feedback prior to final design development.

Instructions

1. Partnership development. Identify a community partner that needs to create physical models of a new product to test with community members. Be clear about the goals of each group involved, and pursue overlapping objectives.

2. Preplanning. Defining desired outcomes can take time, especially in a cross-cultural context. Account for the communication techniques (do they prefer phone, email, meetings?) and capacities of the community partners, who may be working after hours to collaborate, or have specific grant funding for such a project. In addition to the specific project goals, consider logistics. What preparations are required for all groups? How can cultural awareness and sensitivity be raised? Is the new product likely to benefit the community?

3. Meeting. Organize a face-to-face, kickoff meeting with all groups involved. Confirm the project objectives and introduce all of the participants and their potential roles in the process. This can happen formally or informally. It is useful to identify a person to document this meeting. The person should be able to transcribe the conversation into written notes. This can happen by writing during the meeting, or by video or audio recording (with permission in advance) and transcribing notes later.

4. Immersion. Work with local community representatives to immerse the outsiders in local culture. In this case, focus on the needs of the people the group will be serving, and on the ways local people make things: the arts, crafts, and local industries. These can inform the design of prototypes. This immersion process can happen formally through lectures, demonstrations, and presentations from local experts. It can also happen informally through observation, "shadowing," journaling, and the like.

5. Assessment. Develop a format for sharing experiences and lessons learned in a manner that empowers visitors and local participants to provide feedback on how the process met, did not meet, or redefined the initial goals of the project. The assessment does not need to focus only on "successes." It can include conflicts and unanswered questions to address as a group. The assessment can also provide the basis for continued exchange between cultural insiders and outsiders as they move to subsequent project steps.

6. Engagement. Combine project participants per the needs of the effort. Secure a consistent meeting place and work area where everyone will design together. Identify skill sets and resources available. Brainstorm the desired design artifact, combining the earlier stated local need and possible innovations based on existing skills. Set timetables and intermediate deadlines that affect production. Use photographs, drawings, and other abstractions to develop concepts, but reserve the majority of the time for making models for testing with people.

7. Testing. Invite people who will be served by the design to try the prototypes. A party or locally appropriate social gathering is a good way to combine local practices with the needs of the testing session. Begin by introducing the design prototypes and inviting people's interaction and use. Assign a participant to document how people use the models, as well as the questions and comments they make. Ask permission if you need to take photographs of the testing session. Conclude with some directed discussion about the strengths, weaknesses, and potential areas of improvement for the models. Summarize findings from the session and report back to the group.

8. Delivery. Repeat the testing process as possible to refine the prototypes into final design products. Deliver the products and a document outlining the process to all groups.

Case Story

Cross-Cultural Prototyping was used in the Playtime in Africa project, a collaboration between North Carolina State University College of Design's Ghana International Design Studio and the Mmofra Foundation. The Foundation was interested in developing sites that combined the creative play and learning that are integral to healthy childhood development in fast-growing African cities. Mainstream education in Ghana is largely based on colonial British approaches and limits the self-directed discovery time that play outdoors affords. Yet, despite the shortage of formalized parks, play was already going on everywhere in the streets, plazas, and markets that remained from the days when Ghana cities were primarily for trade and business.

Another goal was to develop educational play elements that could be reproduced and located around Accra, the location of the site, and other Ghanaian cities. With these goals the Studio team studied traditional forms of play as well as art and craft in different regions of Ghana. They also held a workshop with schoolchildren where they talked with the children, wrote down their ideas, joined in shared drawing activities, and learned Ghanaian games.

The Studio team applied the results of their new knowledge to the creation of prototypes for creative play equipment that adapted local values, skills, and available resources. The outcomes of the prototyping work included full-scale physical models of a range of creative play elements derived from direct interaction with Ghanaian children and artisans. These included up-cycled wire-spool seating and book storage, a scale and weights inspired by Ashanti gold weight traditions, and a giant abacus with units inspired by bead culture in the Volta Region. The models were co-created with Ghanaians and tested with children at the Playtime in Africa site (now known as Mmofra Place).

Figure 7-10: Responding to Mmofra Foundation's request for educational play experiences that respond to the traditions of Ghanaian traditional culture, the design team adapted the aesthetic of bead making to counting devices, such as an abacus, using on-site materials (wooden discs).

Reflection

The technique was successful in making the design process less abstract and more concrete to local participants. In this case, children enthusiastically engaged in the testing phase, using the physical models in both anticipated and unexpected ways. A significant list of prototypes resulted, about half of which the Foundation is using.

The success of the Studio team's interaction with local social and design networks was mixed, however. The visiting designers hung out in community places and went to parties, but it was unclear whether they overcame the insiders' perception that they were visitors from a wealthy country. Local people sometimes deferred to their visiting colleagues, predominantly middle-class and affluent Americans. Despite the effort to build a common culture of design, socioeconomic perceptions sometimes manifested themselves in the interpersonal power dynamics of design decision making. More time in the local context, as well as additional cross-cultural work with the local participants (to mollify their prejudices of American visitors), could improve this technique in terms of its effectiveness.

Figure 7-11: The Foundation asked that the play concept also be used to define the edge and separate the public part of the site from the private part. The design team proposed expanding the abacus idea to double as a fence to divide the two parts. Participating children also invented and tested new ways of playing with the beads, including races testing who could push the beads the fastest over the length of the fence.

Technique 7.6

DESIGN/BUILD SERVICE LEARNING STUDIO

Daniel Winterbottom

In a Design/Build Service Learning Studio craft and design are integrated. Learning by doing increases students' building knowledge. Through collaboration with marginalized communities students transform underutilized landscapes into nurturing spaces. The process of building offers a way of engaging the community that is less intimidating for the community than a typical workshop or public meeting. The process of building requires collaboration, mutual dependence, and continuing communication. This builds trust, social bonds, and ownership of place among community participants and designers because local people are often skilled in some aspects of building; they are unintimidated by the design/build process.

Instructions

1. Sign a memorandum of agreement with a community group or nonprofit organization that has the resources, capacity, and commitment to the participatory process. Define roles and responsibilities of all the partnering organizations.

2. Offer a design studio (one or two academic terms), with the first three weeks devoted to research, site analysis, and the stakeholder participatory design process. Discuss the participatory strategy with the student team and prepare the participatory design exercises to solicit inputs from community members on concepts, programs, design features, and so forth.

3. Prepare and conduct the workshop.

4. After the workshop, review stakeholder feedback. Develop multiple alternative designs with detailed models and material samples.

5. Hold another workshop to solicit inputs and preferences from community members on alternative designs.

6. Based on stakeholder feedback, synthesize the designs into a single preferred alternative.

7. Develop a construction schedule, prepare materials, and calculate final cost estimates. Identify the teams according to construction tasks.

8. Train the team and community members in basic construction and safety methods.

9. Implement site demolition; establish the site layout; and install footings, utilities, base courses, foundations, and all subsurface elements.

10. Fabricate off-site elements, including welding/finishing steel, wood forms/laminations, and prefabricated structural members.

11. Pour all above-grade walls, footing, and flat work. Install structural elements, paving, site amenities, and so on.

12. Prepare the soil and install irrigation, lighting, and water features.

13. Install plantings, apply finishes, and complete any remaining tasks.

14. Evaluate and celebrate the completion of the project.

15. Conduct a postconstruction and postoccupancy evaluation of the project at a later date.

Case Story

The Rab Psychiatric Public Hospital offers a residential living environment for 450 patients. Patients receive treatment for addiction, posttraumatic stress disorder, dementia, forensic psychiatry, and other mental illnesses. From 2012 to 2016 the Department of Landscape Architecture at the University of Washington was invited to transform 50 percent of the campus into a series of therapeutic gardens for patients and staff.

The studio ethic focused on sensitive, responsive design that derived from an intimate, visceral understanding of, and empathy for, those coping with mental illness. Finding effective methods to cross the divides of cognitive comprehension and communication challenges was essential to the design process. The participatory process offered strategies to increase familiarity and attachment, imbue the site with appropriate meaning and activities, and create an environment offering psychological, physical, and emotional comfort. To better prepare the team to work in this setting and to understand the illnesses patients may have, we hold a few initial preparatory sessions where staff from the medical school explain the causes and symptoms of a range of mental illnesses, and how to better understand and interact with patients.

Patients and staff participated in a series of focus group discussions and reviewed design proposals. Those who couldn't physically or mentally participate drew pictures of their ideas for the gardens. Students in our team were torn between wanting to include every patient and staff idea and the reality of the site. Everything simply couldn't fit because of the size and carrying capacity of the spaces. Eventually we edited to one final set of things to be built: the pavilion, a gathering area, a walking path, and play structures.

The relationship with the patients continued throughout construction. To improve patient participation, we consulted with the medical staff and scheduled meeting times when side effects of medication would be minimal. We learned that for patients the models were more accessible than trying to interpret drawings, and we held separate, shorter sessions with the patients that correlated with their limited attention spans. Many patients felt

Figure 7-12: Members of the design team socializing with a patient despite the limited common language.

the design stages required a level of elite professional expertise that they lacked, but many knew how to dig, plant, and install things. Feeling qualified working in the trades, and honored as they shared their knowledge, the participants' attitude shifted, and they became more relaxed and engaged.

The peaceful, safe, and tranquil gardens increased residents' access to nature. They are adaptable for group and individual activities and universally accessible. They have been used daily by residents for mental, emotional, and spiritual well-being, as well as social-ization, physical exercise, and family visits. The staff facilitates group activities, including arts and crafts, drum circles, games, celebrations, and horticultural, occupational, and pet therapy.

Reflection

Integrating the patients into the participatory process can be a significant challenge. Many had limited attention spans and had trouble focusing. Some were heavily medicated or unsure if they should state their true impressions. Yet there are roles for everyone in a design/build project regardless of anyone's experience, which heightened patient interest. The intermingling between participants organically evolves through large-group activities, such as concrete pours, wood framing, and planting. At Rab, the patients were engaged in all of the building activities; some were required to do so as a component of their therapeutic regime and others because of the social and cross-cultural exchange that they found interesting and fulfilling. A minority of residents had prior experience in gardening or landscape construction, and they were very engaged in the process and in critiquing concepts and schematic designs. The staff also participated, spending a half day a week volunteering, and in some cases serving as intermediaries between the students and the most challenged patients.

Figure 7-13: Patients and designers planting together. Interestingly, the female patients came to work only when the plants were being installed.

Figure 7-14: One of the resulting gardens on the Rab Psychiatric Public Hospital grounds.

Patients commented that they found the act of building therapeutic. Many said they gained a sense of purpose, renewed self-confidence and self-esteem, and an appreciation for the garden work as a respite from the mandated intensive and exhausting therapies. As one patient participant said, "I started working when they asked me to. I started working of my own free will and from the very first day I wanted to be a part of it because I believe that each person should contribute to this project. It wasn't difficult or hard for me and I felt useful. Nobody forced me to work, but I wanted to. I felt positive here. I was surrounded by positive people."

This project required a long-term commitment and collaboration. In four years, we built five gardens. We were able to learn from the previous projects to better inform the subsequent ones. The ability to observe the uses and flaws, for example, the need for more seating and swings, directly informed the new designs and enabled us to retrofit prior projects, thereby increasing patient satisfaction and use. Thoughtful, sensitive editing is the strength of responsive, successful design. Providing what is most necessary, valued, and used is best gained through participatory design and postconstruction analysis. To truly improve a community, you have to stick with it, learn, and improve decisions over time.

8

Testing, Testing, Can You Hear Me? Do I Hear You Right?

Every design is a proposition to be tested. Every concept is a hypothesis. Every detail, big or small, is an intention to be evaluated. The designs we create are merely potential environments; how they are actually used, how they perform relative to the intentions and larger democratic goals are the only measures of the effective environment that count. If major mistakes have been made, they may be expensive or impossible to repair. Postoccupancy evaluations inform the reflective designer, who learns from mistakes and successes, and also the community members, who can initiate changes to correct problems and improve the long-term effectiveness of their project.

Most of us who have completed many projects are haunted by memories of costly failures. Those memories have spurred some designers to reform the process to design-by-inquiry, evaluating design alternatives early on with users. Included in this chapter are methods that will make better memories.

EVALUATE NOW, NOT LATER

As helpful as postconstruction evaluation can be, it is even more important to have assessment points early on and throughout the design process. Transparent and informed evaluation of design hypotheses as they emerge, take form, and are concretized as policy decisions and contract documents needs to occur long before implementation. When well done, the gap between potential and effective environments narrows. The process clarifies which hypotheses have been verified and which need more testing. This forces participants to think deeply about how the new proposals create or change the sociospatial dynamics—the evolving relationships between an activity and a place. As cultural activities change over time, they demand new settings, which, if not provided, leave a place misused, unused, or vandalized. If a newly designed space is to function well for an intended use, the space must graciously accommodate the primary use, its nuances, and related secondary uses. It is especially important for participants to test the nuances of the proposed form of the place to determine if the space fits their particular cultural, life-cycle stage, or other social factors. Precise evaluation of these sociospatial forces leads to environments that meet the users' needs. For example, tables and benches may be designed for a state forest to create a place for the growing number of Latino families to picnic. But will Latino families use the picnic area? Will they have enough tables close together to accommodate extended families? How big do the tables really need to be? What other activities need to be close by? These types of questions can be answered by doing preconstruction evaluation but only after the community articulates precise objectives and performance measures for each design hypothesis. This not only reduces costly mistakes but also leads to far more socially suitable, effective, and locally distinctive design. In many cases this process of design-by-inquiry creates design that goes far beyond efficiency and beauty to transform a place and community. We all want to make such transformative places, right?

Nods, Smiles, and Looking at the Floor

So, how do we start? Obviously at the beginning. Careful listening and inventory lead to precise objectives and informed disagreements described in the earlier chapters of this book. Those techniques serve as the basis for measuring, adjusting, and maximizing the design. The designer needs to share what has been learned as the first litmus test for whether listening has been effective in helping the community comprehend itself honestly and wholly. If this is met with nods, smiles, maybe embarrassed looking at the floor, or even angry interruptions, you have advanced the design hypothesis. The community and the designer can begin to correct spatial misconceptions, give form to common values, and paint a noble picture for the future through critical transactions. The early, honest give-and-take begs for more.

REFORMING DESIRES WITH SPATIAL PRECISION

Almost all of the techniques in the previous chapters build on this foundation and provide continuing opportunities to evaluate ideas. The designer begins to pose questions from the users' points of view, and community participants probe with detailed design questions. As abstract objectives become more spatially precise, user participants make increasingly concrete, culturally informed suggestions that were impossible in the ethereal world of words. Likewise designers and citizens with special expertise can interject challenging imagination, creative directions, and essential practical critique. These interactions provide the opportunity for insights to blossom. Testing, testing, testing. One resident may suggest a setting for a desired activity; another draws it to see if that spatial arrangement does indeed enable the desired functions. Each interaction refines the sociospatial form and creates metrics for policy strategies. Add poetic transactions between designer, experts, and participants, and preliminary ideas reform as visionary and possible alternatives. These alternative futures, once clearly articulated, can be tested by comparing each alternative to the others, and performance measures can be set. A prototype might then test the preferred alternative. Political will, carefully measured, might foretell more assertive, long-term actions.

UNTIL WE HEAR EACH OTHER RIGHT

In this chapter we provide six techniques for evaluating alternatives, creating precise measures of sociospatial dynamics, designing by inquiry, testing alternative choices, and determining ways to measure effectiveness. In "The Spatial Design Game: A Design Game that Teaches and Tests" Henry Sanoff, the master of such games, incorporates principles of design that enable citizens to make complex spatial tradeoffs on their own, in turn evaluating previously proposed but unpopular plans. In "Anticipated Archetypes and Unexpected Idiosyncrasies" Randolph T. Hester Jr. describes his method of drawing expected and unexpected patterns of daily life as a way to test how different spatial layouts will function in a particular place and culture. Victoria Chanse offers a technique that uses site-specific sea level rise data to allow communities to determine actions at the most local level. Her technique, "Raise Your Own Sea Level", dispels debilitating despair, tests practical mitigation strategies site by site, and encourages thoughtful, proactive plans. In "Machizukuri: Visualizing Sequential Futures" Naomi Uchida and Shigeru Satoh build on the tradition of Donald Appleyard's simulation work, enabling people to experience a place before it is built. Their realistic architectural models coupled with a small camera and computer allow participants to test multiple design plans simultaneously, change the model parts, create new designs, and see the results immediately. In "Preemptive Comparison" Randolph T. Hester Jr. provides a way to evaluate multiple proposals using objectives, performance criteria, and activity settings developed earlier in the process through intense back-and-forth exchanges between designer and potential users. Emily Risinger and Sara Egan provide a method for determining a community's highest priorities using play money, accurately tied to real costs. In their "Participatory Budgeting" technique community members vote to allocate money for their most preferred facilities. Although these techniques vary in emphasis, each helps the designer to develop appropriate proposals and helps community members make critical design decisions in democratic ways that transform potential environments into effective ones that fit their particular needs.

Technique 8.1

THE SPATIAL DESIGN GAME: A DESIGN GAME THAT TEACHES AND TESTS

Henry Sanoff

The Spatial Design Game is a small-group decision-making process that builds competence through the transfer of design principles. Participants, aided by game pieces prepared in advance, make choices about activities, hold positions, debate priorities and spatial arrangements, and create a plan for design action. There are three interconnected stages in the process, with accompanying rules that require consensus decisions at each step. First, participants make individual choices, followed by group discussion and agreement about objectives. Then they match activities to satisfy their objectives. The activities and objectives are used to do space planning where participants place graphic symbols representing the activities on a plan.

Instructions

1. Create lists of likely activities and objectives. In order to engage participants effectively and offer a wide range of possibilities, identify objectives and activities that are most relevant to the specific task depending upon what type of facility is being planned. Are you designing a community center, park, or other public place? It may be necessary to conduct interviews in the community to assure that all likely activities are represented.

2. Make game pieces that represent how much space each activity takes and how many people can be accommodated. We often use one-inch squares so they can be located on a plan with a comparable grid. Develop rules for how the game is to be played. Be sure the rules guarantee that every participant has an equal opportunity to voice personal priorities and concerns. Incorporate architectural decisions in the rules to allow laypeople to design quickly and professionally. This can include which activities need to be adjacent to each other, such as children's play areas and restrooms, or qualities such as north-facing windows to naturally light an art studio. Create sheets with lists of possible objectives, a sheet with activities, and another sheet to record decisions each group makes regarding the objectives and activities.

3. Pretest the game before the workshop.

4. At the beginning of the workshop form small groups of no more than five people. Explain the rules, identify each of the three stages in the process, and emphasize the requirement for reaching consensus before proceeding to a successive stage.

5. In stage one, group members individually select four objectives from a prepared list, take turns describing individual objectives, then by consensus agree to a final list of four. In designing a community center, for example, the objectives might include a meeting hall for large groups, places to hold art classes with storage for supplies, a place for teenagers, and outdoor art fairs.

6. In stage two group members match each objective with four corresponding activities and their representative graphic symbols, which were prepared in advance for each activity. The activities related to a place for teens might include a full basketball court, a stage for dance competitions, a recording studio, and vending machines. Objective and activity consensus choices should be entered in the record sheet, which serves as a group memory.

7. When agreement is reached about the appropriate activities, the symbols can be selected and then fastened to a site base plan or within the footprint of an existing building. This exercise can be adapted for use in land or facility planning. The selection of four objectives and four activities for each objective allows the process to be completed within two hours and usually reveals the most important issues and priorities. The result is a design that is accurately scaled and arranged thoughtfully on the plan.

8. Help the group prepare a finished plan to lobby for its completion.

Case Story

The port city of Nanao, Japan, filled an eight-acre area as a symbolic "greenland." Local government prepared the basic plan without consulting citizens, who then rejected several proposals. Consequently, a citizens' group submitted a request for a public process to the mayor. Subsequently people of all ages were invited to participate in planning the new uses for this reclaimed area. I led a three-day workshop, which began with a chartered boat tour that took 60 middle and high school students, teachers, and parents around the future edge of the land to visualize the scale of the site. Adolescents and teenagers participated in this tour because they had been excluded from previous discussions about the future of this reclaimed area.

The planning team consisted of community volunteers as well as people from various parts of Japan interested in learning about the process. These 30 people organized into work groups to prepare the necessary workshop materials, which included a list of possible recreation objectives, graphic symbols to correspond with different recreational activities, and a base map of the filled area. Symbols were identical in size, each corresponded to a specific unit of area. Activity data sheets included the population capacity of each recreational activity, the area requirement, and the number of symbol units that would need to be fastened to a base map of the landfill.

Eighty community members came to the workshop, which was held in a shopping mall adjacent to the proposed site. Small groups were randomly formed, but the youth grouped together. The two-hour workshop began with participants identifying community objectives and linking them to appropriate recreational activities. Key objectives, for example, included the need for a landscape with the use of water, recreation, and a place to hold regular events, such as concerts.

Figure 8-1: After each group established objectives for the Nanao waterfront, participants chose recreational activities to meet their goals, then cut out and attached graphic symbols to a scaled site plan for the activities the group most desired. Note how the premade symbols allowed residents to create their plan with activity settings at accurate sizes and adjacencies.

All groups produced spatial layout solutions for the landfill area. Representatives from each group concluded the workshop with a brief presentation of their ideas. After a break for lunch approximately 400 community members convened at the local museum for a presentation of the workshop results. The planning team organized the event and introduced the process. Representatives from each work group presented their proposals, which coincidentally were very similar. While it was assumed that each group would opt for activities suited to their age, participants were surprised that students selected recreational activities for their parents as well as for their own interests. This alerted community members to the value of including youth in other community-planning activities.

Following the community presentation, a design team developed models based on the workshop results for presentation at the local high school for student and resident comments. The design team refined the design proposal based on those comments, which was favored over the city plan that had been created without community input. Surprisingly, the differences were slight; however, there was a strong sense of ownership in the ideas presented by the community planning teams. City officials were pleased with the results since their process had gone on for two years without resolution, and the workshop created a consensus plan in only three days. The press documented the process and the major results, informing the public of the events and decisions that had taken place. Finally, the results of the community workshops were endorsed by the city officials and implemented. Communities throughout Japan have subsequently used the "gaming technique" approach.

Reflection

Spatial games instill an awareness of a design process that informs decisions regarding size and compatible activities. Being engaged in such a process teaches competence in the design language and concepts, allowing participants to be more effective collaborators with design professionals. Small-group design games have been used effectively for many years in various cultural settings, often to test the appropriateness of existing plans. Games for small groups defuse aggression often evident in large groups or public hearings and create agreement about an explicit design.

Technique 8.2

ANTICIPATED ARCHETYPES AND UNEXPECTED IDIOSYNCRASIES

Randolph T. Hester Jr.

Anticipated Archetypes and Unexpected Idiosyncrasies is a technique for discovering the life patterns unique to a community, how those activities utilize space, and the implications for designing the future, expressing what is particular about a place. Designers typically rely on stereotypical assumptions based on past projects, our own experiences elsewhere, precedents, government standards, status objects, and research. Working from this information, however, often leads to design disasters that are insensitive to the particular way a community inhabits places. This technique tests such assumptions with users, opening opportunities to create places that satisfy their unique needs. This is done by drawing what the designer and community expect sociospatial patterns to be, then comparing those patterns with actual and desired activity settings. As an example, in a recent project all the participants agreed that swinging was a desired activity. But disagreements were exposed when each person drew his or her preferred setting for swinging. Most drew standard candy-striped metal swing sets like those in the school playgrounds of their youth. Two people drew tire swings hanging from large trees. One envisioned a porch swing, another grapevines over a creek in a hardwood forest. After a laughter-filled discussion they settled on tire swings supported by metal frames. Which would you have drawn? The expectations are anticipated archetypes; the community's distinctive life patterns are unexpected idiosyncrasies.

Instructions

1. List activities in the client's program. Typically this program will include standardized activities for such things as streets and sidewalks, community centers, neighborhood or regional parks, or other settings based on the client's experiences. Standards sometimes will be disputed. When city recreation officials included tennis courts for a park we were designing in a working-class neighborhood in North Carolina, residents immediately challenged us. They demanded that we allocate more space for basketball courts, none for tennis. They stated that the few tennis players in their neighborhood drove to a club, but dozens of carless teens needed basketball close to home. Get community members to add other desired activities and draw simple sketches of how each activity is "performed" in their community. The designer should do this before the residents do. Ask community participants

to draw how much space each activity requires, essential adjacencies, and spatial qualities. Get them to diagram social factors like territoriality, symbolic ownership, class, and life-cycle subtleties that seem important to them. Help those who insist they cannot draw. Do not be surprised at how spatially articulate many people are if you create an atmosphere of nonjudgmental safety. For example, residents of South Central Los Angeles were concerned about gang warfare. Collectively they drew explicit boundaries where each gang's territory overlapped another. These areas, they informed us, were the most dangerous flash points and were to be avoided in making initial community improvements. Expect that many of your assumptions will be erroneous; share them with the community anyway, and be open to critique.

2. Circulate these drawings to community members, going out of the way to engage people who do not ordinarily participate. Get them to modify drawings and add new ones based on their special needs. Compile the results. Keep in mind that some deeply held attachments to place remain to be discovered, which may require you to probe more deeply.

3. Before participants become satisfied with their compendium of activity settings, map the sacred places in the community. This requires explaining because most people think of sacred places as religious sites, but every community has activity settings that are fundamental to the sense of community, everyday life, collective identity, and cherished values. Ask participants to call up these places and draw them. These places are often hidden in the subconscious and must be teased out by unfamiliar and unorthodox methods. Likely some of these places were mentioned in previous lists. This mapping most challenges archetypes and reveals meaningful idiosyncrasies. Compile these places into a "Sacred Structure" map and add these diagrams to the compendium.

4. Undertake fieldwork. First, develop a protocol for checking the activity settings for spatial accuracy and to add nuances of informal interactions that may have been overlooked. We usually budget for our staff to do the fieldwork, but increasingly citizen scientists are eager to help. Be sure you train all involved to follow the protocol and to use standardized maps, formats, symbols, diagrams, and notes. Revise previous diagrams as necessary based on this field verification.

5. Test the original program and activity settings on the basis of steps 2, 3, and 4. Redraw the complete array of desired activity settings in a similar manner, note which are universal and which are truly particular to this community, and attach these to the program. These are treasures that will inspire previously unimagined futures.

Figure 8-2: Campers filled out questionnaires, which provided the designers with precise descriptions of desired activity settings for various campers, ranging from car campers and Hmong hunters to Latino family reunions.

Case Story

Demonstration State Forests, established to develop best practices for the California timber industry, provided the only free, unregulated camping anywhere in the state. Campsites were developed to serve only nuclear family car campers who, for a long time, were the only users. For several decades our firm updated recreation plans for these forests, responding to countless conflicts between forest staff clients and users who were "misusing" the forests. These "abuses" were almost always deviations from the standardized single-family model of recreation. This forced us to discover and design to accommodate unusual cultural variations in camping.

The client program envisioned more nuclear family campsites. When forest staff and our design team drew preferred camping layouts, the small privacy-seeking family dominated. We all drew a single picnic table, campfire ring, several tents and a car, surrounded by vegetation. But when we did behavior observations and surveyed users about their desired camp facilities, no one wanted the stereotypical campsite. Hmong squirrel hunters wanted no developed facilities, just a clearing about 30 feet wide in the forest to cook and eat what they hunted, squatting in a circle around their fire. Mexican Americans needed spaces for family reunions with dozens of large picnic tables in a row, with expansive places to park and play informal games of soccer, no privacy required. South Asian mushroom pickers sought small camping sites in remote locations; fiddlehead pickers wanted no camping at all.

One of the most successful camp areas was developed with large groups of horseback riders whose ideal camp included simple things we would never have thought of, such as a sign giving equestrians priority. We held a meeting on-site and walked off the dimensions

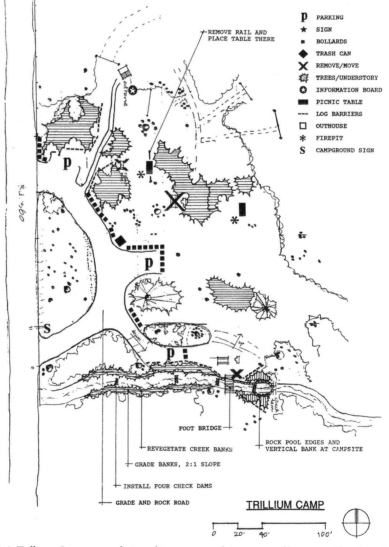

Figure 8-3: Trillium Camp was redesigned to accommodate groups of hunters with private tent spaces and a large, communal cooking area enclosed by natural vegetation.

for trailer turnaround and storage. This camp is extensively used; it meets the test of their needs. Over time we could construct maps of most cherished places to various users to create sacred place illustrations where selective cutting could create perfect recreational settings or places where no logging should occur.

For forest staff one of the most troubling trends concerned homeless people who camped permanently through the summer. Our field maps of activity patterns confirmed the permanent encampments. For example, an extended family had inhabited a hidden campsite illegally at Jackson Forest with enough firewood stacked for a month, a truck raised on makeshift stumps, its engine disassembled, parts scattered about. Adjacent was a pen with mother and puppies nursing. Several clotheslines captured brief pockets of sun under giant redwoods. A handmade sign proclaimed "Home, Sweet Home." There were other similar homesteads. But it turned out that these residents were not homeless. They were descendants of families who for generations had joined logging husbands who lived full time in the forest during logging season. Camping here full time in the summer was

Figure 8-4: The "homeless" campers were not homeless, but they had created homelike campsites. Precise behavior drawings revealed many idiosyncratic camping patterns that challenged the archetypal, nuclear family layout.

a sacred ritual to these families. Part of the problem was solved by explaining to staff this long-standing ritual. Because these users knew they were always breaking some forest rules, they disappeared into the forest when forest staff appeared. How could design help? This family's encampment spilled into surrounding sites. The area was simply not large or flexible enough, plus the appearance of homelessness offended other campers. Our plan gave Camp One, the entrance and most visible public camp facility, a traditional layout, with Roundhouse and other campgrounds designed to accommodate homestay and other less conventional users. Simple interventions, such as screening with native understory vegetation, allowed incompatible adjacencies to work. But testing the traditional camp layout against idiosyncratic "misusers" created a whole new vocabulary of campsite designs that accommodates those we discovered and many that have come to light since.

Reflection

Typically a community is more stable than backwoods campers and easier to assemble as a whole, but the precise drawing of activity settings can overcome problems of words in even temporary communities. We often think that when users say they want basketball courts, nature play, or any number of common activities, we know what they mean. Most often we do not. Identifying life patterns unique to a community requires three things: first, skill in sociospatial observation and recording; second, assertive empathy, which means genuinely acknowledging that you understand and identify with another's situation; and third, the capacity to help communities to overcome their own stereotypes of proper facilities. Following the foregoing instructions can help, but deep digging through trusting transactions is needed to get to valued idiosyncrasies buried in the community's subconscious.

Technique 8.3

RAISE YOUR OWN SEA LEVEL

Victoria Chanse

Raise Your Own Sea Level is a technique that enables residents to visualize precise impacts of sea level change in their community and be proactive at the local level. It combines climate change models and detailed analysis of site topography with a participatory process that involves (1) translating complex and large-scale climate change modeling into projected impacts along the local shorelines; (2) examining potential impacts from different dimensions, including social, economic, and ecological aspects; (3) exploring a wide range of solutions that may include retreating from, rearranging, and revegetating the shoreline, to building up the shoreline; and (4) engaging residents and other stakeholders in exploring a range of these options to decide what actions to take. Until recently, sea level change visualizations were available only at scales too large to be pertinent in terms of anticipating projected local impacts. Online visualization tools make these large-scale scientific data more accessible, easing the translation to the site scale. We can now show things like the number of buildings that likely will be lost in low- to high-risk areas. Showing participants visualizations of sea level change impacts and responses at local scales helps shift the conversation away from "Oh no, this is terrible" to "Oh, here are possible solutions in our community."

Instructions

1. Prior to the event generate the sea level rise impact visualizations, demonstrating time frames of 20, 50, and 100 years; sea level rise in feet; and storm surge levels. Prepare accurate topographic plans showing inundations over time. Make sections and perspectives of potential impacts at local sites; these seem easier for residents to understand. Show levels, locations, and damage forecasts of low- to high-risk areas. Be advised that this will take more time than the participatory workshops themselves.

2. Keep stakeholders informed as the data are translated from climate models to design ideas. Preworkshop meetings and conference calls are essential during this time.

3. Generate a range of specific planning responses to sea level change at different scales. Ask residents and local leaders to prioritize different areas for planning.

4. Generate interactive design games for workshop participants to identify key areas and preferred planning responses to sea level rise. We have created simple techniques, such as having residents map where they live and places that they value which might be threatened by the changing ocean level. Another tool asks them to choose between alternative ways to prevent damage from storm surge.

OPTIONS FOR THE BUILT ENVIRONMENT

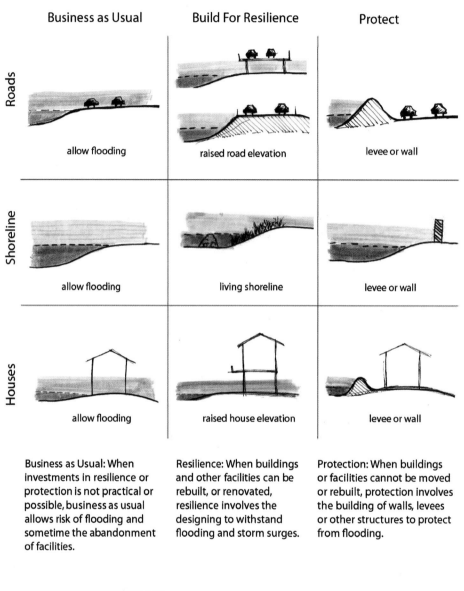

DORCHESTER WORKSHOP

Figure 8-5: Communities often respond to the fearful abstraction of sea level rise with panic, but precise science for the particular coastal location enables reasoned discussion, giving residents some measure of control over their future. Simple diagrams help citizens test ideas about alternatives.

5. Develop an agenda to present background research about sea level rise. Plan for drop-in hours for people with different schedules to discuss and choose preferred alternatives. We usually do this in two-day workshops with enough staff so we can personally walk people through the alternatives when they drop in.

6. Develop a flyer; email to collaborators and stakeholders to publicize the event.

7. Hold the workshop/meeting on-site if at all possible.

8. At the meeting facility set up visualizations of potential sea level rise in a progression. Do not present the most frightening visuals first. Instead, show, for example, the impacts of one-foot sea level rise before three-foot scenarios. Remind participants that these are only speculative projections. We show the research about potential impacts the first day, sometimes followed by an open house allowing people to discuss the research findings and projections. This introduces the public to the projected impacts on the landscape and their daily lives; they then have time to digest the information before the second day of the workshop.

9. On the second day, review the background research for newcomers; show everyone the planning strategies and direct them to workshop stations to discuss their concerns. Show the initial site-specific design strategies. Have people do a series of prepared exercises to elicit answers to critical issues and subconscious desires about the future. Ask people to vote for strategies they prefer.

10. After the two-day workshop develop more specific site-specific designs based on community input. Present these design strategies at a meeting no later than a month after the workshop. Encourage discussion that leads to specific local actions. When possible, continue to share meeting results and design strategies with follow-up meetings with different stakeholder groups.

Case Story

Rural Dorchester County is characterized by wetlands and farms, with the Chesapeake Bay bounding the western portion of the county and Blackwater National Wildlife Refuge to the south. Sea level along Maryland's coast is projected to rise 1.4 feet by 2050 and 3.7 feet by 2100, making Dorchester County one of the most at-risk counties in the United States, a terrifying and debilitating future.

Using the Maryland Department of Natural Resources Coastal Atlas and the National Oceanic and Atmospheric Administration (NOAA) Digital Coast Sea Level Rise Viewer our team developed visualizations (described earlier in the instructions) of projected impacts for key sites in the county. We consulted Olaf Schroth at the Collaborative for Advanced Landscape Planning at the University of British Columbia and Chris Haynes from the National Oceanic and Atmospheric Administration. This required about three months.

Before the workshop, our team met with US Fish and Wildlife staff to understand the wetland loss in Blackwater National Wildlife Refuge and to identify priority areas within the refuge. The team then studied vulnerable sites in other parts of the county. Our team led a two-day workshop with residents and other stakeholders. Key components included developing communication materials and other visuals as well as interactive exercises to identify priority issues and "ground truth" some of the initial areas identified as critical within the county. "Ground truthing" to check the accuracy of topography is essential because the data provided in NOAA models may be incomplete. The team led the kickoff event on the first evening, giving an overview of sea level rise in the county, showing current conditions as well as 2050 and 2100 time frames.

Our team developed seven stations to elicit answers to key unknowns about local beliefs and values as well as actions that people would likely support. At each station participants played a different design game that we had prepared in advance. Although the first day began with a kickoff orientation event, both days were structured for participants to engage with our team at stations. The first station included an activity designed to identify where participants lived and spent time. The second station asked people to identify their ideal community. The third station included visual choices with four types of preferences— environmental interventions, built form, natural features to be protected, and response to flooding. The fourth station asked participants to identify which of several selected statements in terms of environmental, economic, housing, and community development were most important. Station five identified preferred recreational activities. Station six asked participants to examine the potential areas of concern initially identified by the team members. The seventh station asked participants to identify their favorite places relative to sea level change. Issues identified included roads near home becoming unusable, wells and septic systems, and flooding; property values were less important than these three issues.

One of our team's design recommendations called for the Blackwater National Wildlife Refuge to shift inland as wetlands were lost. This clarified the rationale for large-scale planning responses to dramatic coastal changes already happening. By moving Blackwater National Wildlife Refuge, retreating as wetlands are inundated, new wetlands can be established on previously higher ground, retaining a balance of ecological zones, most valuable habitat, and recreational opportunities central to the local economy.

Reflection

We have learned a lot about how to frame a discussion. For example we use the term *sea level change* rather than *sea level rise*. This avoids becoming mired in debates about whether sea level rise is happening at all. Residents seem to relate to more immediate time frames, such as 20-year forecasts, rather than distant ones. One proposal is to examine potential impacts and solutions using 15- to 30-year timeline horizons of a home mortgage.

Figure 8-6: Using the best science available Blackwater National Wildlife Refuge chose a resilient retreat strategy while making new habitats for wild birds and tourism that are already being lost to rising seas. Source: Edwin Remsberg, ©remsberg.com.

Although we strive for our models to show specific impacts on specific places, sometimes a generalized graphic that is not locale-particular can avoid arguments of a place loaded with political or emotional baggage. This is especially pertinent in Dorchester County, where people grieve over their losses as sea level claims cherished places. There, and in some other communities, residents cannot think objectively about such spots. They may favor sacrificing the land of some owners to preserve the property of friends. Or they may be attached subconsciously to certain landscapes and want to keep them exactly as they are. It is easier for them to consider solutions in the abstract and develop policy based on universal principles or nonlocalized best practices.

Since this workshop, sea level rise visualization tools, such as the Maryland Department of Natural Resources Shoreline Atlas and the NOAA Digital Coast Sea Level Rise Viewer, have become increasingly precise and available for more areas. The NOAA Digital Coast Sea Level Rise Viewer beta version and NOAA Sea Level Rise and Coastal Flooding Impacts Viewer are continually being improved. These facilitate our providing participants with accurate information to examine local scale impacts of sea level rise and storm surge.

Technique 8.4

MACHIZUKURI: VISUALIZING SEQUENTIAL FUTURES

Naomi Uchida and Shigeru Satoh

The *Machizukuri* Visualizing Sequential Futures is a simulation technique for presenting alternative design proposals at eye level. The technique uses building models with the pictures of actual facades on them and a small camera to create realistic, moving pictures. It is most effective in testing sequential spaces, such as streets, sidewalks, linear parks, and townscapes, where people move through and stop along the way. Models with realistic facades and furniture can be photographed to simulate motion to help people evaluate choices before construction. We are now using a charge-coupled-device (CCD) camera, but other cameras can be similarly effective. There are multiple advantages of a CCD camera: it is small enough to move about in a model, it allows participants to change the design, it is realistic enough that participants can test the feasibility of specific activities that they want to include in the place, and it provides eye-level and bird's-eye views simultaneously. But these devices are expensive. As technology changes we continue to experiment to find suitable, affordable equipment.

Instructions

1. Prepare the base model in advance of the event. Take pictures of actual facades of the planning area. Correct distorted horizontal and vertical perspectives of facades using a photoediting application. Paste the corrected pictures of facades on the surface of models made from Styrofoam or other material so that the models look real when seen through the CCD camera (sometimes we also paste pictures on the side surfaces to make them look even more real). 1/100 is the appropriate scale for testing streetscape and street design; also, for using the CCD camera, a model has to be as big as 1/100 to look real and provide space for the camera to move around it.

2. Make several patterns of models to show the community alternative choices for the future.

3. Make street furniture, power poles, and trees to discuss design details.

4. Record moving pictures of going through the models with the CCD camera system. Edit the pictures in a split screen mode to compare and evaluate the different visions on the screen at the same time.

5. At the event show the community members the moving pictures, which have been created in advance. Show several patterns of models to the community.

Figure 8-7: The base model needs to be big enough to move the camera around it. With photographs of the actual facades pasted to the model, it appears realistic when photographed.

6. Connect the CCD camera to a monitor to display the eye-level view. The CCD camera is small enough to move through the model as though people were actually walking through it.

7. Discuss the designs and change the models freely to try new ideas that people suggest as they are inspired by the moving pictures.

8. Generate new ideas, rearranging the street elements using the CCD camera to see the eye-level view on the display. Record the preferred alternative and details of furniture placement and report the results to the community.

Case Story

This technique was used in the Numabukuro area, Nakano Ward, Tokyo, Japan, to discuss a street-widening project. In the area, public projects were being implemented to move trains underground while building a new station and widening a 500-meter-long (1,640-foot-long) shopping street to create the main access to the station. The existing street was about six meters (roughly 20 feet) wide with a single car lane and no sidewalk. The City wanted to widen the street significantly.

We made moving pictures of several models to demonstrate future visions of streets at different widths and layouts in a split-screen mode; in this case, the moving pictures were edited as a quadrisection with the current condition and three alternative ideas. It showed the different "after" views simultaneously. The first was an 8-meter-wide (26-foot-wide) street with a single lane, the second was a 12-meter-wide (39-foot-wide) street with a snake-shaped single lane, and the third was a 16-meter-wide (52-foot-wide) street with double lanes. We used the technique long before the official city planning decision, so the design idea was open at that time.

After the discussion using the simulation, the government decided that it would choose a 14-meter-wide (46-foot-wide) street, taking into consideration the community's opinion, which preferred to have a 12-meter-wide (39-foot-wide) street. Even the 14-meter-wide street was unusually narrow for a road that meets planning standards. The simultaneous simulations influenced not only the community's ideas but also the government's decision.

Figure 8-8: The existing street and three alternatives depicted in moving pictures are shown on a split screen so that residents can compare the differences between street widths.

Figure 8-9: Participants rearrange street furniture and trees to improve the designs or create new alternatives, which are filmed at eye level and immediately projected for all to evaluate.

In another case the city also planned to widen a shopping street, but the plan changed after workshops using a similar simulation technique. The community and government opted to create an altogether new style of design for the street to revitalize the shopping district instead of widening the street. Both the local government and the shop owners preferred this alternative after using the technique to test their choices. This type of visualization system is suitable not only for designing infrastructure but also for discussing the management of an area because the visual power helps participants imagine the future lifestyle realistically.

Reflection

Scale models are useful for a community discussing ideas during the decision-making process because people can change the models more easily than with computer simulation models. They can move the streetscape with their hands, and the CCD camera immediately allows them to see that future at eye level. It is useful for planners as well to quickly adjust designs in the workshop, responding to the community's ideas.

The split-screen mode, such as the quadrisection, makes comparison easier and pushes the discussion ahead. It looks real with the CCD camera, so the community can examine the ideas more seriously. This system is one of the most effective ways to discuss physical design coupled with lifestyle because it is detail oriented, and alternatives are easy to compare.

The drawback is that preparation—including making models and filming and editing moving pictures—is time consuming. Using a 3-D printer for making models can help by saving labor and making the models more durable and more easily transportable to the workshops. (Styrofoam models are fragile and easily deteriorate.)

Smartphones can also record moving pictures, although most are presently too big to record a go-through movie of a small model. However, those advancing technologies can reduce labor and equipment costs, making the use of this technique more widespread for professional practice.

Because of the strong visual power of these moving simulations caution must be exercised about the timing of their use. They are good for comparison between alternative choices after the community has had wide-open conversations over a long time and has clear objectives. On the other hand, if a planner shows them too early in the community participation process, the movie simulations may rush people to judgment without considering deeper needs, bias decisions, and preclude more thoughtful and inventive designs. This method is best used in the middle of the process after several workshops, after participants have shared ideas and discussed future visions but before they have made a final decision.

Technique 8.5

PREEMPTIVE COMPARISON

Randolph T. Hester Jr.

Preemptive Comparison is a technique to evaluate the costs and benefits of alternative plans before construction to determine which best meets the specific needs of the community. Developed from methods of postoccupancy evaluation (POE) that reveal failures after construction, preemptive comparison seeks to produce a plan that fulfills community aspirations and avoids costly mistakes. To be effective, such testing before construction requires creating performance criteria based on community goals, diagrams of activity settings, and alternative plans along a spectrum of the most salient competing interests in the community. These allow the designer to think like a community member and community members to think like a designer so that both can test ideas transparently, give honest criticism and praise, discover potential flaws and brilliance in design alternatives, and find opportunities for adjustment. For example, a goal to integrate affordable housing into existing single-family neighborhoods might be made explicit with diagrams of alternatives ranging from town or row houses to garage or in-law apartments. This should result in frank discussions about what would work best in a particular community. In one case a standard was developed by which place-appropriate progress could be measured. The community opted for performance criteria of two accessory units per every 10 single-family homes, with tax incentives for the two units.

Instructions

1. Compile a list of objectives, performance criteria, and diagrams of activity settings based on previous steps in the community design process.

2. Develop a number of alternative plans. Usually three to seven are considered appropriate. Fewer provide too little choice. More are difficult to compare. Alternatives are best developed in public workshops, but we sometimes add plans to create a complete continuum. The continuum may pit megaforces (e.g., cultural preservation against virtual-capital-driven extraction), but it can be as local as sports fields versus nature play. Include some alternatives that benefit each polar opposite over the other, some compromises, and some that maximize competing values.

3. Decide on the appropriate forum for the community to test the alternatives. This may require multiple events with different publics to include marginalized groups. Newspaper and online surveys can reach different groups, but at some point community members need to evaluate plans face to face.

4. Prepare appropriate graphics. We always make large wall graphics and letter-sized handouts in black and white for unbiased comparison and media duplication. Draw plans and sections of each alternative. Write a narrative that describes each alternative. Point out key activity settings accommodated in each alternative. Neither plan nor text should advocate one alternative over others. We are testing not advocating at this point. Include the performance criteria in a simple form to focus attention on evaluating costs and benefits already determined as most significant. Make a form with objectives with space for participants to write evaluative notes, rank performance criteria they consider most important, and vote for the alternative they prefer.

5. Evaluate the alternatives in public. Present each alternative plan, asking participants to individually evaluate the plans using the letter-sized handout. After participants have completed the handout, divide into groups of six to eight people, each with a design team facilitator. Tell participants to listen to, but not debate, differing points of view. Taking turns, ask each participant to say which plan he or she prefers and to briefly explain the criteria underlying the choice. Do not let participants interrupt each other. After everyone has spoken, ask if participants have ways to improve preferred plans. Do not seek agreement. When the discussion wanes, have each person put dots on the wall graphics as votes for the plan the participant prefers. Use sticky notes to write comments. Reconvene the whole group and note if there is an overwhelming favorite or a wildly split vote. Explain the next steps in the process. Collect all evaluation forms to mine the data later.

6. Attend to sociospatial details. Most participants will test alternatives on the basis of a few performance criteria and activity settings. But to achieve a splendid design, attention must be paid to all the criteria and spatial implications of proposed activities. A subcommittee can accomplish this.

7. Tally all of the evaluations. The letter-sized handouts provide comparable data to determine the overall top choices. It is easy if there is overwhelming agreement, but even more useful are critical comments from thoughtful participants. These can lead to a refined plan or dramatic revisions. Review the results for trends and minority insights. Prepare a summary for participants. Include a revised design plan based on the evaluation. Point out key improvements based on the rigorous testing the public did.

Case Story

Yountville, California, is "the path less trodden" in Napa Valley. Residents expect to be actively engaged in testing alternatives, be they minor sidewalk repairs or multimillion-dollar capital improvements. This forced our firm to continually create more sophisticated methods for pretesting proposals with simple diagrams that clearly showed the choices and trade-offs.

In designing the community center such diagrams facilitated testing alternatives, from an addition shoehorned within existing facilities to a greenfield relocation. The shoehorn tested best and was ultimately built. But the details of the architectural program required an iterative process of developing alternatives, testing them, and generating refined choices; this entailed dozens of workshops to narrow the choices to three. Floor plans at quarter-inch scale were provided to every participant at workshops targeting different groups from youth to residents of the veterans' home. A worksheet focused on "things that would work" and "things that would not work" for each of the three choices. Participants had to

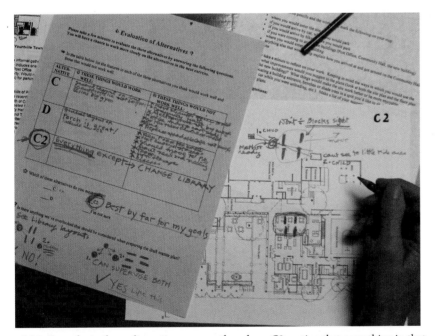

Figure 8-10: To evaluate three alternatives one mother chose C2, noting that everything in that plan worked well except the library. The layout blocked her view of some areas of the room, making it impossible to supervise young readers in different locations. She diagramed on her worksheet exactly how to change the design.

imagine themselves in each plan to make judgments about what would work. Then they were asked to select which of the three alternatives they preferred. The one most preferred by a significant majority of residents was refined.

The plan participants felt was the best was then evaluated in a community meeting, using a planning worksheet that asked participants to select specific activities they wanted to do and measure how well the plan performed for those activities. They were asked to draw ways to improve activity settings directly on the plan.

Figure 8-11: Some residents drew a larger gym to accommodate basketball and dozens of other activities. The enlarged multiuse room is heavily used for classes and events. Source: David Wakely.

Figure 8-12: During one pretest several residents envisioned large barn doors between the multipurpose room and the barbeque patio, creating indoor–outdoor interactions that became a most cherished aspect of the new building. Source: David Wakely.

The resulting community center evokes resident desires for multitasking use of the town center; a gym provides a basketball court but opens through oversized barn doors to increase the flexibility for indoor and outdoor events. A sheriff substation makes community policing an everyday reality. One mother redesigned the library so she could supervise children throughout the library. Getting residents to test plans from both a user and a spatial design perspective created a distinctive community center, serving local needs somewhat unorthodoxly.

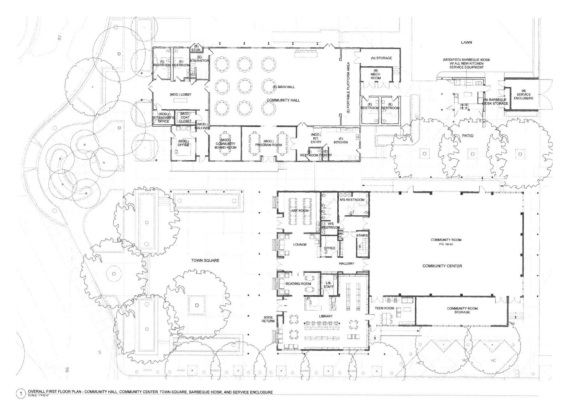

OVERALL FIRST FLOOR PLAN - COMMUNITY HALL, COMMUNITY CENTER, TOWN SQUARE, BARBEQUE KIOSK, AND SERVICE ENCLOSURE
SCALE 1"=40'-0"

Figure 8-13: In the revised plan for the library Susi Marzuola, the architect, shifted the adult reading nook to a central spot, enlarged the gym, and created indoor–outdoor spaces under an arcade that connected the new and old buildings. Source: Siegel & Strain Architects; Susi Marzuola, Principal.

Reflection

From years of testing before construction it is clear that it is worth the time and money to generate distinguished design and avoid costly mistakes. But to some it seems to be unduly expensive and time consuming at the time. In reality, the iterative and detailed testing in the case of the Yountville Community Center cost only about $20,000 in design fees for a much improved building and public space costing in excess of $6 million. The real time expense is the hours residents volunteered to go far beyond just voting. Instead they carefully evaluated plans by projecting themselves into the spaces as users and designers. The challenge is balancing feedback from many participants with the extensive evaluation of a thoughtful few who listen to other opinions face to face and contribute nuanced design ideas through extended engagement. Both are important to democratic design. The redesigned ideas from the few produce designs that particularly fit the needs of the users.

Figure 8-14: An open layout provides a view from the art room and lounge through the reading room to the library, superseding requests for an open, inviting floor plan. Source: David Wakely.

Technique 8.6

PARTICIPATORY BUDGETING

Emily Risinger and Sara Egan

Participatory budgeting is an activity in which citizens are provided play money and asked to spend it on project elements. How the money is allocated indicates items most supported and preference for design scenarios. This exercise puts participants in the decision-making role, helping stakeholders, decision makers, designers, and clients to understand costs, think critically about how to best apply limited funds, identify trade-offs, and determine the elements most valued by the community. Participatory budgeting creates dialogue regarding the magnitude, importance, and experiential qualities and elements of a project; it can be applied during many phases of a planning process and at various scales.

Online versions of this technique enable participants to allocate money to project elements, with graphics representing those elements changing in real time, allowing participants to see how their preferences rank in comparison to those of others.

Instructions

1. After initial design concepts are created and before the event, conduct a cost analysis that allows the planning team to craft a budget exercise based on feasibility studies.

2. Gather supplies: colored paper and boxes, totes or trays to collect votes.

3. Create a meeting agenda that includes adequate time for the exercise. Time needed for the exercise will vary based on the size of the group.

4. Develop a template for "play money." Use a template that features several colors (or patterns) so that different categories of currency amounts (e.g., hundreds, thousands, millions, billions) can be easily communicated. Gather "money" and bundle amounts that will be given to each participant. Make extra bundles to eliminate the risk of running out of supplies at the meeting.

5. Gather boxes (or trays) for participants to place their money in as they vote with their dollars. Make a sign for each box that lists the project element to be voted on and how much it costs (e.g., new playground—estimated cost $50,000). Consider having a descriptive presentation board associated with each element and have facilitators nearby throughout the exercise to answer questions.

6. At the meeting facility, lay out the bundled amounts for participants prior to the start of the workshop. Set up the boxes so that participants can easily walk along to place dollars into each according to their priorities.

7. The meeting facilitator should explain design elements being considered, their associated costs, and how each bundle of money may be allocated across projects of their choosing. Then announce the beginning of the budgeting exercise.

8. Have participants drop funds into collection boxes correlating with project elements. Photograph the process.

9. Collect boxes and record amounts allocated. Post results on a wall so that as the final dollar amounts are being transparently calculated they are displayed for real-time review by participants.

10. Discuss elements that received the most dollars.

12. After the event summarize the results of the exercise in a memo or graphic display.

13. Share the results and photos of the exercise.

Case Story

Design Workshop applied participatory budgeting during its Lafayette Park at the Horse Farm project, a master planning effort for a 100-acre tract of land in Lafayette, Louisiana. The Horse Farm has a rich history and is the last remaining significantly sized piece of undeveloped public property located within central Lafayette. For years, advocacy groups, neighbors, and businesses supported the municipal government's plans to purchase the

Figure 8-15: Although Lafayette Park was large enough to accommodate many facilities, citizens needed to study alternatives carefully to determine the highest priorities and eliminate facilities inappropriate for the park. Source: Design Workshop.

Figure 8-16: Using participatory budgeting, participants voted with bundles of play money to choose park elements. The most highly funded elements gave community leaders clear direction for expenditures. Source: Design Workshop.

land for a new city park. Design Workshop engaged the Lafayette community to gain feedback regarding which park programs and facilities the community envisioned. Through participatory budgeting, the community prioritized programming and plan elements. The community weighed in on design alternatives for the park, featuring different program elements: a playground, farmer's market, amphitheater, dog park, pedestrian bridge, mini-golf course, or carousel. Participants received an overview about each alternative and were provided bundles of money to vote for their favorite park programs.

After attendees "spent" their money, the planning team calculated the results, which were shared during the concluding presentation of the workshop. This exercise tested program alternatives, ensuring inclusiveness, full transparency, and recommendations that emerged from the desires of the people. Five workshops and online surveys revealed that, across all constituents, the playground, pedestrian bridges, and farmer's market remained the most highly "funded." These most preferred elements formed the foundation of the park design.

Reflection

Participatory budgeting is flexible; it can be used during many project stages, including analysis, idea generation, prioritization, and narrowing down larger sets of options. In larger groups, the anonymity of the process can enable everyone to have an equal say; in smaller groups, the technique can feature in-depth discussions about how to best implement "funded" projects.

We have learned some lessons the hard way, for example, to be conservative and transparent about the cost of items to be voted on. While the cost of some projects may seem large to citizens, getting an inaccurate or inadequate budget can have long-term consequences. The method of calculating the results needs to be explained before participants vote with their money. Will results be based on the number of times an element is voted for or the actual dollar amount? Also, as part of the introduction, it is critical to explain how results will be used in real life to implement projects. Additionally, voting exercises need to be aligned with online voting platforms. It is necessary to ask identical questions and provide the same quantities of play money for every workshop and online participant or the process may be discredited by conflicting information.

For fine-tuned results, appropriate increments and amounts of monies should be provided in each bundle. Make sure money categories are sufficiently varied so that participants can vote across projects and are not forced to put all of their money into one box (e.g., if only "million-dollar bills" are provided to vote on capital improvement projects, participants are unable to vote for smaller projects that may cost $100,000, $250,000, or $500,000). Allow time to count the money in the meeting so that results can be shared without exceeding the allotted time. This usually takes no more than 15 minutes. Several design team members can count the money while others lead additional workshop exercises. For example, small groups might brainstorm strategies for implementing the plan (30 to 45 minutes) or break for snacks (15 minutes). But be sure to bring everyone back together to share the results of the budgeting session.

9

Putting Power to Good Use, Delicately and Tenaciously

Design is a political act. The politics of design determine who gets what, from parks and housing to landfills and freeway pollution. The politics of design determines if a bench prevents a homeless person from sleeping or if a park includes facilities for all in the neighborhood to enjoy. The politics of design determines whether land resources essential for a heathy ecosystem are enhanced or destroyed. Participatory design is one of the most effective means in a democracy to create cities and landscapes that distribute resources and shape places to be sustainable, representative of diverse publics, well informed by local wisdom, and just. Transactive design processes empower participants and designers with information, skills, and self-confidence as well as the recognition that there is much to be gained by change. This chapter provides the tools to dissect, develop, and put power to good use.

The Power of Design Itself

A transactive process is one means to develop political strength, but design itself has transformative powers. It may resolve what seemed intractable through spatial distancing or time sharing, reuse resources in ways never before considered, connect people to the moral authority of their values, or inspire a possible future grounded in the everyday. And after it is implemented, the design takes on a life all its own. It has the capacity to accommodate local needs, represent community identity, welcome those previously excluded, create an atmosphere of dignity, inspire further improvements, and concretize advances in environmental justice. None of these occurs automatically; each requires the highest denominator of design acumen.

WHO HAS POWER AND HOW IT REDISTRIBUTES

Getting almost anything positive done, especially in marginalized communities, requires changing the political status quo. The change, big or small, may be graciously accepted, violently resisted, or anything between the two. Each action changes the distribution of power between those with more power and those with less. Those with more power typically monopolize virtual and local capital and maintain direct access to and control of the decision-making structure and important resources. Additionally, this privileged access is generally protected by favorable laws, the police, and the military. They seldom give up these privileges voluntarily, relying on progressive stasis and public fear of uncontrolled change. Their strategies exhibit in trickle-down economics and playing less powerful groups against one another, placating those groups with stakeholder activities and token improvements.

Those with less authority, however, are not without potential power. They are often experienced in making do with the capacity to improvise using local resources and skilled labor. If connected with sympathetic experts, they combine their native wisdom with science to create knowledge. They often occupy the high moral ground and can expose injustices that force remedial action. If unified they have large enough numbers to vote, resist, boycott, and ultimately disrupt, causing uncontrolled change. If they marshal these strengths and master transactive design techniques, those with less power possess all the same negotiating skills of the powerful—from cooperation and win-win innovations to conflict mediation and shuttle diplomacy. Plus one strategy the elite lack—nonviolent civil disobedience.

APPROPRIATE ACTION TO EMPOWER THE VOICELESS

Giving voice to the voiceless is a rallying force that has long been a guiding principle of participatory design. Almost always when a subculture is oppressed there is an associated endangered ecosystem exploited by the same forces that oppress the human community. Like powerless people, the land cannot speak for itself against dominant authority. The community of land has little or no legal standing, necessitating advocacy and proactive design strategies. In those cases principles underlying conservation biology and spatial sociology need to be introduced into the design and empowered in the political fray. Similarly, sustainable green strategies often lack political support, and the designer must be their advocate.

How the techniques in this chapter are applied depends upon the context. In poorer communities strategies to "reduce, reuse, and recycle" may be part of every-day life that only need to be championed, whereas more affluent communities may need encouragement to use their power for conspicuous nonconsumption and sen-sible status-seeking. Coalitions between polar ends of the economic spectrum can achieve affordable housing, healthier shopping, or improved civic places, requiring less confrontational strategies than redistributing unwanted land uses and health hazards from poorer neighborhoods.

STRATEGIC THINKING

Putting power to good use requires strategic thinking throughout the planning pro-cess, even the smallest decision. The manner in which a meeting is run is strategic. The choice of one technique over another is strategic. How the design itself evolves is strategic.

To be effective at transformative design requires the ability to recognize and assemble all the forces the community possesses in order to see their plans through to completion. It means being able to decide which strategy to employ by assessing whether the group is trying to prevent a bad thing from happening, attempting to remove or redistribute some bad thing that has already happened, reclaim some-thing lost, conserve something valued, or create something good. This is the essence of strategic thinking. Some designers eschew strategic thinking because they are only the designer, politically clueless, or satisfied with the current state of things. Others are simply naturals at strategic thinking and action. But strategic thinking in design is both an art and a science that can be mastered with practice.

TECHNIQUES FOR DEVELOPING POWER

This chapter contains seven strategic techniques essential for putting power to good use. We include techniques that are most effective at changing power imbalances. We think these go beyond the trendy uses of the word *empower(ment)* and actu-ally change political outcomes and gain measures of control. Randolph T. Hester Jr. describes "Mapping Environmental Injustice," the foundation for addressing inequities and redistributing resources. Diane Jones Allen's "Kitchen Table Work Session" designs in the most familiar haunts of residents. By also connecting to experts remotely, she shows how home field advantage increases the odds for effective action. Hester contributes the time-tested tool "Power Mapping" to uncover potentially hidden spheres of influence, draw them, and reshape status quo outcomes. In every process the designer exercises power knowingly or unknowingly—positively and negatively. Shalini Agrawal and Shreya Shah offer a means to make your unknown power known. "Positioning Yourself on the Spectrum of Power and Privilege" enables self-awareness in order to maximize the positive impacts of the designer's presence. Laura J. Lawson shares a technique she uses in the most powerless communities. Her "Build Small, Think Structural Change" shows how to turn ambitious projects into modest but achievable, "bite-sized" undertakings that build the confidence and power to take on more improvement efforts while keeping eyes on the bigger prize of structural reform. In the last techniques Hester explains methods employed in pursuit of the bigger prize. "Conflict in Its Time and Place" shows how to expand the community's political roles beyond facilitation by practicing a full house of tactics that confront, deflect, and accommodate conflict appropriately. "Organizing a Place-Based Campaign" is a primer in community organizing around social issues that are grounded in locality, requiring a particular use of design skills. Together these methods are a substantial basis for empowering community to see transformative design through to completion.

Technique 9.1

MAPPING ENVIRONMENTAL INJUSTICE

Randolph T. Hester Jr.

Injustice mapping creates a spatial record of inequities in accessibility, distribution of public resources and hazards, and exclusionary design. The maps are particularly powerful in raising public awareness in ways that written reports alone do not; they make the invisible visible, embarrassing authorities and spurring action.

Inaccessibility to the necessities of everyday life, information, and decision making prevents many people from an opportunity to thrive. For example, land-use segregation and remote employment centers handicap those without cars. A map of these locations overlaid by carless households can be compared with a similar map for households with cars showing the burden of inaccessibility. Similarly, distribution of desired resources and unwanted land uses is typically skewed. Maps showing relative distribution of parks, decent housing, healthy food or water as well as polluted air, dangerous industries, or toxic sites usually reveal patterns of environmental classism and racism.

From restrictive zoning to the shape of benches, design encourages some to use and excludes others from using public facilities. Mapping the geography of exclusion based on class, race, migrant status, or other marginalizing factors shows patterns of discrimination with blatantly missing activity settings or subtle messages telling "others" they are unwelcome. All of these can be effectively mapped.

Instructions

1. Clearly identify the environmental injustice you want to assess and available resources for drawing the data. Are the data easily accessible in secondary sources, such as census data and GIS layers in government files? What must be mapped firsthand? Are these skills available in your group, a university, or a nongovernmental organization? How many citizen scientists can be counted on? Involve as many as possible; nothing empowers like mapping injustices that affect you directly. Do you have adequate equipment to measure the injustice? Although the process is similar for access, distribution, and exclusion, precise distinctions determine the course of action. To map transit deserts, particulate pollution, or exclusionary facilities requires different strategies. For example, access and distribution can often be mapped from secondary sources, but inclusionary design usually relies on field research by local citizen scientists.

2. Map data from secondary sources first—they are often free, easily compiled, and visual. Make the maps at a scale that conveys the inequity in the target neighborhood relative to the community to which it is to be compared. Determine metrics for the extent of discrimination, risk, or other critical factors.

3. Determine which additional data are needed to accurately measure the injustice. Find an expert in associated risks and metrics of the injustice. Ask the expert to explain the best field methods for volunteers to map the problem. Cultivate a long-term relationship that benefits the expert and the community.

4. Get the expert to train local citizen scientists in scientific protocols to gather and record data rigorously enough to withstand public and scientific scrutiny. Secure the needed equipment; learn how to use it and how to code and input field observations. Different inequities require different technologies. Some monitoring equipment downloads and compiles data by location automatically. In contrast, psychological exclusion requires citizen scientists to record "extent of unwelcomeness" on a paper map, then "download" their findings by hand onto a group map. In such a case it is important to record not just location but also race, gender, and other social factors to be analyzed by cultural category.

5. Exclusion at the site design level requires answering multiple questions. Review the documents of the process and plan for the facility. For whom was the project designed? What activity settings were left out, excluding certain people? Sleuthing the facility itself offers other clues. Is it Americans with Disabilities Act accessible? Do benches invite or preclude sleeping? Are there places to sit in sun pockets to warm old bodies? Is the facility dominated by a single use, preventing new uses? Is there enough emptiness to accommodate unanticipated activities? Is there symbolism that disinvites some? Map as many of these factors as possible. Decide on a way to simply analyze and map these complex data. Monitor citizen scientists to guarantee the quality of the data.

6. Draft the map. Discuss what it conveys. Be sure the map is accurate before it goes public. Nothing prolongs an injustice more than an inaccuracy. Finalize the map through a rigorous review.

7. Ensure that the map is in an appropriate form for the essential audiences. This is tricky. A hand-drawn pictograph, presented by youth suffering ill heath resulting from the injustice, may communicate to the impacted community or city council. But agency experts and lawyers typically take seriously only professional, computer-generated maps.

8. After presenting the map, keep the pressure on targets who can address the injustice.

Case Story

The most diverse and poorest area in Oakland, Fruitvale had less than two-thirds of an acre of parkland per thousand people in contrast to residents in the affluent hills, which have over eight acres of parkland per thousand. And it was getting worse. Fruitvale open space was being converted to portable classrooms for overcrowded schools, community gardens were being paved. Competition for soccer fields among Latino clubs led to confrontations. Without water access, Vietnamese residents trespassed to fish. The Spanish Speaking Unity Council, one of the most effective local community organizations in Fruitvale, decided something had to be done immediately. The Unity Council assigned Michael Rios, a staff architect, to coordinate a strategy with neighborhood groups, public agencies, and faculty at the University of California, Berkeley. The Department of Landscape Architecture and Environmental Planning at Berkeley researched the issue of public park distribution in Oakland and produced a report warning that the lack of access to open space in the Fruitvale/San Antonio District was a crisis with grave consequences to health and child development. Rios, Jeff Hou, and a team of designers sifted through available data to determine the most appropriate measures of park distribution and access to open space. Distribution was easily mapped, but access varied, depending upon car ownership and transit lines. By all measures Fruitvale was underserved. For years, leaders had been aware of this but took no action until mapping made the inequity impossible to ignore. Data to make the map were easily accessed from city documents and converted to GIS overlays. The most effective map showed each district of the city color coded from dark to light, depending on acres of parkland per thousand people. The area around Fruitvale was the lightest, indicating the fewest parks. Armed with undeniable visible evidence the community mounted a campaign—Let's Dream It! Let's Build It!—to attain a waterfront open space that could accommodate priority activities of all cultural groups. They successfully acquired nine acres of land from the Port of Oakland to create Union Point Park. Today it is a cherished open space, but more park land is needed before this story has a truly happy ending.

Reflection

Mapping injustices is undoubtedly a source for the community via the process and map itself. Injustice is no longer "out of sight, out of mind." It instigates action. But, even with the visible document, attaining a measure of equity requires extraordinary effort beyond the stamina of most designers. Mapping Injustices is only the beginning. Powerful interests reluctantly relinquish the resources to address inequities. In Fruitvale, Rios spent months organizing community groups to demand action from the City of Oakland. At the same time he met with administrators from the City and Port of Oakland who were most

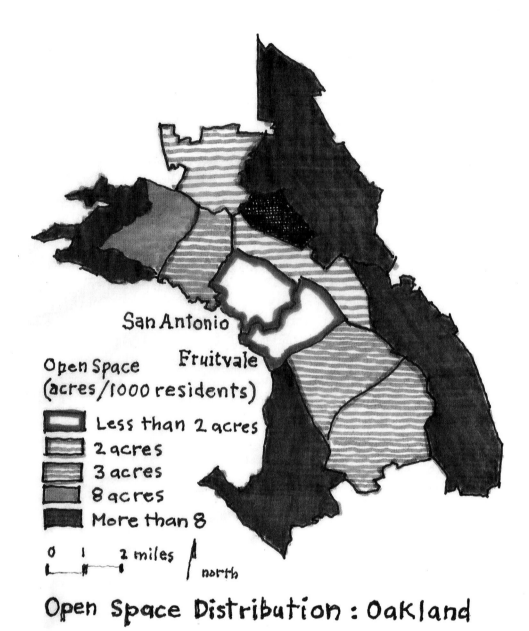

Figure 9-1: Mapping injustice makes the invisible visible. Some Oakland neighborhoods have over eight acres/1,000 residents, and Fruitvale and San Antonio have less than two acres.

resistant to surrendering land for a public park. He finally hammered out acceptable details of land transfer. Who would pay for park development was the next barrier. He worked out an arrangement with the University of California Crew Team to build part of the park in exchange for crew access to the estuary, but they demanded the prime park land for their boat house and restricted public access to the water. That deal fell apart. Rios persisted. He met weekly with the Berkeley designers to revise the master plan and the funding sources. His creative financing was persuasive. He got the land and the money.

There are all kinds of maps that could be made to tell an injustice story. The following are just a few examples:

- Images to Enrage; Maps to Enact. These two maps give maximum effect in addressing environmental injustices. They should clearly show relative inequities in a factual way; this communicates to the objective brain. On the other hand a passionate poetic depiction may better stir emotional commitment to fairness. There is a place for both.

- Experiencing Injustice Personally. Most of us are concerned about injustices, but nothing makes us more intensely committed to justice than to be treated unfairly ourselves. Recall an instance when you were unjustly treated. Remember how you felt. Draw the feeling.

- Just Environments in My Own Community. Discover subtle injustices by observing just and unjust environments in your community. Make two lists—one "Just" and the other "Unjust"—and categorize local places. Then look at them in terms of inaccessibility, distribution of resources, and exclusion. Make notes about their physical characteristics. Develop your own vocabulary of environmental justice.

Technique 9.2

KITCHEN TABLE WORK SESSION

Diane Jones Allen

The Kitchen Table Work Session investigates a situation, strengthens existing communication networks or builds new ones, and affords people a degree of control at the most local level by providing venues that go beyond public meetings and stakeholder interviews. It can tackle issues that need to be addressed on a grassroots level requiring input of the community that will be most impacted, for example, where to locate a new facility or whether it should be developed at all. This might include undesirable uses (e.g., a dangerous industry) or desired improvements (e.g., affordable housing, a grocery, or a farmer's market). The technique brings a community designer to a small focus group for a dialogue. Together they develop plans around the kitchen table, or other personal space, of someone in the community. The designer seeks concerns, desires, and visions of those living in or directly impacted by any proposed development in their area. Simultaneously, the group uses remote technology to inform their discussion, bringing outside data into the safety of their homes, where they combine local wisdom with external expertise to develop effective political strategies for community improvements.

Instructions

1. Once it is determined whose homes or establishments will house the work sessions, those hosts invite friends, neighbors, and other community members with whom they are familiar. This creates an ease and openness for expression of ideas. Hold the Kitchen Table Work Sessions at a set time one or two days a week throughout the project.

2. Create a comfortable and nonjudgmental atmosphere to ease participants' fear of asking questions or expressing opinions regarding the project. Homemade food helps. Get everyone to talk about the issue. Do not judge divergent points of view. After people have comfortably expressed themselves, introduce the computer technology, such as Skype, Go to Meeting, or other programs that allow community members to "conference in." These can also connect the neighbors to outside professionals who have expertise unavailable within the neighborhood group. Depending on the issue, those gathered around the kitchen table might call on the outside help of a land-use lawyer, the city parks director, or an environmental engineer practiced in mitigating storm surge threats. The Internet can also bring Google Earth or a geographic information system (GIS) right into the kitchen to provide real-time locations, pictures of the existing conditions, or layers of mapped

data. If the kitchen table discussion has all the expertise it needs, great! Use the technology to simply record the discussion and conclusions.

3. Arrange beforehand to have experts "on call" in remote locations, available to answer questions. This brings essential outside knowledge to the group without having to leave home, makes that knowledge local, and allows professionals to continue work in their offices until their consultation is needed.

4. Alternatively, we have experimented with a centralized information exchange center in the community, where we convene a group of outside professionals as a "think tank" to offer research tied to inquiries likely to emerge from the kitchen table discussions. From this location they still connect by computer technology. This is especially useful when the experts need to hear each other's information in order to advise the community, and when multiple kitchen table sessions are going on simultaneously throughout the community. Include professionals with expertise related to the issues, representatives of the client and other successful grassroots efforts, and government agency staff with knowledge about local initiatives. The panel need not agree with each other or residents. Their role is to answer questions, interject new ideas, and help the project group to learn from different perspectives. They also serve as a catalyst for greater dialogue. The think tank allows for multiple kitchen table workshops to be held at the same time and for each to have access to the outside expertise and ideas from other kitchen table discussions.

5. When using the on-call or exchange center advertise the time so all will follow a schedule to access the outside and local expertise at the same time.

6. Use laptops, iPads, iPhones, large flat-screen monitors, or even residents' televisions to display up-to-the-moment information, external databases, digital images, and drawings. It is essential for individuals to see their ideas expressed expediently. Just as important, the processes of inquiry are demystified in familiar surroundings. This is also an easy way to capture information and record the discussion.

7. Make the technology user friendly. Use what people have in their homes if possible. Often people, especially older adults, are intimated by digital technology, but being in a familiar setting with a small group of neighbors can create a desire to explore unfamiliar methods. This especially empowers people.

8. The designer's role is to quietly ensure that everyone participates, legitimize local knowledge, interject questions, steer the group to essential sources, move the discussion to conclusions, and keep a record of the decisions made.

9. When the group reaches agreement on a tactic, help implement it. (This will be a longer-term commitment beyond the scope of the kitchen talk.)

Case Story

DesignJones, LLC, has worked with residents in the Lower Ninth Ward of New Orleans for many years, helping community groups plan and implement various improvements. One of the most effective techniques has been the Kitchen Table Work Session. Recently the Port of New Orleans proposed to change the zoning of a key parcel in the Warehouse District. The parcel had long been zoned mixed-use, which accommodated community as well as port functions, but the Port wanted to preclude all uses except industrial ones. There was concern among residents, but few knew much about the potential restrictions of the zoning. We held several Work Sessions in the homes of Holy Cross residents who lived closest to the site.

The workshops attracted people who seldom attended formal zoning hearings. Kitchen talks seemed like everyday neighboring, producing a candid sharing of ideas about the site. Several essential outside experts, including representatives from the City of New Orleans Environmental Office and a landscape architect from Louisiana State University, volunteered to attend the sessions in person. The landscape architect brought Google Earth and GIS to the table. He could access via Internet basic facts that strengthened the confidence of residents. Everyone learned from each other and the design professionals about the basics of the zoning process, how they could intervene, and the potential of the site to serve more community needs if it retained the mixed-use zoning.

The results of these sessions manifested in two ways. The main focus was to determine if the Holy Cross/Lower Ninth Ward neighborhood could use the Warehouse Waterfront District as a viable site for sustainable food security, economic development, and cultural livability. Almost everyone agreed it could. Through the Kitchen Table Work Sessions we got a clear understanding of the type of development community residents wanted. Secondly, and most importantly, we were able to galvanize opposition for the upcoming zoning change that would have prevented any development that was not industrial or port related. After several Work Sessions, residents gained a thorough understanding of zoning issues, they organized, and many attended their first planning commission meeting. They spoke with kitchen-table honesty, informed by their own local knowledge and what they had learned from each other and the planning experts. They won a major victory, defeating the industrial rezoning and maintaining the existing zoning that allowed community use.

Reflection

This is the most effective technique that we have used to get at deep community desires and needs. Through the Kitchen Table Work Sessions we now use an incremental approach to develop greater community interaction and receive greater clarity about people's

Figure 9-2: The Holy Cross/Ninth Ward in New Orleans has long been neglected by city officials, in part because residents do not attend intimidating formal proceedings. The Kitchen Table Work Session was invented to take neighborhood rezoning to the homey comfort of everyday places.

intimate aspirations. Different than other techniques in larger forums, the Work Session occurs in home territory where local expertise is foremost. Residents speak their thoughts and express their ideas, learn, question, and exchange without the judgment or influence of a large and formal audience. This gives community members confidence, so that when they do participate in a larger group, they are armed with knowledge and the strength of their ideas.

One difficulty with this technique is maintaining consistent messaging aligned with the objectives of the project. The informality makes it hard to maintain focus. Determining how the community desires to see a particular project manifested sometimes takes a backseat to neighborhood gossip. Another difficulty is that the demand for the Kitchen Table Work Sessions grows as word spreads of the opportunity to participate in meaningful, personalized dialogue that focuses so centrally on a particular local opportunity. A clear monthly schedule of dates and times of the Work Sessions partly solves this, but we anticipate and budget for increasing demand.

Technique 9.3

POWER MAPPING

Randolph T. Hester Jr.

Power Mapping diagrams the people who have the ability to make a project happen, prevent it, or cause it to have a certain outcome. The map records the type and extent of power and relationships between people and agencies. It notes formal and informal authority. It is not static; it evolves as more is learned. Do not undertake a project without making this map because every design is an expression of power. We need to know if power is transparent or hidden. Drawing the transparent is easy because it is legitimized as "stakeholders," but even among stakeholders personal agendas and long-standing disagreements can disrupt collaboration. Power brokers who work in secrecy and are much more difficult to identify need to be revealed and mapped to uncover greedy plots. Excluded or marginalized publics who lack recognized stakes but have vital interests that will impact project outcome need to be on the map as well.

Instructions

1. Start by mapping the obvious—elected officials, neighbors, and activists. Diagram them using big circles for the most powerful. Draw lines to connect alliances. Use arrows to show direction of power and whom it impacts. Date this and each subsequent map.

2. Conduct private, one-on-one interviews because listening is the best way to learn about and understand power. Privacy is the key. Begin by talking with key players in the community, local activists, then agency representatives and elected officials. If you know about conflicting goals in advance, talk to people from both sides. After you have discussed all your other questions, ask a question like, "Imagine your dreams have been fulfilled for this project. Who was central in making it happen?" Add these people to your list to be contacted. Listen between the lines, and add the unspoken information to your map.

3. Hunt for hidden information. Ask project supporters to help you understand the political landscape, especially things that do not make sense to you.

4. When opaque political pressure threatens your effort, look for predictable explanations, such as real estate interests, exploitable resources, and environmental racism. Consider how the project may upset the status quo—opaque power has likely been activated. Be cautious but do not be intimidated. Follow leads to expose resistance to public disclosure. Draw your suspicions on the map.

5. When big shifts occur, draw a new map and date it. Track down the cause of dramatic changes and unexplained exercises of strength. Circle back with more questions. Confirm explosive information. Draw your own emerging role in the power structure.

6. Balance the public right to know about your map with individual rights of privacy. A power map is an internal document. Some information is privileged. Do not expose sources. Make the information data, not tabloid intrigue. Accept help from reporters and sympathetic expediters cautiously.

7. Use the map to tell you which strategies to employ to further your goals. Depending on what you need, you may have to meet with agencies you did not know existed, find experts in fields outside your expertise, conduct shuttle diplomacy between warring parties, set up a meeting with unexpected allies, or organize a boycott.

Case Story

When we first met Taiwanese Chigu fishermen, alarmed by a proposal for an industrial plant in the waters where they fished, it seemed to be a classic case of a big company exercising its muscle over a powerless group to enrich itself. My preliminary ecological analysis of the plan to build the Binnan plant raised red flags, and I believed a careful scientific assessment would kill the project. I envisioned two players, David and Goliath, with environmental laws swooping down, preventing the destruction of the lagoon. My colleague, John Liu, quickly corrected me. The Binnan plant was supported by all levels of government.

He convened an emergency meeting of National Taiwan University's Building and Planning Institute (NTUBP). An architect on the team started drawing on the chalkboard. Instead of one Goliath there were dozens, including the KMT ruling party, the Ministry of Economics, Tuntex Corporation, the YeiLun Consortium, and scientists paid to find a no-effect assessment of the industrial project.

We declared the situation hopeless and went to dinner. Hsia Chu-Joe, the most strategic and politically connected of the group, offered a long-shot tactic: coordinate local protest with an international boycott. He argued with his colleagues. I challenged them to try. After dinner we added Hsia's ideas to our diagram. Still no one could visualize a positive outcome. Then John proposed experimenting with a few local ecotourism interventions to bolster the fishermen's cause. Things got more creative. Someone drew a big box on the map to represent the middle class, adding, "As it becomes more concerned about pollution, the middle class will question dangerous industry." Then someone shouted, "The shorter work week! Demand for nature tourism will expand." Taiwan was reducing the work week from

Figure 9-3: Because mapping out power uncovered so few vulnerable spots in the Binnan proposal, saving the lagoon and the fishermen's jobs required finding unconventional ways to influence the outcome.

six days to five. More middle-class citizens would be expected to travel domestically from Taipei on two-day weekends. Chigu would soon be readily accessible. John Liu's idea for ecotourism seemed more realistic. "A thousand moons on a thousand rivers," another colleague called out in Mandarin. Everyone nodded in agreement. I was later told that this was a best-selling novel in Taiwan, an old-fashioned romance set near Chigu. The characters paid homage to the sky, the earth, and the gods in traditional rural lives, living in rhythm with the seasons. The book, reprinted over 60 times, sparked nostalgia for exactly what the fishermen could offer urban visitors. The novel lent support to Liu's plan. The evolving middle-class values, shorter work week, and a popular book suddenly challenged outsized powers. Drawing power relationships had stimulated inventive strategic thinking. A deal was offered. John would oversee the local strategy if I would organize the international campaign. Making power visible broke the impasse.

Within weeks John's team was in Chigu strategizing with the fishermen. They started a restaurant with an environmental education center in the prime location for bird watching. An elder fisherman, Uncle Gao, organized expeditions to take visitors in his boat to fish in the to-be-filled lagoon. Outings ended with dinner followed by briefings on Binnan. So popular were the events that the fishermen built a center to serve visitors now arriving by the busload. But most Chigu residents supported the Binnan industrial project until a local lawyer, Huan-Chih Su, shaved his head and bravely marched throughout the county to protest the proposed project. He took the fishermen's cause to the electorate and was narrowly elected to Congress. Updating the power map required weekly additions.

Internationally recognized scientists told us that filling the lagoon would send the rarest of all spoonbills into an extinction vortex. We created Spoonbill Action Voluntary Echo (SAVE) International to prevent this. SAVE was and remains a nonprofit research, planning, and action group housed within the Earth Island Institute. The Institute guided the fledgling SAVE organization to essential expertise. We had no idea how to organize a global protest, but several San Francisco Bay Area nongovernmental organizations did. The bird now occupied a prominent position on the map. The threat to an endangered species shook all the authority invested in the existing power structure.

Then SAVE turned to its internal capacity for regional development, entering an alternative plan into the political fray, one that created more jobs over 15 years than Binnan would. The fishermen negotiated the plan with skeptical neighbors. SAVE members flew to Taipei to present compelling data at congressional hearings. We organized nonviolent protests and staged spoonbill "migrations" in Berkeley to raise public awareness. The Taiwanese press covered each event; the controversy sold news. Su was threatened, his supporters beat up. His bodyguards assured they could keep us safe. Over 400 international organizations signed on to support the movement. More people visited Chigu to see for themselves.

Additions to the map led to bolder actions. Some were disasters. I tried to persuade the pro-Binnan county magistrate to consider SAVE's alternative. He attacked us in the press. Then SAVE found scientists studying global warming who challenged Binnan for excessive CO_2 emissions. New dams that were needed for water supply threatened a rare ecosystem in Meinung, several watersheds away. We formed an alliance. Central government officials were now confronted with regional and national protests. The power map began to swell with equalizing forces.

Pursuing another tactic we met covertly with Taiwan's EPA director when he was in San Francisco. Charged with overseeing Binnan's environmental impact assessment, he explained that government-funded scientists had concluded that filling the lagoon would not impact the spoonbills because they did not inhabit those waters. We knew their science was flawed. Uncle Gao had already mapped where he had seen spoonbills, and the world's leading spoonbill scientist reached the same conclusion. Our science was indisputable in the face of alternative facts. But the director was being squeezed between the international science and the Goliaths back home. In due time he guided the assessment to a reasoned conclusion. The environmental impact assessment was approved, but with 30-plus conditions, some of which could never be met. The project died.

Figure 9-4: Over the course of the fight the map changed dramatically. The first map, when it seemed like a "simple" David versus Goliath battle in which the Environmental Protection Agency would rule in favor of the fishermen.

Figure 9-5: After the strategy session with National Taiwan University's Building and Planning Institute it was clear that all parties with significant power were strong supporters of the Binnan project, including every government agency from the central government to local officials. Opponents declared the effort hopeless.

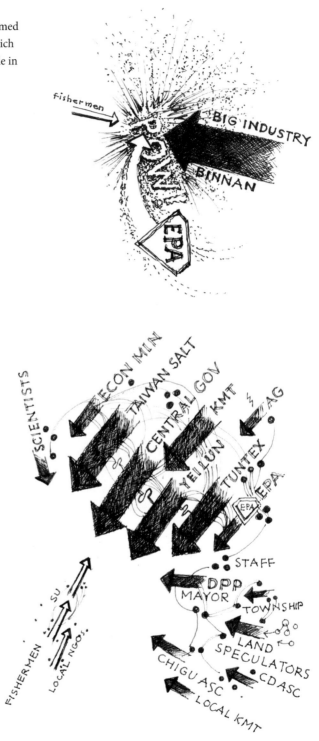

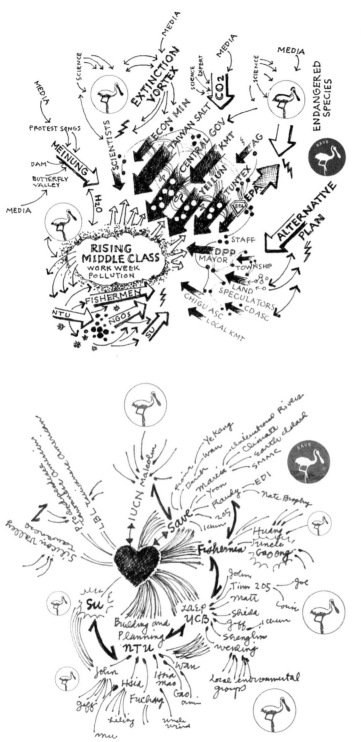

Figure 9-6: When planners met to brainstorm creative ways to defeat the plan to fill the lagoon, they added the spoonbill's international appeal and Taiwan's rising middle class to the power map. These forces unsettled the political status quo.

Figure 9-7: As Binnan died a slow death, the economic development ideas proposed in the alternative plan were implemented by local innovators, and power became shared by many.

Su was elected Tainan County mayor and over the next decade implemented the alternative plan. The spoonbill became a symbol of national pride. Today a national park and scenic area provide protection for the birds. Domestic tourism has risen, largely initiated by local entrepreneurs. Specialty fish products, restaurants, bed and breakfast facilities, ecological tours, and cultural events have created thousands of jobs, drawing young people back to previously dying villages. Bird-watching towers recalling cultural history have invited volunteer efforts and tourists as well. SAVE began new campaigns in Japan, Korea, and China, with the power map expanding throughout the East Asian–Australasian Flyway.

Figure 9-8: In Shin-Tsen Village residents hold a festival for their god to ask for input on a plan to create local jobs through cultural and ecological tourism.

Figure 9-9: One project that emerged was the re-creation of a gun tower in the new park, designed and constructed by villagers. Source: Fu-chang Tsai.

Reflection

Power mapping is essential for any design endeavor. It consistently makes invisible authorities visible, spurs thinking about power beyond official structures, and unleashes unforeseen strategies. It has dramatically changed the outcomes of many of our most important projects. But it requires political acumen and willingness to seek a broad public good beyond the political status quo. Many designers ignore the ill forces of power. It is more profitable to merely serve the powerful, no questions asked, claiming, "I'm just the designer." Power mapping makes me constantly ask, "Whose politic do I serve?"

Figure 9-10: The function of the gun tower is now reinvented to serve local ecotourism and educational needs as well as a bird-watching tower. Source: Fu-chang Tsai.

Technique 9.4

POSITIONING YOURSELF ON THE SPECTRUM OF POWER AND PRIVILEGE

Shalini Agrawal and Shreya Shah

This technique helps designers understand how they may be perceived as outsiders who have experienced power, privilege, and oppression differently than the community with whom they will work. It uses a self-reflective framework developed by Saltwater Social Justice Training (www.saltwatertraining.org) to expose power imbalances that are especially salient when working with underserved and historically exploited communities. Design practitioners place themselves in a spectrum that identifies various societal privileges and distributions of power. This technique should be used before starting a community-based project and in a group of no more than 30 participants.

Instructions

1. Establish an inclusive and judgment-free environment. This requires a facilitator who begins by personally describing his or her own privilege and power. The facilitator's vulnerability encourages the participating designers to genuinely reflect, which benefits the group's learning. Next, write the following community guidelines in a visible place:

    Practice active listening.

    Be brave—speak truthfully and authentically.

    Stay present and responsive to your impact, even when different than your intent.

    Verify that access needs/requests (emotional, physical) for the space have been met.

    Review these with the group to determine agreement.

2. Display the diagram to walk participants through the spectrum of power, privilege, and oppression. Discuss it. The facilitator should point out that these are simplified generalizations to help understand complex interrelationships. Ask participants to mentally place themselves within the spectrum of each category as explained. The goal of this step is to increase awareness of the many facets of identities defined by society in the United States.

3. Split participants into pairs to discuss (1) an experience where they held privilege and (2) an instance where they were more targeted or oppressed. Ask participants to discuss the multiple categories they identify with, and which they share with their partner. Allow a total of 20 minutes: 10 minutes for each prompt, 5 minutes per person. The facilitator should keep track of time and provide reminders to switch partner sharing.

Intersectional Spectrum of Spectrums: Identity, Power and Privilege

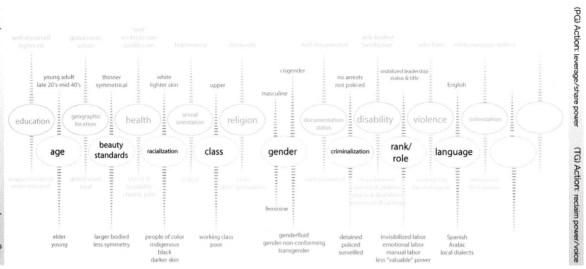

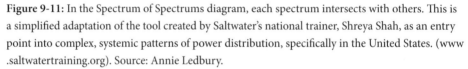

Figure 9-11: In the Spectrum of Spectrums diagram, each spectrum intersects with others. This is a simplified adaptation of the tool created by Saltwater's national trainer, Shreya Shah, as an entry point into complex, systemic patterns of power distribution, specifically in the United States. (www.saltwatertraining.org). Source: Annie Ledbury.

4. Reconvene as the whole group and ask the pairs to voluntarily share individual reflections and, with permission from their partner, insights from their discussion: What was learned? What was unexpected? How might this help or hinder working with a community? How might this influence the way a designer engages with communities? Allow 20 to 30 minutes for this discussion.

5. Give each participant a copy of the Spectrum. Have them enter other instances of power imbalances as they recall or experience them. Discuss it with the team periodically.

6. Take action, better prepared to engage with the community in meaningful ways.

Case Story

An interdisciplinary designer team from California College of the Arts was preparing to work for the Mission Neighborhood Resource Center, a nonprofit organization providing resources to homeless populations in San Francisco. The facilitator presented the Spectrum to the team before they met with the community partner. Team members reflected on it, then shared insights that surfaced regarding their personal positions. The most frequently mentioned was race. Young, white designers acknowledged their privileges. Designers of color appreciated this being acknowledged within the team. Several were surprised to learn someone else on the team was Jewish, and they discussed the advantages and discriminatory experiences they held in common. This led to a discussion about privileges relative to the homeless community. The young designers openly expressed assumptions, biases, discomfort, and uncertainties about working with the homeless community, allowing them to be more honest within their team. One repeated, "Identity, power, and privilege of race are always present but seldom openly recognized or addressed."

The identity awareness vocabulary of power and privilege supported a beneficial shift in language and design approach. Our team became mindful of stereotyping language that stigmatized simple things, such as instead of referring to "the homeless" they began to say "the people experiencing homelessness." This humanized the community we were working with. One interior designer's journey started with her asking, "Why don't the homeless just get a job?" Her initial proposal was to redesign the interior of the Resource Center. After rethinking the issues she had discovered in the Spectrum, she realized that her aspiring design identity was blinding her to more appropriate actions. Her proposal shifted to building on an existing jobs program for the organization. She designed an employment support system in collaboration with the site case manager that included a "pre-resume," best practices for job searching, and motivational tips. This project was implemented by the organization.

Throughout the project the power and privilege lenses helped alter expectations and adjust to unforeseen challenges. For example, the team felt it had full access to the Resource Center—it never occurred to us that our presence was disruptive. At some point the design team realized staff at the Resource Center was constantly shorthanded. They did not enjoy the privilege of time we took for granted. We adjusted our behavior so we would place fewer burdens on our community partners yet still provide them solutions for critical problems they faced.

Reflection

The Spectrum has uses in any community where the participants are "foreign" to the designer. Privileges of race, class, religion, and gender must be understood to be effective. Add distinctions of life-cycle stage, seniority, national origin, or date of immigration for murkier expressions of power. Beyond the obvious, this technique creates a personal power map, likely to reawaken designers to distinctive means of control, even in communities we consider "just like us."

Technique 9.5

BUILD SMALL, THINK STRUCTURAL CHANGE

Laura J. Lawson

Put simply, this technique is about making some tangible, small physical improvement as a means to affirm a longer-term plan. It is particularly appropriate in disadvantaged communities working toward change that requires extensive power and resource redistribution. In such contexts, the big changes needed—new housing, more parks, better schools, infrastructure improvements—take time and can often overburden a community that faces immediate needs as well—repair to housing or a well-used park, cleaning trash from school grounds, signs for pedestrian crossings. This technique provides a quick change that improves existing conditions, encourages ongoing resident participation, and activates the political will of the neighbors. With limited funds, time, and experience, the building project is usually simple, yet it encapsulates the intention of the larger project, grounding it in what is possible now. Building something small is never intended to placate or substitute for the bigger issue; instead, it is a commitment to make change and an opportunity to get into action.

At a different level of empowerment, making something levels a previously unbalanced political playing field. This technique creates a direct opportunity for the design team to work side by side with the community. Building moves the conversation away from the drawing, where the designer is expert, toward problem solving that engages a broader range of skills and acknowledges those skills, be they welding, carpentry, cooking, or team building. This redistributes interpersonal authority.

Instructions

1. Identify a small piece of a larger planning project that can be quickly implemented. The project may arise from observations of how the community uses space and an opportunity to improve an existing pattern. The project should be one that can be designed and built quickly with minimal funding or red tape that might stall enthusiasm. For example, the community may discuss the need for signage to discourage illegal dumping, or the design team may observe many people waiting at the spot where the bus stops and see an opportunity to build some benches and provide shade there.

2. Propose, discuss, and set a workday to build the project. Involve a mix of design professionals and community members.

3. Be sure someone on the design team assists in coordinating workdays so the materials, tools, and labor are all available to build the project.

4. Make handouts that highlight the location, materials, tools, and other things needed as well as procedures for construction.

5. Think of ways to make the process fun, efficient, and social. For instance, arrange music and food during the workday, provide colorful t-shirts to volunteers, or give awards to work groups based on some of the funny interactions that occur over the course of the workday. Include ways to recruit more people to take political action. This might require passing around a sign-up sheet for future events, asking participants to list additional neighbors whom they will contact, or discussing the next steps and what local businesses might contribute materials for construction. You might ask everyone to commit to bringing two additional volunteers to the next workday.

6. Invite local media to raise public awareness of the effort.

7. Take before, during, and after images so that everyone can appreciate the improvement.

8. Since these projects are often built quickly and inexpensively, return to repair and update the improvement as necessary so that it stays looking good and working for the community as the longer-term project continues. Take advantage of the improvement to persuade doubters and naysayers to join the bigger cause.

Case Story

In 2004, a landscape architecture design studio, part of the University of Illinois East St. Louis Action Research Project, began working with the 41st Street Neighborhood Coalition to design a new park that the group had proposed to build on a vacant lot in their neighborhood. Because the city's park department had very few resources to provide, this group was preparing to build the park without municipal support. The neighbors were eager to create the park as a way to eliminate its abandoned state that made it vulnerable to illegal dumping and other undesirable activities and also to provide places for children to play and seniors to exercise.

The faculty and students initiated a participatory design process. The team met with residents to discuss goals for the project, conducted fieldwork, presented their analysis, and developed several design alternatives based on the key goals residents had identified. At the final meeting when students presented finely rendered alternatives and perspectives of what the park could look like, rather than generating excitement, the images generated concern because the scope seemed too big for the small group. While residents acknowledged many important reasons to promote a park, they were daunted by the reality that the construction and maintenance would fall on them. This stalled the process. Residents and designers had to step back and consider the goals from a different angle, asking not just what did the residents want, but also what could the group do now to start this larger project? Design ideas were revised into a modest interim strategy with key priorities to deter illegal dumping from vehicles, develop a walking path for residents, and put up a sign to convey ownership.

The Build Small project was not initiated by the design team but rather by two residents who took matters into their own hands and constructed bollards topped with planters that blocked trash dumping. This immediate change inspired the team. With students ready and able to work, several other doable projects were started. People acquired free plants from a local nursery to reinforce and beautify the bollards. Students and residents worked together to acquire in-kind contributions and a small grant to build a gravel walking path around the site for seniors. The group named the site Pullman Porter Park, in honor of the Pullman porters who had served for decades on the adjoining railroad line. Students designed and built a sign for the park entrance. A couple years later, a new parks department director saw the work under way and negotiated to acquire the land with the idea that the expanded park would someday become a reality. Only then could residents actually see the results of their activism. They had actually claimed their control of this small piece of land and the City recognized it.

Figure 9-12: The 41st Street Coalition has so many neighborhood inequities to address that it is difficult to know where to start. The Build Small project transformed this vacant lot into a park with little more than removing trash, installing bollards and plants to prevent illegal dumping, and making a walking path.

Figure 9-13: A handcrafted sign invokes pride in the community because it celebrates the history when Pullman porters settled the area. Completing such small projects empowers neighbors to undertake additional improvements and possibly structural changes.

Reflection

The most important takeaway for this technique is that it should not be seen as a placebo to the real goals at hand. Nor should this technique be used without conscious reflection on the issues of power and access to resources that make such techniques required. It would be far better if the community had the ability to achieve the larger goal at hand—the park, the new housing, and so forth—but if this isn't the case, this technique helps to move toward change. This technique should be used in conjunction with others described in this section.

Another key issue is the impact of a small intervention. To the design community, a simple gravel path or sign may be considered mundane design, eliciting a "so what?" response. If developed with the community, however, the small intervention has meaning to its users. To garner larger interest and political support that may lead toward the long-term goal, it is important to document the process that affirms its connection to the larger project.

Technique 9.6

CONFLICT IN ITS TIME AND PLACE

Randolph T. Hester Jr.

This technique develops the proper use of conflict to make transformative design possible. It trains one to deal forthrightly with confrontation and empowers community by employing the full range of strategies, from individual to collective creativity, from servant to advocate, from partnership to disobedience, from mediation to disruption.

Why are extremes necessary? First, most designers develop a single role or mode of operation that is comfortable, relying on that even when inappropriate, becoming one-dimensional like an American football team that is only run oriented. This diminishes effectiveness. For example, powerful interests assess whether you are facilitative or disruptive and take advantage of the tendency. Second, conflict avoidance rules design society, dominates planning approaches, stifles thoughtful debate, and undermines the imaginative alternatives that civic conflict spawns. Third, democratic design requires maximizing competing interests without compromising the deepest values; therefore, the designer must play multiple roles in order to bring out conflict so it can be addressed with originality. If, like Muhammad Ali, you can both float like a butterfly and sting like a bee, you will be more effective. Fourth, no truly transformative design occurs without confronting status quo powers. For these reasons it is useful to become accomplished in each role. This technique will expand your tactics.

Instructions

1. Make a list of the interactive roles—whether facilitator or instigator or some other—you think useful in various contentious situations from conflicts within the community, between you and other personalities, or with external forces you wish to change. Make lists independently; then share this with others.

2. For each role you list, find an opposition at the other end of the spectrum; pair these in your list, forming two columns. Understanding the pairs is important because we frequently have to switch tactics quickly.

3. Circle the one that is your "go to" mode and others that you are pretty good at. Underline ones you avoid. Decide which underlined one you want to focus on.

4. Write down the behavior characteristics you think necessary to practice the role you want to master. You might note that you want to be a stronger advocate without being condescending, or more accomplished in disobedience without being violent, or better at stimulating communal creativity. Let's say you want to master the latter, but you realize that you become defensive when a resident challenges

Figure 9-14: Designers have a full arsenal of tactics with which to engage in conflict.
Source: Marcia McNally.

your professional expertise. You might then decide to practice these behaviors: (1) before a meeting repeat a mantra like "Collective creativity inspires my design," (2) think of residents' ideas not as challenging your authority but as elaborations of your intervention, and (3) rehearse saying "Interesting idea! I had not thought of that. Let's draw it and see how it works."

5. Choose a design project you are doing for practice. With a teammate, role-play a situation in the project requiring the skill you want to master. Consciously try the behaviors you wrote down. Then complicate the situation; switch back and forth between this role and others. Practice this enough so you are ready to test yourself in a heated disagreement about a specific design priority. When comfortable using one new mode, practice another.

6. In the community situation, get a team member to take notes on your effectiveness. If conflict avoidance prevents you from designing creatively amid contentious clashes, try a set of calisthenics inspired by James C. Scott. He prepares himself to confront intolerable authority or disobey unjust regulation by practicing like he exercises regularly to keep fit. With humor Scott practiced jaywalking. In

that spirit these eight stretching exercises might help prepare for confrontation: (1) take the first step, (2) break out of your own prison, (3) assume responsibility, (4) resist, (5) vote, (6) take a bigger risk, (7) reach beyond your limits, and (8) climb the mountaintop. (See diagrams to get a sense of how to begin each radical stretch.) Vary as needed to overcome your specific conflict avoidances. As you practice, concentrate on particular strategies for (1) encouraging conflict when it has been "swept under the rug," (2) maximizing core values of competing parties, and (3) supplementing courage with tactics to take on adversaries over stakes that matter.

7. Put your skills to proper use to outflank those who profit at public expense. Their strategies play out over time. Prepare for prolonged battles. Expect personal attacks. Test public sentiment for proper and timely action.

Figure 9-15: Practice these radical calisthenics daily to prepare yourself for managing conflict to creative advantage: (1) take the first step, (2) break out of your own prison, (3) assume responsibility, (4) resist, (5) vote, (6) take a bigger risk, (7) reach beyond your limits, and (8) climb the mountaintop.

Case Story

All the real estate investors needed was to extend water and sewer several miles beyond the growth boundary of Roanoke Island, North Carolina, in order to make millions of dollars in second-home development at public expense. With local connections and deep pockets to discredit sound planning, the speculators targeted the Coastal Plan Update as the battleground by which they would enable their personal enrichment. Our design team had been hired by the local government in Dare County to undertake the Update, which was required by North Carolina Coastal Act legislation, and found ourselves in the developers' crosshairs. They named our design team as their adversary even before we began the Update. This story is about the tactics we practiced to overcome their attacks on issues that mattered deeply to the community.

Each of our staff had to prepare for ugly public confrontations. Conflict avoiders practiced presenting facts firmly without being intimidated. Rehearsing through role-play for several weeks strengthened staff confidence. When the speculators, arguing for their development below sea level, bullied staff in meetings, staff forcefully delivered facts like "hurricane storm surge with rising sea level poses unacceptable risk to the speculators' low-lying development site and costs the community can never afford." (On the other hand, I practiced avoiding screaming matches with the developers. We all have different Achilles' heels.)

Because we knew the attacks were forthcoming, we also turned the Coastal Plan into a tactic for itself. We implemented four strategies:

1. Confirm local objectives through the most extensive community goal-setting process in the island's history; extension of water and sewer services to flood-prone sprawl violated 8 of the community's 10 most deeply held planning values.

2. Frame the public debate around factual data from reliable sources about the community objectives. For example, staff diagrammed for residents how a most important goal, to protect wetlands on the island, held additional value to dissipate storm surge and reduce damage from sea level rise.

3. Employ state regulations requiring that land-use designations account for specified sea level increases, based on the best scientific projections available. (These science-based regulations have since been discarded by the Republican-controlled North Carolina legislature.)

4. Develop a workshop focused solely on where water and sewer should be upgraded to serve anticipated growth. We gambled on a tactic to confront the developers directly about their intentions, which they tried to hide from the public. Workshop participants were asked to study three alternative residential growth scenarios,

select their preferred scenario, then locate that growth in the area they preferred. We created a game in which the scenarios with potential locations, and acres of anticipated residential growth, could be quickly understood. Each participant was given the same fixed number of acres cut into squares and a map showing available land (total squares based on the 8.5 percent growth rate, existing density of 0.16 residential acres/person) and then asked to affix the squares to their individual map. The game took about half an hour, after which residents compared their maps. Only the land speculators located future growth in hazard areas vulnerable to sea level rise.

The immediate result of these tactics was the solidification of community support for concentrated infill growth on higher ground—a strategy more desirable for permanent residents than for seasonal residents. The Coastal Plan was adopted by the Town Board of Commissioners with stronger than ever commitments to mitigate sea level rise through wetland enhancement.

Figure 9-16: On Roanoke Island the conflict over developing lowlands imperiled by rising seas played out in public. Design staff practiced responding to intimidating threats with forceful facts. Using a growth scenario game, civic-minded residents confronted land speculators by choosing ecologically informed growth scenarios.

Reflection

In our office we often ask if we should do only work that is important enough to warrant high-stakes conflict. "Mostly," we respond. Sometimes you facilitate settlement, sometimes you maximize opposing goals, sometimes you win graciously or lose disastrously, sometimes you create the unimaginable.

TABLE 9-1: RULES OF POWER TACTICS	
Rule 1	Power is not only what you have but what the enemy thinks you have.
Rule 2	Never go outside the experience of your people.
Rule 3	Whenever possible go outside the experience of the enemy.
Rule 4	Make the enemy live up to their own book of rules.
Rule 5	Ridicule is man's most potent weapon.
Rule 6	A good strategy is one that your people enjoy.
Rule 7	A tactic that drags on too long becomes a drag.
Rule 8	Keep the pressure on.
Rule 9	The threat is usually more terrifying than the thing itself.
Rule 10	The major premise for tactics is the development of operations that will maintain a constant pressure upon the opposition.
Rule 11	If you push a negative hard and deep enough it will break through into its counter side.
Rule 12	The price of a successful attack is a constructive alternative.
Rule 13	Pick the target, freeze it, personalize it, and polarize it.

Source: Saul Alinsky's *Rules for Radicals.*

Technique 9.7

ORGANIZING A PLACE-BASED CAMPAIGN

Randolph T. Hester Jr.

Organizing a place-based campaign builds the political capacity to implement a community improvement or change a local policy, relying heavily on the skills of designers to observe the unseen, to draw attention to a pending catastrophe or a possibility not to be missed, to make a situation comprehensible to the community, and to prompt political change.

Instructions

1. Identify the problem or opportunity in terms of how it will impact the community. Draw simple diagrams to explain the situation and likely impacts.

2. Get the support of active community members to address the problem or opportunity. Check the accuracy of your assessment and invite their partnership to form a core group; collectively determine the degree of difficulty you face. Be prepared for discouragement because anything worth doing will threaten some power structure.

3. Begin a power map to help guide you through troubled waters. (See Power Mapping technique earlier in this chapter.)

4. Check with the technical experts. Many a local campaign dies as a result of basic factual errors exploited by those resisting change. If the core members include experts, great. If there is no one, go to the nearest university. Ask your questions, take notes, seek clarification when experts use terms you do not understand. Get them to help you draw the ecosystem and social intricacies of the issue.

5. Determine what role the experts will play. Will they express opinions publicly? Are there research articles you should read, especially ones the expert has written?

6. Pursue other experts like city staff with procedural questions. If you are challenging city policy, do not expect support, but good public staff will provide maps, reports about the project, environmental review, funding, and schedules of meetings and construction.

7. Get the facts to the community. Summarize everything you have learned in maps, charts, and brief text. Make a two-page summary that you can post on websites and through list servers, publish in neighborhood newsletters, and hand out at community meetings or by going door to door. Most people will appreciate your effort because it likely impacts them as well. Invite them to join you; give them specific things to do. If someone is hostile, be especially charming. This takes practice.

8. Only when your position is well formed should you contact local media. Neighbors may tolerate half-baked ideas, but the mass media audience will not. Time the media coverage to your best advantage. Focus on essential facts and human impacts. Publicize your schedule of activities and invite public participation.

9. Hold a meeting to share tasks among increasing participants. Additional community members likely joined your group as you got them the facts personally or through the media. Flex that power through an open meeting. Prepare a precise but flexible agenda and a list of next steps. Choose a place with two rooms available, one seating about 20 people, another for 50 to 100 people. Begin in the small room; move if necessary. Efforts die in a room so large that it exposes a lack of support. They thrive when a crowd must relocate to a bigger space. Serve something to eat. Get people to sign in, provide contact information, and fill out a brief survey about their priorities. Allow people to vent frustrations, but accomplish something concrete. Get everyone to voice opinions. Select interim leaders. Name the group. Set a primary objective with widespread support and make a plan to achieve it. Appoint groups to take on key tasks to research the issue in more detail, develop better communication, and get the unrepresented involved. Vote on some motion. Set a time for the next meeting, noting that task groups will report.

10. Get the most organized person to coordinate the work of the task groups. If the situation has reached crisis stage, get one group to quickly develop tactics to obstruct the unwanted action. Remember that you will need to put forward alternatives so form another task group to create alternatives with your experts. More people will pitch in when a threat is imminent, but some people are best at long-term planning so engage them in a special task group for future projects.

11. Plan strategies with a core group and implement them with as many people as possible. Strategy is the exercise of power so realistically appraise the nature of your power. Is it a better idea? new knowledge? numbers? Evaluate the power against you. Who would be hurt by your success? Who *thinks* they would be? Draw this on your power map. Be sure you know how the system works in regard to your project. There are complicated procedures for community gardens, freeway construction, or self-help housing. Learn the formal process and plan tactics to intervene at points most vulnerable to your power. Consider outrageous, fun, or exciting tactics. Alinsky can help you here. He might suggest dumping a barrel of dead fish on the doorstep of the company whose coal ash polluted the river. Choose one strategy that the group thinks will be quickly successful and involve a lot of people. Every group needs decisive early success to build morale and legitimacy. Find a strategy that will "cost" the least but get the job done. If a respected participant can

call the city manager and quietly redirect an unjust policy, don't choose instead to demonstrate at city hall demanding the city manager's resignation. But do credit all the participants who were prepared to demonstrate. Make the final strategic decision inclusively and transparently.

12. Take action; escalate as necessary. An inappropriately harsh tactic will cost you public favor; slow escalation will build support and is usually most effective—like shuttle diplomacy in reverse. Show force, used sparingly. Demand action from the responsible agency. Boil demands down to their pointed and reasoned essence. Speak to the agency in their language, but do not violate the intentions of citizens in the community. Community concerns can easily be lost in translation. Attend to details such as where, when, and how elected officials will conduct a decision-making meeting. At this point you may want to consider a time-tested alternative put forward by Dr. Martin Luther King, Jr. His approach uses six steps, the fifth of which is direct action.

13. Be persistent. If a bureaucrat tells you he will do something, check it out to be sure it is done. Do not get sidetracked. Keep a watchful eye, even after a success is achieved, to be certain it is not undone. Remember, "Eternal vigilance is one price of our liberty."

14. Advertise positive outcomes to existing and potential supporters.

15. Celebrate success with an event that people will remember as a "big time."

16. Undertake other projects across scales. Evaluate your previous strategic process, positive and negative. Get the task group for longer-term projects to present to the larger group. Now is the time to act because you have the community's attention. However, expect some of the hardest workers to have burned out; they may retreat for a time. Maybe you need a brief break yourself.

Case Story

In 2015 a partnership of intercity passenger and freight train officials in Durham, Raleigh, and Chapel Hill, North Carolina, completed a study of grade separations. Grade separations keep various modes of transportation apart by placing them at different topographic elevations, or grades. In this case bridges and tunnels were proposed in order to separate freight and passenger rail tracks from automobiles on streets. Realigning tracks and streets at different grades is typically done to increase speed and efficiency of both rail and car traffic and improve safety. The study was hailed by all as an essential step toward implementing a light rail system to link the Triangle cities. Counties passed tax increases to support light rail. Engineering consultants garnered praise for successfully separating trains from automobiles, but a citizen was alarmed when he studied the plan. The citizen deciphered the

TABLE 9-2: STEPS OF NONVIOLENCE	
Information Gathering	To understand and articulate an issue, problem, or injustice facing a person, community, or institution you must do research. You must investigate and gather all vital information from all sides of the argument or issue so as to increase your understanding of the problem. You must become an expert on your opponent's position.
Education	It is essential to inform others, including your opposition, about your issue. This minimizes misunderstandings and gains you support and sympathy.
Personal Commitment	Daily check and affirm your faith in the philosophy and methods of nonviolence. Eliminate hidden motives and prepare yourself to accept suffering, if necessary, in your work for justice.
Discussion/ Negotiation	Using grace, humor, and intelligence, confront the other party with a list of injustices and a plan for addressing and resolving these injustices. Look for what is positive in every action and statement the opposition makes. Do not seek to humiliate the opponent but to call forth the good in the opponent.
Direct Action	These are actions taken when the opponent is unwilling to enter into, or remain in, discussion/negotiation. These actions impose a "creative tension" into the conflict, supplying moral pressure on your opponent to work with you in resolving the injustice.
Reconciliation	Nonviolence seeks friendship and understanding with the opponent. Nonviolence does not seek to defeat the opponent. Nonviolence is directed against evil systems, forces, oppressive policies, unjust acts, but not against persons. Through reasoned compromise, both sides resolve the injustice with a plan of action. Each act of reconciliation is one step closer to the "Beloved Community."

Source: *Letter from Birmingham Jail,* Martin Luther King, Jr.

engineers' calculations for grade changes and drew cross sections at key points in Durham. It was true the engineers had successfully divided cars from trains, but their marvel created a 22-foot wall through the heart of the city, cutting apart neighborhoods the city had long worked to connect: rich and poor, black and white, young and old, invested and disinvested. Pedestrians would be forced to walk along narrow automobile tunnels, through pockets of underground pollution 300 feet long. In some places the slope of walkways exceeded 12 percent, inaccessible to wheelchairs and most elderly people. Existing grade separations of trains and cars were lost. The citizen shared his drawings with other professionals who checked his calculations; they did similar studies by cutting sections at other points along the route. The wall extended for miles, dissecting the city. Light rail was inaccessible from the street. What to do?

The small group of concerned citizens showed the drawings to a few other professional designers who met monthly as a public service group called Durham Area Designers (DAD). DAD took up the cause. They divided tasks, organized a campaign to question the grade separation plan, and prepared an at-grade alternative for light rail accessible at street level. Two members consulted a member of the authority governing freight trains. A regional planner provided procedural and technical data. One group studied the entire corridor to determine system-wide urban design impacts hidden in the engineers' abstractions. Another group contacted neighborhoods and business interests that would be negatively impacted. A neighbor created "Up Against the Wall" via Facebook. DAD leaders began a quiet effort to inform decision makers. Everyone who saw the evidence was concerned, but no one wanted to "derail light rail." City staff insisted it was not as bad as DAD suggested.

A landscape architect drew six-foot-long cross sections (at a scale of 1 inch equals 10 feet) showing the wall in red, cars in depressed "street sewers," people dwarfed by concrete channels longer than a football field as they tried to walk from Main Street to the Performing Arts Center, two districts that the city council had invested millions of public dollars to connect. The wall laid waste to all that investment. The drawing was accurate, dramatic, and impossible to dismiss.

DAD concluded that the city council had to be confronted. The tactic was to simply present a brief fact sheet of negative impacts along with the big drawing, titled the "Great Wall of Durham," at a council meeting where other citizens and the media would see the "Great Wall" writ large for the first time. Council members gasped aloud; they had been vocal proponents of the grade separation study but were unaware of its impacts. The council reacted with the same alarm as citizens. The tactic had its desired impact.

However, staff continued to defend the plan as necessary to achieve light rail. Transit planners stated funding would be lost unless the grade separation plan was adopted immediately. One senior agent said the problem could be covered up with nice murals. All of these turned out to be false.

The "Great Wall" campaign had turned the tide of public opinion and city council support. The city transportation director began attending DAD meetings to draw alternatives. The group organized design workshops to develop plans to maximize access to light rail, create an at-grade system using existing grade separations, and better serve underserved,

Figure 9-17: The "Great Wall of Durham" drawing prepared for the public record caused a stir.

poorer neighborhoods. The city council allowed the grade separation study to die a quiet death. A year later the regional agency charged with planning light rail produced a new, preferred alternative with no wall and at-grade access to each transit stop.

Reflections

Place-based organizing is grounded in particular land with specific resources and cultural idiosyncrasies. Topography and climate must be considered precisely. Two lessons from this case stand out. First, the ability of designers to draw complex abstractions is a powerful tool for organizing. Drawings that are simultaneously rational and provocative serve as change agents. Second, no staff person in the city, county, or transit planning agencies had comprehended the spatial implications of the engineers' work. Shocking! This serves as a warning that illiteracy of topographic and other place-dependent design expertise invariably leads to catastrophic decisions.

Conclusion

Hindsight Seeking Tomorrow

Having compiled this book to serve a not-so-hidden agenda—to collect participatory techniques into one volume accessible to a large audience—we made unexpected discoveries. We planned the book to be for and about you, the designer, and to serve as a tool that enables you to successfully build community. We knew we had to find techniques to both reform and re-form the design process, the built environment, and society. We searched for and found reflective, experiential, and procedural means to achieve those reformations within the near future.

But as we worked together to evaluate, select, and make collective sense of the techniques submitted, our editorial discussions—honestly they were more often soul-bearing admissions or loud arguments—revealed insights that merit recounting. By curating participatory processes serving a range of contexts and communities, how could we not also turn to look at ourselves? The techniques and case stories, the editorial meetings, the merging of text with images—each step provided us mirrors of reflection and revelation. The book was no longer just for you but for you and us, appropriately the collective we. We summarize these insights as five mirrors because they will help you as you reflect on and use the techniques, and grow as designers too.

THE MIRROR OF HONEST ASSESSMENT

Many of the techniques focus on preparing planners and designers to do community design well or better by reflecting their essential selves back to themselves. This forced us as editors to see our own motivations clearly—what do we seek in self-reflection among designers, and for ourselves as well? We can now admit that "knowing thyself" is for every-one, no matter how much or little experience you have. We conclude that we must contin-ually invest energy to understand or learn again how we see, analyze, and design "against," "for," or "with" others. Worldviews matter. Stereotypes matter. Actions based in hidden biases matter. How we think and are perceived in light of class, race, ethnicity, gender, religion, and science matter, and the reflected image changes as we get older and the world confronts us with new challenges. These factors, however, are rarely part of design training or continuing education, and few of us are equipped to deeply reflect on their impact, either personally or professionally. The editors are close colleagues, yet our own basic perceptions of truth, good-ness, and necessity grounded in these aspects of society arose each time we worked together. All of us struggled to relearn to be sensitive to these differences, empathic without pity, and to remain true to our authentic selves. This mirror reflected the need for newcomers to see self clearly, but maybe more importantly for seasoned activists to engage in "do overs."

The mirror of honest assessment requires lifelong work in order to do meaningful community design. As such we express surprise at how the techniques of self-assessment, programming, and policy seem to dominate. Our original vision was for a cornucopia of techniques that show how to design transactively, you know, with a base map and a pen. We, and hopefully you, will spend time in the foreseeable future creating methods to truly create ambitious, spatially explicit plans with others and take the time to write down how you and we did it.

The Mirror of Self in Community Context

The amazing ability of a mirror is that it reflects oneself undistinguished from the sur-rounding background. We become one with the everyday landscape we inhabit and the communities we contribute to. Such holism makes every participant the designer. Sure, we knew this before. *You* becomes *we*. *He*, *she*, and *they* join *we* in the collective creativity of democratic design, but so many of the techniques we included in the book invent ways to truly transact, sharing the joys and responsibilities of the design process as never before.

We cheered these emerging methods to go to the people, legitimize native wisdom, utilize local expertise of people who historically never participated at all, and draw explicit futures together. The contributors offer sophisticated ways to uncover common values embedded in place, describe unique patterns of habitation, and celebrate both the shared and the distinctive values in built projects. Part of what we saw in this mirror was our own growth. The great joy for the editors, we agreed, is the never-ending learning that partici-patory design offers. Beyond broadened horizons, we saw brilliant studied and unschooled design solutions that challenged us to act with increased oneness with community.

THE MIRROR OF NEW AND OLD

We set out expecting to chronicle new transactive and transformative methods, and indeed we were introduced to many, from evoking to co-generating. This is encouraging because it shows how community design pulses with life's expectations and is never content with the status quo. Reform! Re-form! Luckily there is saneness to this newness. The baby has not been thrown out with the bathwater. Many of the techniques we reviewed and included are modest improvements to active listening, the Nominal Group Technique (NGT), gaming, and design–build with volunteer labor. These foundations, we decided, were too essential to exclude in spite of their age. In fact we found they are aging well. For example, the NGT remains the foundation of democratic intelligence. It requires thinking alone and together, listening without interruption, respectful debate, and transparent decision making.

The ubiquitous workshop illustrates another facet of new and old. In participatory design, meetings are a foregone conclusion—we have lots of them. Many of the techniques described in this book happen as workshops, but, as we learned, the workshop is no longer a soft happening. It has transformed into a design problem itself. How it is structured is based on previously collected data, the designers' reads on the context and stage, and explicitly intended outcomes. Carefully crafted agendas strategize the use of particular methods best suited to fully engage people and activate them.

We observed that the workshop in an institutional setting no longer monopolizes participation like it once did. *Carritos*, scored walks, and kitchen table sessions more often take to the everyday landscape to experience it firsthand, saturate the participant designers with the nuances of the place, and ultimately make decisions in situ rather than abstractly. It is heartening to be reminded that the time we spend walking around, recording daily events, eating at a local café, or sketching ecological processes helps right the world. These are not only legitimate opportunities for collecting information and engaging but also essential aspects of our job. These allow us to learn and help people to see their places afresh. Such shared experiences often spark moments of epiphany, unthinkably shared visions where discord previously ruled, and inspired insurgencies. The workshop certainly does not belong in the trash pile of untransactive public hearings, but the shop where the work takes place now takes many settings to work effectively.

This mirror reflects still recognizable participation but exposes worry lines caused by intractable old problems, present ones misunderstood, and emerging ones ignored or denied. We are encouraged by innovations that go to the people, maximize remote involvement, and recruit through public performances of making. However, we still need methods to gather these participants together from time to time into a collective democratic whole to address local issues and boundary-crossing crises.

The Mirror of Multiple Roles

The clarity that the editors gained in their attention to individual chapters became a dizzying whirlwind as we came together for the first time to read a rough draft of the book in its entirety. It left us breathless, in part because, at that moment, we first imagined the comprehensive value of our effort—the "glocality" it reflected, the opportunities each technique conveyed, the optimism of the case stories. But we were more winded by the range of techniques that one must incorporate in order to master the often contrary roles that democratic designers must play. Daunting. We are participant and protagonist, listener and instructor, facilitator and strategist, professional and activist, often simultaneously. In this mirror we see not our single familiar portrait; rather the same face reflected under so many different hats that the image unsettles us, pushing us out of comfort zones.

Our roles seemed so much simpler years ago, but ours is an avocation of ever-increasing difficulty. One example is how many different scales democratic designers now work at. The traditional view of bite-sized projects as the upper limit of participatory capacity has been debunked. Sure, many projects are faithful to the neighborhood or the village. But the stories also suggest a dramatic "scaling up," from Los Angeles to the Karuk Nation, from Hua-lien to the Research Triangle, from the Delmarva Peninsula to the East Asian–Australasian Flyway. Techniques like the *Renkei* method, Designing Life, Power Mapping, and In-House Aha! break unexpected limitations of scale by moving back and forth from microscope to telescope.

The book highlights techniques in all phases of the design process—to exchange expertise, to order, to calm and prioritize, to create together, to test, to generate and build, to put power to good use, and to steward. Each technique was born from various necessities: to listen more attentively, to learn hidden truths about community, to work efficiently as groups, to create a better-informed democracy, and to get things done. As designers we constantly make and remake techniques to support the backbone of a planning process. As with recipes in a cookbook, the chef-designer experiments, tests, and adapts methods until they are his or her own. Designing the technique to fit the project is an act of design thinking. The tasks multiply. "Is there anything else you need me to do?" each designer asks the mirror.

The Mirror of the Future

One of the few good things about driving is the ability to see the road ahead simultaneously with the road gone by. The rearview mirror affords this unique perspective. Likewise, making this book helped us grasp the needs of the future informed by the past of participatory design. This book is a call to action grounded in the creativity and efficacy of the contributors. Each has bolstered the capacity of democratic design. This collection is a seedbank for genuinely transacting around issues, redistributing power, transforming community, and protecting the planet through tenacious placemaking. Hopefully seeds of structural change are also sown herein.

However, as we complete this book, we feel a special urgency beyond current practices. Environmental problems have a way of keeping us a generation behind. Democracy tied to place suffers. For too many, democracy is only about freedom. Youth reinvent or neglect it daily. New immigrants seek instant lessons in civics to claim a place at the table and express identity. Unrecognized injustices become visible, but their reality is denied by the powerful. At a time when participatory democracy is challenged daily by fiat and tweets, you and we together will create the next phase of a deeply democratic world.

But are we prepared to? Do we have the stomach and stamina for it? We must acknowledge how few contributors offered methods to put power to good use. The claim that participatory design empowers has currency today, but how much of this work really delivers? Yes, there is an appropriate emphasis on collaboration. But inattention to the design of resistance, disobedience, and redistribution of power worries some of us. We call this out because the story of participation is graced with contentious design, with elegant homemade beauty, challenging established powers. Sometimes conflict is unavoidable.

We believe this collection offers the essential art, science, and politic to produce design excellence that counters a world in crisis. Unique among professionals, only participatory designers actually realize futures that erase misplaced phobias, that include the many not just the few, and that transform inequities into fairness. The techniques presented here release subdued voices, champion diversity, and bend the arc of the universe toward justice. Our hope is simply that you and we will collectively employ these methods both to address the challenges the world faces and to shape democratic places that are irresistible.

Contributor Biographies

Shalini Agrawal is the director of the Center for Art + Public Life at California College of the Arts. She has more than 20 years of experience engaging diverse communities in the design of their shared spaces. Trained as an architect, she teaches interior design, interdisciplinary studies, and the First Year program.

Shin Aiba is a professor in the Department of Urban System Sciences at Tokyo Metropolitan University. He specializes in city planning and community design and has practiced as a planning supervisor. He is the author of *Folding Up a City* (2015), a book that examines the problem of shrinking cities in Japan.

Austin Allen has participated in 11-year recovery efforts in New Orleans as an associate professor of landscape architecture at Louisiana State University, as a principal of Design-Jones, LLC, and as chair of the Department of Landscape Architecture at the University of Colorado, Denver. He also taught at Cleveland State University.

Diane Jones Allen has 27 years of professional practice experience in land planning and varied scales of community development work. She is principal landscape architect with DesignJones, LLC, in New Orleans, Louisiana. DesignJones, LLC, received the 2016 American Society of Landscape Architects Community Service Award. Allen wrote the introduction for Chapter 3.

Richard Alomar is a landscape architect and assistant professor at Rutgers University. Alomar uses sketching to record ideas on place and design, focusing on the connection between sketching, walking, and cognition. He holds a BS in agronomy from the University of Puerto Rico and an MLA from Louisiana State University.

Noah Billig is an assistant professor of landscape architecture and planning in the University of Arkansas's Fay Jones School of Architecture and Design. His research focuses on participatory design and planning, adaptive urbanism, generative design, and informal settlements. His forthcoming book is *Istanbul: Informal Settlements and Generative Urbanism* (2018).

C. L. Bohannon is an assistant professor in the Landscape Architecture Program at Virginia Tech. He received his PhD and MLA from Virginia Tech and his BLA from the Fay Jones College of Architecture and Design, University of Arkansas. His research focuses on community engagement and design pedagogy, community narrative, design activism, and social justice.

Kofi Boone is an associate professor of landscape architecture at North Carolina State University, College of Design. He teaches in the areas of environmental justice, site analysis and planning, community engagement, and media. His focus is on participatory design and innovating tools for engaging communities in the design and planning process.

Victoria Chanse is an associate professor in the Department of Plant Science and Landscape Architecture at the University of Maryland. She specializes in community-based responses to sea level rise and stormwater issues. She holds a PhD in landscape architecture and environmental planning from the University of California, Berkeley.

Terry Clements is a professor and the chair of landscape architecture at Virginia Tech. Her work addresses community engagement practices and impacts within the built environment disciplines. Her recent work includes research on the history of women in landscape architecture, and the evolution of landscape architecture education and practice in the United States.

David de la Peña is an architect, urban designer, and assistant professor of landscape architecture at the University of California, Davis. His work and practice explore methods by which citizens and designers co-produce urban spaces, with a focus on sustainable architecture, self-managed communities, and urban agriculture in the United States and Spain. De la Peña wrote the introduction for Chapter 2 and coauthored the Introduction.

Andrés Martínez de la Riva Díaz is an urbanist architect and a member of the Raons Públiques cooperative based in Barcelona. He has published articles on the evaluation of urban participatory processes and has participated in different congresses on urbanism and participation in Spain and Europe.

Christian Dimmer is an assistant professor in architecture and urban studies at Waseda University, Tokyo. He earned his PhD from the University of Tokyo on the conceptual history of public space in Japan. He founded the civil-society initiatives Open Architecture Collaborative, Tokyo Chapter (formerly Architecture for Humanity), Tohoku Planning Forum, and Tokyo Transitions.

Sibyl Diver is an environmental scientist. Taking a community-based approach, Sibyl spent the past 10 years studying collaborative management between indigenous communities and state agencies in Pacific Northwest salmon watersheds. She received her PhD from the University of California, Berkeley, and is currently researching indigenous water governance as a postdoctoral scholar at Stanford.

Masato Dohi is the president of the Ecological Democracy Foundation and an associate professor in the Department of Architecture and Building Engineering at Tokyo Institute of Technology. He is the coauthor of *Community Design Primer* (Japanese edition, 1997) and the translator of *Design for Ecological Democracy* (Japanese edition, 2017).

Paul Duggan holds a doctorate of planning, design, and the built environment from Clemson University. His research interest includes the effects of physical planning and urban design on the quality of life in small towns and urban environments. His doctoral research investigated the effects of involuntary relocation and participation in El-Gourna, Egypt.

Sara Egan is a landscape architect and urban planner focused on linking design and community engagement. As an associate and project manager of Design Workshop, Sara has implemented all scales of planning and design, resulting in award-winning community change in the western and midwestern United States as well as internationally.

Lauren Elder is an environmental artist and landscape designer based in Oakland, California. She practices sustainable design for school and community gardens in the Bay Area and throughout Latin America. Community design–build is her preferred method, and art is a key element. She has taught at California College of Art (2005–2016).

Javier Fraga Cadórniga is an architect with wide experience in participatory design process, which he has developed in different countries and contexts. Since 2015, he has been an associate and cofounder of the cooperative Raons Públiques from Barcelona, working on the empowerment of communities through cooperative design.

Alex Gilliam is the founder of Public Workshop, nationally recognized for redefining the way youth and communities participate as citizens and leaders in the design of their schools, neighborhoods, and cities. His work has been featured on NPR's Studio 360 and in *Metropolis, The Architect's Newspaper, Architect Magazine,* and *Fast Company.*

Randolph T. Hester Jr. champions cultural and biological diversity through his writing and built work in complex political environments, from Manteo, North Carolina, to Los Angeles and the East Asian–Australasian Flyway. Hester wrote introductions for Chapters 8 and 9 and coauthored the Introduction and Conclusion.

Jeffrey Hou is a professor of landscape architecture at the University of Washington, Seattle. His work focuses on design activism, public space and democracy, and engagement of marginalized social groups in design and planning. He is the editor of *Insurgent Public Space: Guerrilla Urbanism and the Making of Contemporary Cities* (2010). Hou wrote introductions for Chapters 6 and 7.

Hirotaka Ikeda is a professor in the graduate school of Environment and Disaster Research, Tokoha University. His research interests include city planning, disaster mitigation planning, and disaster recovery planning. One of his major projects is a series of community tsunami evacuation planning projects in Numazu city since 2014.

Jing Jin is a PhD candidate in the Department of Urban System Sciences, Tokyo Metropolitan University. Her majors are urban planning and community design. She specializes in creating academic opportunities that promote cross-cultural exchanges in East Asian communities. Since 2014, she has been hosting community design study tours in Japan.

Yeun-Kum Kim received her PhD from the University of Seoul. Her work and research focus is on community design, landscape architecture, and life world. She has published several books, including *Place Making with Communication* (2009). She currently runs her own firm, Wul Landscape Architecture Office.

Maren King is an associate professor in the Department of Landscape Architecture and director of the Center for Community Design Research at the SUNY College of Environmental Science and Forestry in Syracuse, New York. She facilitates programs and projects that engage students and the public in community design and participatory action research.

Isami Kinoshita is a professor in the Department of Landscape Architecture, Chiba University, Japan. He received a PhD in architecture from Tokyo Institute of Technology in 1984. He has been a leading scholar in children's participatory design in Japan, featuring techniques such as Three Generations Play Maps, Street as a Museum, and Gulliver Map.

Laura J. Lawson is the dean of Agriculture and Urban Programs and a professor of landscape architecture at Rutgers, The State University of New Jersey. Her scholarship and teaching focus on urban agriculture, community open space, and participatory design. Lawson wrote the introduction for Chapter 5 and coauthored the Conclusion and the introduction for Chapter 1.

Sungkyung Lee is an associate professor in the College of Environment and Design at the University of Georgia. Her teaching and research focus on community-based design and the issues of preserving community history and collective memories in Asian urban development practices.

ChenYu Lien is an assistant professor in the Department of Landscape Architecture at Chung Yuan University, Taiwan. Since 2009, he has been promoting collaboration between nongovernmental organizations and neighborhood residents through participatory design of temporary green spaces. His current projects include "Building Local Community through Community Networks" and "Space Share, Taipei."

Amanda Lovelee is a visual artist working as the City Artist for Public Art Saint Paul in the City of St. Paul. Lovelee acts as a translator between the city's ideas and its residents, with the goal of building a city everyone wants to live in.

Kota Maruya is an assistant professor of School of Regional Development Studies at Kanazawa University. He received his PhD in engineering from Tokyo Institute of Technology. His specialized field is the cultural landscape and tourism. He has been engaged in community revitalization projects focusing on the relationship between traditional crafts and natural resources.

Kousuke Masuo is an architectural and regional designer at Alsed Architectural Laboratory Co., Ltd. He has studied the regional design of architecture, and has written on the subjects of local housing production and preservation standards for farm villages in Japan.

Milenko Matanovic began his career as an experimental artist in the late 1960s in his native Slovenia, exhibiting worldwide as part of the OHO collective. He founded the nonprofit Pomegranate Center in 1986 to develop an effective model for helping communities using collective creativity and powerful collaboration.

Marcia J. McNally is a recognized leader in international environmental mobilization and on-the-ground citizen participation. She retired from the University of California, Berkeley, in 2010 but continues to teach at Berkeley and in Taiwan. McNally now lives in Durham, North Carolina, where she runs The Neighborhood Laboratory, an on-demand community design center. McNally wrote the introduction for Chapter 4 and coauthored the introduction for Chapter 1.

Joe Mulligan is a chartered civil engineer and associate director of Kounkuey Design Initiative. He has worked for over 10 years on sustainable infrastructure, water management, and rural and urban development planning, with extensive experience in India, China, Nigeria, Malaysia, El Salvador, Kenya, United Arab Emirates, the United Kingdom, and the United States.

Hala Nassar is a professor of landscape architecture at Clemson University, honorary professor at Huazhong Agricultural University, China, and principal at HewittNassar Studio. Her broad international understanding of design and culture reflects her research and scholarly writing focusing on historical and cultural landscape transformation of the Middle East and North Africa.

Chelina Odbert is an urban planner, cofounder, and the executive director of the award-winning Kounkuey Design Initiative. Chelina leads multisectoral, urban, and rural development projects throughout Africa and the United States. Her research, writing, and practice focus on the intersection of participatory planning and design, and economic and social development.

Yu Ohtani is a doctoral candidate at the University of Leipzig. In 2011, he founded the nonprofit organization Das Japanische Haus (The Japanese House), which occupied a vacant building in Leipzig. As a community organizer, he manages cultural events, international architecture and urban design workshops, local art festivals, and academic symposiums in Japan and Germany.

Patsy Eubanks Owens is a professor of landscape architecture at the University of California, Davis. She holds an MLA from the University of California, Berkeley, and a BLA from the University of Georgia. Her research focuses on the relationships between people and place, including youth and adult engagement in design and policy development.

Emily Risinger is an urban planner specializing in participatory design and public engagement. Her work has been recognized through numerous awards and speaking engagements. As an associate and project manager of Design Workshop, she helps clients explore, design, and implement creative plans through DW Legacy Design.

James Rojas is an urban planner, community activist, educator, artist, and founder of Place It! He has developed an innovative community visioning and outreach method using storytelling, objects, art production, and play. He is a nationally recognized urban planner who examines Latino cultural influences on urban design and sustainability in the United States.

Sago Network is a small not-for-profit team of built-environment and community development professionals who specialize in community-centered development projects in Papua New Guinea. Projects focus on village-scale water and sanitation infrastructure. The Network collaborates with communities who are motivated to address these challenges as a crucial stepping-stone toward improved village health.

Henry Sanoff is a professor emeritus at North Carolina State University. He is best known for his publications *Democratic Design* and *Community Participation Methods in Design and Planning* and as one of the founders of the Environmental Design Research Association. Sanoff has been a visiting lecturer at universities in Australia, the United Kingdom, Japan, Greece, Turkey, Korea, and Qatar and has received numerous awards, including a Distinguished Fulbright and Senior Specialists Award.

Shigeru Satoh is a professor and director of the Institute of Urban and Regional Studies at Waseda University. He has spearheaded the *machizukuri* movement in Japan. His contribution to the town planning field in Japan has been awarded the Prize of Architectural Institute of Japan in 2000.

Shreya Shah is a liberation-seeking facilitator, trainer, coach, graphic designer, and artist. She gives workshops and speaks about social justice, creativity and creative design, and embodied leadership across the United States and internationally with grassroots groups, nonprofit organizations, universities, and beyond with Saltwater Training & Consulting.

Hideaki Shimura is a professor in the Department of Architecture at Shibaura Institute of Technology, Japan. He developed many workshop methods, including the Community Design Simulation Games. He is an architectural designer and town planner and an author of numerous books on town planning,

Akihiro Soga received a master's degree in urban system sciences from Tokyo Metropolitan University in 2016. He currently works in the Business Development Department at Tansei-sha Co., Ltd., a design consulting company that provides services to public offices.

Julie Stevens is an assistant professor of landscape architecture at Iowa State University. Her research and teaching focus on improving human and environmental health by creating mutual stewardship through engaged design. She directs a partnership with the Iowa Department of Corrections to create restorative and productive landscapes in Iowa's prisons.

Chip Sullivan is a professor of landscape architecture at the College of Environmental Design, University of California, Berkeley. His latest book, *Cartooning the Landscape*, concerns the metaphysics of drawing and learning how to "see." Chip received the 2016 Jot D. Carpenter Teaching Medal from the American Society of Landscape Architects.

Yoko Tsuchiya is a director of the Ecological Democracy Foundation. She is an active participant in the Pacific Rim Community Design Network.

Naomi Uchida is an associate professor in the Faculty of Economics of Saitama University, where she teaches classes in urban planning and urban theory. She is the coeditor of *Machizukuri Kyosho* (2016) and *What Is the Kanazawa-ness?* (2015). Her current research topics include gentrification, local revitalization, and community development.

Daniel Winterbottom has research interests in landscape as a cultural expression, ecological urban design, community participatory design, service learning, and restorative/healing landscapes. He developed a design–build program in 1995 and was inducted as an ASLA Fellow in 2011. His awards include ASLA Community Service 2007 and EDRA Great Places Award 2010.

Chao-Ching Yu is a professor emeritus and the former dean of the School of Design, Chung Yuan Christian University, Taiwan, and is currently the director general of the Institute of Historical Resources Management. Trained as an architect, he has worked professionally and academically in urban design and community design in Taiwan for over 40 years.

Index

Page numbers followed by "f" indicate drawings and photographs.